MY BROTHER IN ARMS

The Exceptional Life of Mark Andrew Forester,
United States Air Force Combat Controller

THAD FORESTER
- WITH MATTHEW GLENCOE

My Brother in Arms published by **Triumph Press**
www.TriumphPress.com

Cover Artwork: Jana Nielsen
Layout and design: ipublicidades.com

10 9 8 7 6 5 4 3 2 1

Triumph Press is a resource for those who have the passion to tell their life stories and change the world. If you have a true and inspiring story to share visit www.TriumphPress.com to learn how we can help you publish and join our library of inspirational books.

This was taken April 4, 2010 and is the last picture of Mark (left) and me before he deployed to Afghanistan. We were not divided in life and now in death we will not be separated.

CONTENTS

Preface

When I set out to write this book on my brother's life, I intended to have it completed and ready for publication in June 2011. With its release in September 2013, it seems I was a little over ambitious in my planning. I have devoted every available moment to promoting Mark's legacy, and the effort has taken many forms, this book being only one of them. Also, I think the book is more complete and effective than it could have been much earlier. Far more information is available recently than it was in the weeks following Mark's death. Most importantly, though, is that the time has given us perspective to determine the true purpose for this book. I am satisfied that the final product, at minimum, provides our family a personal account of Mark Andrew Forester—son, brother, friend, patriot, and hero. However, I have a greater goal that it will serve as not just a memorial in print, but as a tool for perpetuating Mark's legacy of service, sacrifice and excellence.

First and foremost, any time I write or speak of Mark, my desire is always to speak the truth. I don't make unrealistic assumptions, especially about the times I wasn't present. I have always wanted to make sure details about Mark are accurate and unembellished. I write confidently about our childhood and the time we lived together as adults. However, when writing of his military life, I've gone to great lengths to verify, to the best of my ability, everything printed. If errors are present, it is not for any deliberate reason. There are some seeming inconsistencies in the book, notably with the spelling of places in Afghanistan. This book exists because so many people contributed to it. Where there are different spellings and formats for dates and time, I followed those used by the contributor.

I've never wanted to make Mark out to be anything he was not. He was an exceptional man—a cut above the rest, and most people agree—but I've never wanted to inflate stories or circumstances to make him out to be a superhero. Mark wouldn't want that anyway. It happens too often that we put someone in exalted status once they die. As if, all of the sudden they never did any wrong and were the best people in the world at everything they did. As his brother, I'm well aware Mark wasn't perfect. Once again, I have strived for accuracy.

From day one, I told those who contributed to this work that I would not print anything they aren't comfortable with and that they haven't approved. I tried to be up front with everyone that I was writing a book, so when I asked questions, sometimes I was thinking of using that info in the book. I never wanted them to feel surprised or "under surveillance". In some cases names have been changed, and in all cases, call signs have been changed (except for Mark's). Air Force Special Operations Command (AFSOC) has reviewed all chapters referencing Mark's military life and suggested few changes, which I made. This was to assure me that I didn't print anything that could cause harm to our military and/or our country.

Since Mark was killed, we have met countless men and women in the military who have impressed me with their commitment to protect America. What's more touching is when they lose their own, they're able to turn off their stern, professional personae and turn on compassion, love, support and acceptance. We have witnessed it first-hand, up close and personal. All have expressed complete support and consolation. But more than this, many have become close to us, some are like family now. They visit us often. We talk, email and text regularly.

We have been amazed at the support from the Air Force, especially the mighty Two-One from Pope Field (formerly Pope Air Force Base), NC. This was Mark's assigned squadron. Anything we needed, or need in the future, they will do. These were not just empty words, but promises they have delivered on—repeatedly. Even those from the Army, Navy and Marines who worked with Mark have kept in close contact with us and have provided valuable insight into his life at Firebase Cobra and what it was like to work with him, in the heat of battle, and slow times goofing off. And I have to mention the great bonus it is that so many have become Alabama football fans, thanks to Mark's die-hard loyalty.

Numerous friends, teammates, and associates of Mark's have contacted us to share their impressions and experiences with him. These are people who came to us on their own, unsolicited, sharing incredible stories about my brother. They will probably never really know how important this is to us. We love it.

Given my desire to learn everything I can about others' experiences and memories of Mark, I applied this to a recent situation when a friend was suddenly killed in a car accident. It was tough on me. I spoke at his funeral. That night after speaking, I wrote down my thoughts of him and our experiences together and sent the letter to his wife. I explained how precious this type of information was and continues to be for me to hear about Mark.

I received a card from her recently. In it she wrote, "The letter had great memories and we all read it and cried a little more. Thank you for doing that. Thank you for honoring Rich.... and for your letter with all the memories. I treasure that. There are no words that I know to thank you..."

As unique as Mark was, which you'll discover in this book, I have to recognize the many other men and women serving our country, or who have served. I am grateful to each of you for your many acts of service and sacrifice. I know it's hard on your bodies, hard on families and relationships, etc. We aren't the only ones to lose a loved one to war. Unfortunately, there are many. Our citizens need to know about the great sacrifices these men and women make on our behalf. Most of them don't want attention, but they deserve our respect and appreciation; and they deserve much more than they currently get from our country—it's citizens and leaders. My Dad always said that someone had to do it; he just didn't want it to be his kids. I think most parents can understand that.

Mark's example continues to touch and inspire others. He didn't talk a big game; he just reliably lived his beliefs in a way that wasn't preachy or judgmental, and it was infectious. He genuinely cared for his friends, and although he may not have agreed with some of their lifestyles and personal choices, he still spent time with them and was a true friend. One teammate summed it up well, "Mark was a great man, and during our time working together—where many people compromise their beliefs in one way or another—I never, ever saw him act in any way that was not completely consistent with his beliefs. He was someone that I was honored to call friend—someone I'll never forget" (David Gross). It's easy to sit back and say he stuck to his principles, but when others share info like this, the validation is powerful.

Immediately after learning of Mark's death, our friend, Michael Shiffler[1] posted about Mark and his heroic death on his photography web site. He did this on his own and if he hadn't, we wouldn't have come in contact so quickly with so many men and women who served with Mark. By the time of his funeral, we'd received numerous stories about Mark—his skill, humor, and love of country. Michael was also in Haleyville for the funeral and documented those few days in a way that is priceless.

---

[1] www.michaelthemaven.com

Mark is the youngest of five children. He is my little brother and I write from that viewpoint. We were the youngest in the family and he was my best friend. There are few things in life that I can speak of with total confidence and conviction—my little brother is one of them. I will spend the rest of my life proclaiming the man and warrior he was. There are many books in print about military heroes, and I have read a lot of them. But Mark's military career was only a small part of his life, so this book doesn't highlight just the last three years of his 29 years on earth, but I've tried to capture his entire life. From his family environment, to his spiritual beliefs, to his trials, and then to his physical talents; these all prepared him to face the most violent battles in one of the most violent areas of the world.

While some family members are not greatly represented in these pages, that fact has nothing to do with their interest, sense of loss, or devotion to Mark. It only means they are less inclined than others to share their deep and poignant feelings in this form. Primarily, this is my book on behalf of my family. It naturally follows that my voice and perspective are dominant. This work is one expression of my love for Mark, my commitment to remember him, and part of the duty that I feel to continue his legacy and protect his name.

Another aspect of his legacy is that in addition to his immediate family, Mark left behind a brother-in-law, three sisters-in-law, and (at this point) 16 nieces and nephews. He left them all with an unmatched example of duty, honor, selflessness, and humility. My new first-born son carries his name because I never want him to forget his uncle's example and always strive to follow it. I often wish Mark were here to see and hold him and celebrate the experience with me. I know he does celebrate with me, but I wish I could have seen his face as he held my son.

Our good friend, Michael Madsen, offered one of the most concise descriptions: "Mark was, perhaps, the most harmonious blend of different character traits I have ever seen in one person. Mark was strong but mild. He was immensely courageous and thoroughly confident but unfailingly deferential and humane; deeply intense but profoundly calm. He was compassionate and mild but utterly unrelenting in defending his principles."

CMSgt Calvin Markham, the chief of Mark's squadron, once told us, "Mark was one of the best Combat Controllers, regardless of rank and experience. As I've said before, I would like to be more like Mark." Whatever you do in your life, I hope this book inspires you in the same way. Nothing can honor my brother more.

Foreword

Note: We are deeply grateful for the concern and overwhelming support our family has received from Mark's Combat Control family. It is fitting that Mark's commander, Lt Col Parks Hughes, authored the Foreword of this book.

In the late summer of 2009, I was the commander of the 21st Special Tactics Squadron (21 STS), Pope Field, North Carolina, when Mark Forester and several other Airmen reported to the unit for their first operational assignment.   They had just completed the two-year training pipeline to become Special Tactics Combat Controllers in the United States Air Force. Special Tactics is a component of Air Force Special Operations, and consists of Airmen who work on the ground, often in conjunction with Army and Navy special operations teams, to bring airpower capabilities to bear. These Airmen are trained in several distinct specialties, one of which is Combat Control. Combat Controllers provide tactical control of airstrikes as well as assessment, establishment, and control of airfields in remote or austere environments. The training for this field is one of the longest and toughest in all of Special Operations, and Mark Forester excelled throughout.

For me, being a squadron commander was, in many ways, not unlike being a parent. I cared for all squadron members equally, I looked out for the welfare of all equally, and I drew great satisfaction from watching each one develop professionally and succeed at his or her respective job. However, in my two years as commander of the 21 STS, some unit members made a larger impression upon me than others--none more so than Mark Forester. And it was not the heroic way in which Mark died, or even that he died for that matter, but rather, because of the extraordinary way in which he lived. Mark was truly one-of-a-kind.

Prior to his arrival at the unit, we received positive reports regarding Mark's performance in the training pipeline, but nothing that prepared us for the remarkable individual who would soon positively influence all of our lives. At first glance, Mark was clearly more mature than most of his peers who arrived each quarter from the training course in Florida, and as I got to know him, I quickly realized how exceptional he was. Sure, there was his record of superior performance throughout training, but beyond that, Mark possessed a degree of commitment, a level of life experience, and a sense of direction that most young Airmen did not possess. From his time as a Mormon missionary, to his completion of a business degree at the University of Alabama, to his deliberate decision to join the Air Force to become a Combat Controller, to his rapid completion of upgrade and combat-mission-ready training (faster than any other Airman in my time at the squadron), Mark was on a different path than those around him. It is difficult to characterize; you simply had to know Mark Forester to appreciate it. And for those who knew him, none were surprised to learn, upon hearing of Mark's tragic death, that he was performing his job superbly, advancing in the face of the enemy, and risking his own life in an effort to save that of a wounded teammate.

The reason Mark was fighting in Uruzgan Province that day and not some other part of Afghanistan, is because I made the decision to send him there. As the commander, I approved the plan that outlined which location each Combat Controller, or "operator" as we referred to them, would deploy to. I and the other leaders at the squadron considered many factors when making these decisions, but above all else, we valued performance. We sent our most skilled operators to the most challenging locations, and at the time of Mark's deployment, the most challenging assignment was Firebase Cobra[2]. For most people, Firebase Cobra, if they know of it at all, is simply another of the multitude of small, austere operating bases that dot the map of eastern and southern Afghanistan. However, in the spring of 2010, Cobra was one of the hottest spots in Afghanistan--a place where you were all but guaranteed to confront the enemy every time you stepped outside the wire. The mission absolutely required our most capable Airmen.

To be sure, Firebase Cobra was not a place where I typically would have sent a Senior Airman on his first deployment, but then, Mark Forester was anything but typical. I talked to the guys who trained Mark, I talked to Mark's team leader, I talked to Mark himself, and in the end I was confident that he would excel at Cobra just as he had excelled at everything else in life. Mark was not the most experienced Combat Controller in the unit, but he was one of the most talented. And of course, as Mark emphatically demonstrated, he was up to the task. In a matter of months on the ground, Mark established himself as a consummate professional and a superior operator.

---

[2]   It was originally named Firebase (or Forward Operating Base-FOB) Cobra until the death of Capt. John Tinsley near there in August 2009. Many still refer to it as Cobra, as we do in this book, however, its official name is FOB Tinsley.

Mark's Special Forces teammates spoke of his professional skill, his courage, his selflessness, and his sense of humor. They remarked how, in a firefight, Mark always made his way to the front of the formation, even when his duties as a Combat Controller did not require him to be there. A month prior to the engagement in which Mark was killed, his Special Forces Team Leader sent me a note recommending Mark for a Bronze Star Medal with Valor for heroism during a separate mission. In it he wrote, "Let me just reiterate how well Mark is doing here. I couldn't ask for a better controller. He has been an invaluable asset to [the team]." Mark was also highly regarded by pilots across Afghanistan. Many have told me that he was the most talented controller they ever worked with. One of those was an A-10 pilot, a U.S. Air Force Brigadier General and Wing Commander, who flew for Mark on several missions. Another was an AH-64 pilot who flew for Mark many times and was actually flying in support of the mission on which Mark was killed. One of Mark's teammates, another Airman from the 21 STS with multiple combat tours and years more experience, was also working out of Cobra with a separate Special Forces team. He remarked to me that not only did Mark teach him how to be a better controller, he taught him how to be a better person.

In the days leading up to his final mission, I spoke with Mark on the phone about the upcoming operation and how he was getting along with the team. Mark was doing exceptionally well and was heavily engaged in planning for the mission. In our phone conversation and in the emails I exchanged with him, it was clear that Mark was exactly where he wanted to be, doing exactly what he came into Combat Control to do. Quite frankly, there is no other way to get there. You do not wander into an Air Force recruiter's office and suddenly find yourself out at Firebase Cobra taking the fight to the enemy on a daily basis. You have to want it, and you have to work extremely hard to get there. Mark Forester was a volunteer many times over, and he excelled throughout two years of training and some of the toughest schools in the Department of Defense. Mark consciously sought the path he was on, and it was truly a path less travelled.

At the time of his death, Mark was engaged in a significant operation to clear a valley in Uruzgan Province. During this operation, he distinguished himself, as he did throughout the deployment, as a skilled Combat Controller, a courageous warrior, and a selfless teammate. On 29 September 2010, while assaulting an enemy ambush site, Mark performed his professional duties superbly. He covered the team with close air support, provided suppressive fire with his personal weapon, killed several insurgent fighters, and maneuvered his element into position to flank the enemy. When one of his teammates was shot by a sniper in the open, Mark paired up with another team member to go get him. As they moved to retrieve their wounded comrade, Mark was struck by a bullet in the upper chest and died shortly thereafter.

Mark could have pursued countless professions that did not involve risking his life in a far-away land, but he did not. In fact, he scorned other options and enrolled himself in the academy of discipline and sacrifice. He braved great dangers knowing full well the risks involved. He did so willingly, and he did not ask for anything in return. I'm not sure it is normal to willingly accept such risks. I'm not sure it is normal to have a smile on your face as you drive into what is certain to be a close fight with a ruthless enemy. But that is how I prefer to remember Mark Forester, and I think the image in my mind is pretty close to reality. It is what he lived his professional life to do. And while I'm not sure it is normal, I'm absolutely convinced that it is vitally necessary if we want this country to maintain its place as the greatest on earth. Someone has to carry that load, and thankfully we've got patriots like Mark Forester who are willing to do it, patriots who conduct the very dangerous and very costly business of confronting our enemies face-to-face so that the citizens of this great nation can sleep safely at night, most never knowing the extraordinary sacrifices that those like Mark Forester make on their behalf.

I often wonder why great Americans like Mark sign up for this duty, when they could pursue so many other, less risky endeavors. Although I don't have a complete answer, in Mark's case, I have a pretty good idea. You need only meet his parents and his brothers and his sister and it all starts to make sense. Like so many of our great warriors, Mark comes from an extraordinary family, a family that is just as committed to this great nation as Mark was. Mark paid once in full, but his family, like the families of so many other Americans who have not returned from this war, continue to pay the price every day. Mark's sacrifice, the sacrifices of others like him, and the sacrifices of their families must never be forgotten. As a nation, we are eternally indebted.

I am honored to have served as Mark Forester's commander, and I consider myself privileged to have been associated with such an extraordinary professional and remarkable human being. Mark inspired the best in all those around him, and he set an example of character, selflessness, courage, self-discipline, competence, humility, professionalism, and commitment that the rest of us can only hope to match. We would all do well to take a lesson or two from the way in which Mark lived his life, and apply it to our own. And by doing so, may we continue to honor the sacrifice that he made.

Lt Col Parks Hughes
Special Tactics Officer
Pope Field, NC
11/11/2011

First There . . . That Others May Live.

On Heroes

The world's battlefields have been in the heart chiefly; more heroism has been displayed in the household and the closet, than on the most memorable battlefields in history.— Henry Ward Beecher *(1813-1887) American politician.*

What is a hero without love for mankind.— Doris Lessing *(1919-) Author*

All heroes are shadows of Christ — John Piper *(1946-) Author*

A good tree cannot bring forth evil fruit, neither can a corrupt tree bring forth good fruit. Wherefore by their fruits ye shall know them. — New Testament, Matthew 7:18, 20

He was a strong, charismatic, funny, opinionated bright beacon of what we should all aspire to be.— YK

If a man does his best, what else is there? — General George Patton Jr. *(1885-1945)*

"I am convinced that life is 10% what happens to me and
90% how I react to it…"
– Ray Forester quoting "Attitude" by Charles Swindoll

CHAPTER 1

Notification

The Afghanistan sun had just broken over the horizon as my brother, Mark Forester, and Calvin Harrison sat on the porch of a village compound for a moment of preparation before heading out. It was the second day of an operation to liberate the people of that village from Taliban control, which had been oppressed by the terrorists for quite some time, allowing them to lead a life free from fear.

Afghanistan was insanely hot; but that didn't stop Mark from wrapping a full size American flag around the front and rear plate of his body armor prior to this mission. This was not standard procedure, but then there was nothing standard about Mark Forester. He was a Combat Controller (CCT), a Special Operations component of the Air Force, which supports other Special Operations Forces. CCTs skydive, scuba dive, are experts of countless weapons systems and serve as the eyes on the ground for commanders and pilots who are far from the front lines. They coordinate all of the aircraft flying in their vicinity, giving final release authority for the bombs and weapons aboard each bird, bringing the most chaos and destruction to the enemy as possible. Combat Controllers must be fully aware of the flight patterns and safety of the aircraft above as well as the positions of the troops on the ground, all while avoiding being shot. The stress and challenge of being a CCT is intense, and Mark was a natural.

Calvin Harrison was a Green Beret Medic, as Mark was attached to his Special Forces team operating out of one of the most violent and dangerous areas of Afghanistan at this time, called FOB Cobra. Cal was loved by his team, with a perpetual smile and ability to serve, not just his men, but their families as well. Calvin would often Skype with their wives, giving advice and assistance, helping with pregnancy and other concerns. He spoke with them from across the world as if he were their personal physician and wouldn't leave until he met their needs; to the chagrin of husbands anxious to talk to their wives.

Mark joined the Air Force and trained to be a Combat Controller at the age of 26, after previously completing a business finance degree. Being deployed three years later made him one of the older members of the team. Although what he wanted most was to marry and have a family, Mark felt compelled to protect freedom and kill terrorists. Mark was five months into his first deployment and had been sent to one of the most active areas in Afghanistan, which is almost unheard of for a CCT on his first deployment. Even before he hit the battlefield, his command knew he was a force to be reckoned with; and, so far, he had proven them right every day.

A moment of tranquility, if you can call it that, was captured when this photo of Calvin and Mark was taken as they sat on that compound porch. Their team had moved into the village the night before, with great success, and were about to run the rest of the Taliban out in the coming days.

Neither one considered the possibility of dying that day, but before the sun would sink below the horizon, they would both be killed; first Calvin (on

left), and then Mark in an attempt to rescue him. This last picture of them together has become highly significant and valued by our families and those they fought beside…….

On the evening of 29 September 2010, I had just settled on the couch to watch a *Seinfeld* re-run with my wife when we heard two car doors close just outside our house. Then the doorbell rang. Wondering who it could possibly be, I opened the door and discovered two men in dress uniforms of the United States Air Force. They called me by name and said they knew Mark, my younger brother. They asked to come in. I said "sure," led them to our living room, shot a concerned look to my wife, and shut off the TV.

I sat alone on the love seat with Rozlynn, my wife, sitting in another chair. Captain Andrew Bair sat down while Sgt Sean Gleffe remained standing. Their somber faces said it all; my worst nightmare had just come true, though my mind refused to believe it. They said my brother had been killed in action (KIA) earlier that day during an intense, close-range firefight. Rozlynn quickly moved and sat at my feet and gripped my leg. The only other details they could confirm were that he was shot through the forearm and into the upper chest, and that he went down fighting.

The men were very calm, soft spoken and clearly upset. One of my first questions was, "Did you know Mark?" (Even though they told me they did at the door). Cpt Bair didn't know him well, but Sgt Gleffe, who was clearly fighting back tears, had been one of his instructors. I sat there in calm numbness and asked the typical questions: What happened? Did he suffer? What was his team doing?

Meanwhile at mom and dad's home, you can imagine the shock and anguish happening at this moment. Dad told mom while she was still in the bed,[3] "Something's happened to Mark." She couldn't grasp it. She remembers most that she needed to comfort dad and said, "You've got to tell the kids." She was also overcome with anger. She couldn't believe that she didn't already know. How could she not know her son was in danger, or more, since they were so close? She regrets her mind

---

[3] Mom was actually watching the new Robin Hood movie with Russell Crowe. She had sent the DVD to Mark at his request, so she figured she'd see what this move was about.

was preoccupied with other things, instead of the possibility of "feeling" something happened to her son. Even when she heard the doorbell ring (both times that day), she didn't have a clue something was wrong. I actually felt this very same way. Even three days prior, on 26 Sept, I had written in my journal that I was excited for Mark to be home in about five weeks and also expressed my worry for him while down range. I never thought of this as a premonition, just constant concern for my brother.

As we talked, the phone rang—it was dad. Rozlynn answered and told him two men from the Air Force were in our home and we would head to Haleyville shortly. She hung up and said dad was sobbing. According to Mark's request, the US Air Force had coordinated notification so my parents and I would simultaneously receive word, sparing us from having to tell each other such awful news. (Later we learned they had watched mom and dad's house all day until dad got home from work. They even knocked on the front door earlier. Mom didn't answer because she was in bed not feeling well and normally, only strangers and salesmen knock on that door. It's an unbelievable blessing she didn't face that without dad.)

Even though I had considered this possibility—because I knew Mark was in a dangerous area—there is no way I could have prepared for that moment. Everything was suddenly surreal, it seemed like I was watching a movie of someone else's life, not living through my own. At the same time, it was all so dreadfully real. I was shocked, sad, a little mad (more anger would follow), but mostly I was heartbroken. It was good to hear he died fighting and moving forward. It helped build my resolve to do the same.

Before we left for Haleyville, I quickly called mom and dad's neighbors, Randy and Judy, to let them know. Maybe they needed to go check on mom and dad since I had a 1.5 hour drive and I lived the closest of all the kids. They didn't answer, so I called other longtime friends, the Bradberrys. Fortunately, they already knew and were headed to mom and dad's. Rozlynn drove while I called Joseph and a few close friends on the drive up. The first thing Joseph said, in a wavering and strained voice, was, "They took our little brother...." I didn't dare call Terri because I couldn't handle that conversation—I knew what a wreck she'd be. By the time we arrived home, cars were parked all down the driveway and along the road. The carport was covered with people—family and close friends. I was amazed at how quickly so many heard the news and were at mom and dad's house. This was just the beginning of extremely generous support from so many. Dad was first to greet me. I then quickly found my way to Mark's room where mom was lying on his bed crying. She spent a long time there that night, even as a flurry of activity went on throughout the house.

Finally, late that night, there was nothing left but to retreat to our beds and try getting some rest—but it really didn't happen. There were brief times when exhaustion and grief gave way to restless sleep, but in between those moments, I could hear crying and whimpering from mom and dad's room and around the house as they paced through the night. Rozlynn slept with her hand on my leg for much of that night to comfort me as I repeatedly muttered Mark's name in my sleep.

During the next nine days, we discovered what a tight-knit group the Air Force Combat Controllers (CCTs) are. We were assigned two CCTs, Barry Crawford and Sascha Kvale, to be with us as much as we wanted. They helped with all the bewildering arrangements—the Dignified Transfer flight to bring Mark's body to Dover AFB, meeting that flight, preparing his Dignified Arrival at Haleyville, funeral service events, preparing for possible protestors, etc. The list went on and on.

Looking back on it, we deeply appreciate the Air Force Special Operations Command's policy to notify families of a loved one's death. They didn't send a USAF representative from a local base—they sent Mark's teammates, instructors and commanders; men who personally knew and worked with Mark. In the bewilderment of the situation, it was a huge comfort to have people with us who mourned Mark as we did and could tell us, from personal experience, what it was like to work with Mark, what filled his days, and how much he was respected. When Mark died, our family lost a son, brother, uncle and friend. His empty place in our home and hearts can never be filled. However, we cannot ignore the fact that because of this dreadful loss, our lives have been filled with the love and respect of countless others we would have never known. These men first came to our homes as strangers, but very quickly became like family. Before Mark's death, he had two worlds: his family and pre-military friends, and the military. Because of his death, those two worlds are now combined; and Mark's not here to be part of them.

A few weeks later, I found a quiet moment and cracked Mark's Facebook password. (I knew some of the passwords he had used years earlier, so it wasn't hard.) Reading through literally hundreds of wall posts and friend requests was comforting in a way. Then, I decided to take a gander at his private messages. What I discovered brought all the shock and pain right back to the surface. It actually broke my heart as much as the news of Mark's death had, but in a different way because I could see mom's worry and foreboding.

While Mark was deployed, mom told us she'd more than once dreamed of him dying. In one, she clearly saw him lying in a casket, but she never saw his face. It was deeply disturbing and she was really upset for a while—she couldn't hide from her fear of what could happen and it gnawed at her.

Among the Facebook messages, I noticed Mark and mom communicated more, the closer it got to 29 September. The increase started when a fellow CCT, Senior Airman (SrA) Daniel R. Sanchez, was killed on 16 September 2010.Even though none of us knew of Danny before his death, the news hit us hard when we heard of it two days later, on a Saturday. It scared mom even more than she had already been. It was a hard day for me too. Suddenly, the war and its costs were much more real; and I feared for my brother.

I'll never forget how distracted and pained I was after hearing about Danny. I wanted to talk to Mark to understand what happened and to get some reassurance he was okay. I had to wait until September 22nd and he insisted, "Bro, I'm fine." Then he changed the subject by telling me not to worry about sending cereal because he only had about five weeks left and by the time it would arrive, he would be leaving. Besides, Mom had done a great job of sending plenty of care packages.

Mom also wanted to know about Danny's death. Was Mark with him when he was killed? Was he okay? Was he *going* to be okay…..? She pressed her worried questions. He finally responded with short, direct answers telling her he was not with Danny, though Danny was a fellow CCT; that he was just fine and would call her soon.

Their messages to each other became more frequent—especially from mom. Mark, of course, was working hard, planning that final mission and doing his job. He was busy "checking baseline" (a code he and I used for "eliminating terrorists"). What caught my attention most was mom's last message to Mark.

She sent that message at 3:32 a.m. on Wednesday, 29 September 2010. Mom had been sick and couldn't sleep, so she wrote a short note and told him she was thinking of him and hoped he was back to his "little hut, safe and sound and getting some rest." (You have to imagine those words with a sweet, motherly doting.)

Since Mark was 9.5 hours ahead of us, when mom sent that message, it was 1302 in Uruzgan and Mark was with his team, engaging the enemy. Within about two hours of her clicking "Send," Mark's teammate, Calvin Harrison, stepped through a doorway in a compound in Shah Mashad and immediately went down. Mark organized his element to assist Calvin, confronted the insurgents directly in the face of their fire, was struck in the hail of bullets, and drew his last breath. According to the record, Mark died at approximately 1036 Zulu, 1506 local, 5:36 a.m. in Haleyville, AL.

When the MEDEVAC helicopter took Calvin and Mark from the battlefield, the gear they carried was gathered up by their teammates and stowed in the trucks. Then they pressed on with the battle. Two days later, **George Earhart,** Mark's friend and fellow Airman on the team, and an Army teammate, Tony Venetz,[4] headed back to base. George needed medical attention, and from Cobra he could catch a flight to the base at Tarin Kowt (TK) which has better medical facilities. Also, he knew a memorial for Cal and Mark was planned while he would be there and that Lt Col Hughes would attend.

As soon as George got on base, he headed for Mark's room. He guessed (correctly) that things like Mark's red Alabama cap and "DONT TREAD ON ME" patch[5] would be precious mementos for our family; he wanted us to have them as soon as possible. He had only a little time before the flight to TK where he could pass the items to Lt Col Hughes who would see to it they got to us as quickly as possible. Glancing around the room, George remembered the armor plates in Mark's tactical vest. Days earlier, he watched Mark preparing his gear for his next, and last, mission.

He watched Mark struggle to squeeze the ceramic armor plates into their pockets. They are tight fit normally, but Mark had wrapped the two breastplates—in effect wrapped himself—in the flags of the nation he loved.

---

[4] Tony Venetz Jr. was also killed in Afghanistan only a few months later in January 2011 from non-combat related injuries. Among those he left behind were his mom, his wife, Debbie and their two children. I communicated with his wife shortly after hearing the news and we've stayed in touch, sharing a common tragedy.

[5] Some of these items had stains from Mark's blood. George debated a moment whether to send them, but then thought of himself, back home having just lost his brother in combat. He knew he would want these things. I am so grateful he put himself in our shoes and sent them along.

Mark had to fold and refold the flags around the plates before he got the tightest fit, and then used zip-ties to hold them while he shoe-horned the bundles into their pockets. He was wearing the flag around his chest plate for dad (mom had sent it to him), and around his back plate for Joseph. Joseph had sent it to Mark because he wanted a flag that had been flown in battle. Mark told Joseph he would fly one from his gun truck and could probably return it with bullet holes from being shot at. Then he said he'd wear it around his armor. Ironically, just three weeks before that front flag was pierced, Joseph said, "Now Mark, I don't want any bullet holes in this one."

George tugged the plates from the vest and cut the ties. Next, he and Tony started to fold the flags in the official manner that produces the star-spangled, blue triangle we know so well. One of the flags, though, would not open for folding. It was fused. Looking closer, George and Tony discovered where the fatal bullet had grazed the edge of Mark's armor before entering his chest. Fragments of its brass jacket were still entangled in the fibers of the flag, some of which were fused by the scorching heat of that bullet.

It seems strange now, but none of us had any premonitions that day. In the same moments my brother was giving his last, I was getting ready for just another normal day. While my daily routines unfolded at work, the battle raged on and Mark's teammates carried him and Calvin from the battlefield. From the official report:

> Mark was *"unresponsive with no carotid pulse. This was at approx. 1036Z. The team sergeant called for reinforcements. Once reinforcements arrived, they were able to recover the team medic who was also deceased [Calvin]. SrA Forester and the team medic were placed on a medical evacuation helicopter at approx. 1130Z and flown back to the surgical facility at Tarin Kowt. Airman Forester was pronounced killed in action by Dr. J.W. Haggerson at 1205Z."*

Next, they were transported to Kandahar where they joined another fallen marine and his escort.

Bobby Bonello, Mark's stateside roommate, close buddy through the training pipeline, and each other's designated escort, happened to be in the operations center (OPCEN) at his base when Mark's last fight played out. He remembers, "As I stepped into the OPCEN, I could hear over the radio (Satellite Radio or SATCOM) that there was a Troops in Contact

(TIC). After about 30 seconds of hearing the radio traffic, I noticed that it was Mark's team because I recognized their call sign. Shortly after that, I heard the call come over the radio and say that the JTAC[6] and the Medic were KIA. Of course, at first I was in denial because this could have been a mistake or another JTAC."

Stunned, but knowing what he had to do, Bobby went to his commanders for permission to escort Mark. Leadership cleared the way for his rush to Kandahar to begin the longest flight of his life. Mom, dad, my family and I had no clue, but the news spread quickly through the close-knit CCT network. Even those who didn't know Mark were shaken in a similar way I had been by Danny's death.

Just the night before, my parents were telling our friend Tyler Knight how concerned they were, but that Mark was like a kid over there, loving riding 4-wheelers (for work of course), and shooting the wild dogs that attacked their pet dogs on base. They were counting down the days until he came home.

Those who knew Mark struggled with their sharp emotions and grief and, to some, the duty fell to simultaneously deliver the news to mom and dad,[7] and to Rozlynn and me. And the first any of us suspected something was out of the ordinary was when unexpected visitors appeared in front of our homes that evening.

---

[6] Joint Terminal Attack Controller (JTAC) was one of Mark's key jobs as a Combat Controller (CCT).

[7] Several times, I've asked dad to explain what happened when he and mom received the notification. He just can't do it.

CHAPTER 2

Growing up Mark

Haleyville is a small community of about 4,100, tucked against the foothills of the Appalachian Mountains in the northwest part of Alabama. The area was first inhabited by Cherokee Indians. Later settlers were mostly mountain people: loggers, hunters and trappers. Slaves were virtually nonexistent among those rugged, freethinking individuals of the early 19th century. During the American Civil War, residents of Winston County, where Haleyville is located, resisted secession and tried to establish the *Free State of Winston*. Dad's roots go all the way back to those people.

Today, Haleyville is off the beaten path and in most ways epitomizes the best of small town, red-white-and-blue America. People know and look after each other. Haleyville High School athletics are major community events, and the football stadium is large enough to hold more than the whole town. It remains a safe and nurturing place to raise a family.

Mom used to buy clothes for us "on approval," meaning she would pick out some things, show them to the clerk, and then take them home to be sure they fit and looked right. After "approval," she'd go back and pay for the items we kept and return those we didn't. I think there is one store where she still does that, only it's for my nieces and nephews now.

In 1974, my mom and dad built our home. Their family was quite young with Terri (8), David (4), and Joseph just a baby. They still live in that house and it remains a very pleasant and hospitable shelter from the world. Visitors are always welcome, especially the grandchildren and their friends who play and enjoy being kids just like we did.

The house is outside town a bit, along a dead-end side road with only a few other neighbors, and sits on 14 acres that includes both woods and open space. The house is big enough to accommodate our large family and constant guests, but it still has a welcoming, cozy feel. Maybe that has more to do with mom's hospitality than a good floor plan—the architect messed up and the kitchen/dining area ended up 4 feet shorter than it was supposed to have been.

Terri has clear memories from when mom and dad were building the house. One day she was there when she somehow disturbed a wasp's nest and they immediately swarmed her. She ran around screaming and finally headed to the area that was to be our basement. A large puddle had formed there from recent rains and she jumped right in, hoping to escape the angry bugs. She got wet and muddy on top of being stung.

Growing up, we had a whole pack of boys, close in age, in our neighborhood. We spent our summers from breakfast until supper, outside, exploring and hunting in the woods, playing games, riding bikes (and later 4-wheelers), fishing and swimming in the nearby ponds and streams, and anything else we could find to fill our time with activity and adventure. I don't know how it could have been a better childhood for us.

Mom mostly seemed to worry that we got our meals, stayed out of trouble, and looked after each other. When it was time for us to come in, mom or dad would ring a bell on the back porch. We came running, as much to enjoy some good food as to avoid trouble for not minding our parents. Looking back at the type of foods mom cooked us regularly, I'm surprised none of us turned out obese. We loved fried honey buns, oats and toasts, biscuits and gravy, and green beans fried in bacon fat, just to name a few of our favorites.

Years later, when Mark got serious about his health and physical preparation for the military, he gave up this kind of diet. However, when he was back home visiting, he didn't hesitate to dive in. Plus, mom always loved cooking for her kids—especially her youngest boy. Mark burned enough calories during the week with all his training that indulging in "Mom's good home cookin'" on the weekends did him no harm.

Sundays were different from the rest of the week. After church, it was our priority to stay closer to home and each other. We nearly always enjoyed a nice dinner together, and often hosted friends, family, or the missionaries from our church serving in the area. Although Sundays were "a day of rest," they were not somber. The priority was on reconnecting as a family while still honoring the spirit of the Sabbath. In addition to Sunday services, family meals and time together (including wrestling with dad), we would also take opportunities to perform certain acts of service for others.

Mark was my buddy from the day he was born. I was four years older, so we were home together for a year before I started school. I always thought he was the cutest kid with his fine, blonde hair, huge smile, and enthusiasm about life and his chance to live it. It was easy to love him and his fearless desire for adventure and fun.

He was also very sweet and close to our mom, but honestly, he had a temper like no other child. When he got mad, a vein in his neck would pop out. I remember it had two bumps on it and we saw them regularly.

Sometimes mom really had her hands full with Mark. She used to read different children's books to Mark every night. One time he brought a library book home when he was no more than six years old. It was about a troll named Tumptin who lived under a bridge. Mom told Mark that Tumptin stayed in the culvert at the end of our driveway, and that he would not like it if boys and girls didn't mind their parents. Mark didn't like that. Mom never implied Tumptin would hurt him; however, just the mention of his name was enough to get Mark to mind. "You want me to call Tumptin? Alright....'*TUMP-tin!*'" With the dreaded Tumptin summoned, and supposedly on his way, mom suddenly had Mark's full attention, and she could get him to do whatever he was supposed to.

I can remember two times in particular when he came up missing as a very young boy. One time we found him asleep under mom and dad's bed, but the other time he was in the woods. He was probably about two or three years old. Our neighbor Randy helped us look for him and mom was hollering and panicking. He had no fear then, but later, when mom introduced him to Tumptin, it kept him closer to home and mom feels it was a true lifesaver, if not for Mark, then certainly for her.

When he was young, our brother David had intentions of becoming a mountain man when he grew up. He spent a lot of time in the woods, learning everything he could about our natural surroundings and how to survive away from home and civilization. Of his three younger brothers, Mark enjoyed a unique relationship with David. Mark loved going in the woods with him, and I'm sure the interest Mark showed in learning from David is a big part of what forged the bond they shared. It also may have contributed to Mark's eagerness to roam.

Forester Family 1984

We spent as much time outside as we could, and bikes were a big part of our lives, especially during the summer. We rode all the time: going to friends' houses, racing each other, trying tricks, jumping ramps—typical boy and kid stuff. I even helped Mark learn to ride without training wheels. I figured out if I pushed him but didn't tell him when I let go, he could go on his own. Soon after showing off for mom and dad, he got his own Murray bike from Wal-Mart for his fifth birthday.

When we weren't riding bikes, there was a good chance we were throwing knives in the red dirt bank, exploring the woods, or overturning rocks in the shallow stream behind our house looking for crawdads and snakes. We would often walk through that stream without shoes or a care in the world. At one spot, the banks are steep and high (maybe seven feet). To cross the stream we would skid down the bank, splash through the water, then scramble up the other side. One day, though, we had a better idea and cut some vines from the trees and used them to swing across the stream. It was a blast and we felt like Tarzan. Our neighbor Randy happened to see us doing this one day and wanted to give it a try. (He was a grown man, but a kid at heart.) We busted out laughing when the vine broke on him and he fell to the bottom of the stream. Fortunately, he wasn't hurt. He came up wet and laughing too.

One of these summer days when Mark was very young, a thunderstorm blew through our neighborhood. Mom called us all in from outside and we waited anxiously for it to pass, clustered together around the bed in her room. The lightning was close and a bolt struck the house right above us, putting a crack in the ceiling and knocking the pictures off the wall. The biggest frame, over mom and dad's bed, fell right on Mark's head. It didn't faze him. Despite being stunned at the loud boom, seeing that happen was funny, especially since it didn't bother him. He was hard-headed, both literally and figuratively.

Mark loved just about all animals. Throughout his childhood, he had parakeets, a gecko, hermit crabs, fish, and of course dogs. He caught animals all the time. He knew their names, characteristics and habits. Even as adults, I would ask him to identify certain animals and birds for me. He always knew what they were. (Not long before he left for basic training, he was explaining to me the difference between crows and buzzards while we drove somewhere.)

For Christmas of 1991, we got go-carts. Two of our neighbors already had them, and to make it even better, two other neighbors got go-carts that Christmas too. It was inevitable that the following months and years were full of dust and throwing objects at each other while riding. Our most common ammunitions were pinecones, rubber balls, water balloons and persimmons. We tore up a lot of grass for the next year or so. Mark had our neighbor, Randy, soup up his cart a little so his was faster than mine. Those were a lot of fun.

Mark was prone to breaking bones at an early age. When he was three, he broke his left arm and had a full arm cast. Terri still cries when she tells us how she remembers him calling her while she was in college and saying, "Sissy, it hu'ts" in that sweet way three year olds speak. (Terri and Mark were very close during his

First Time

first couple years of life, but being 15 years older, Terri was off to school, marriage and her own family as Mark grew up.) Unfortunately, there were

17

three more broken arms before he turned ten. By the last one, his response to it was a matter-of-fact, "I did it again."

Mark was also a typical little brother—he never hesitated to tell on us, whether it was to get us in trouble, or just because he wanted to tell someone he had a secret. Whenever I told him *not* to tell mom, dad or anyone else about something we had done, he would always tell. So I figured out to never say something was "secret." If I didn't point out that he should be quiet, then he would stay quiet.

I proved this to David and our uncle Stephen one summer day after swimming in their pond after our grandparents told us not to. David and Stephen were worried that Mark would tell on us. I told them in private not to say a word about keeping it secret and he wouldn't rat us out. Sure enough, no one ever found out (until now, of course).

We often took in stray dogs. After all, there were several kids on our street, we were always playing outside, and out in the country most dogs roam free. One dog in particular hung around for a couple days in the field across the road from our house. I remember him sitting over there watching us and our other dogs. He looked pretty and white. Finally he stepped across the road into our yard and actually got along with my dog, "Doggie." This was impressive because Doggie was kind of aggressive and liked to fight with other dogs.

Mark took him in and called him Bullet, because his back leg was hurt and it looked like he had been shot there. Mom doctored the wound and Bullet had no more trouble with it. That said, he eventually lived up to his name because years later he wandered off and got shot in the back. The vet said he was fine and left the bullet in him.

During the winter of 1993, Mark was 12, and we got more freezing weather than usual. Mark had been out with his friend, Jonathon, when he showed up at the back door, soaking wet. Bullet was dripping too and both were shivering uncontrollably. Mom was shocked, not knowing what to think, except maybe, "What now?!!"

It turned out that Mark and his friend were playing at our neighbor's pond, which was covered by a sheet of ice—thin ice. Jonathan started throwing sticks, some of them out on the pond. Mark told him to stop, knowing Bullet would follow his instinct and fetch them. Well, one more stick got tossed, Bullet chased it onto the pond and sure enough, the ice finally broke and Bullet went in. The dog struggled, but couldn't get out of the water. In an instant, Mark jumped in, clothes and all, to save him.

I didn't think much of it at the time, but from that day on, Mark and Bullet were more than buddies. Having shared selfless sacrifice and a life-threatening event, they had a bond like veterans. Mark was irrevocably Bullet's master and he became the best dog we ever had. He was very protective of Mark, mom, and the other kids around our house.

Not too long after this, our brother Joseph started dating Patsy Taylor and they married after a short engagement. I asked her to tell me some of what she remembers about Mark. Her perspective is fairly unique, coming into the family late and as an intimate outsider.

> I first met Mark when he was 13 years old. Joseph and I had just started dating. We were married a few months later and Mark was 14 by then. He and I were immediately buddies and we acted like siblings from the start.
>
> The Foresters had a long tradition of arm wrestling and I always would sit back and watch the boys to see who would come out the winner. I recall a time when Mark wanted to arm wrestle me in the beginning, and I actually won. I don't think he liked that, but took it well! Joseph had the "Arm Wrestling Championship Title" for a long time. But after Mark went through his training in the Air Force, Joseph followed Jerry Seinfeld's lead and "went out on top," declining to meet Mark's challenges. It was always a joke around the Foresters.
>
> Mark was raised in a very loving home. There is no doubt in my mind that is largely why he became the man he was. He clung to his values because they were instilled in him as a boy. When he was faced with decisions, he would choose the right because he had a very strong moral core. When faced with challenges, he would act, and was not acted upon. This was what separated Mark from others. He didn't care what others thought. He cared about what he thought and what God wanted him to do. He truly had a strong moral compass. One of the most steady that I've known.
>
> Mark went through an incredible metamorphosis in the time I knew him. It was amazing to see him grow up and change from a boy to a man. Not just a man, but an amazing man who I loved and respected.

As much as he loved being in the outdoors, it's no surprise Mark took to hunting from an early age. Dad used to take him deer hunting behind our home and in the woods behind our grandmother's house. When he got a little older, he went with Joseph and our Uncle William and Cousins Mike, Al and Jon. He went to Crooked Creek Hunting Club with them regularly. In light of the incredible warrior Mark became, it's ironic that back then— in his early teens—he caught a lot of good-natured teasing from the other guys because he was small, young, and couldn't hit a running deer worth a flip. Eventually, though, with tutoring from Uncle Will, Mark became a very good shot. At closer ranges, he virtually never missed his target.

One time when Mark and Joseph were hunting, they were standing near Joseph's Blazer on a dirt road listening to the dogs run when they saw something dart across the road that they were certain was a black panther. They both saw it and were too shocked to get their guns up in time. We know panthers have never been confirmed in Alabama, but to them, that's just what it looked like.

The last time Joseph and Mike hunted with Mark was the winter before he deployed. They went on some of Mike's land at Crooked Creek. Mark let Joseph hunt in his tree stand because he said it was the best place to see a big deer. (He didn't see anything, by the way.) That was just Mark—being generous and putting others ahead of himself. He went to an old tree stand that hadn't been used in a while. As he was perched there, it broke from under him, but he caught himself on a part of the stand that was still secure.

He had to climb 20 feet down, bear-hugging the tree trunk. The rough bark left his chest and stomach skinned up pretty good. When the stand broke, he naturally let go of his rifle to catch himself. Of course, it hit the ground muzzle-first, clogging it with dirt. Mike helped him clean it with a stick, then Mark went to another stand and sat until it was too dark to hunt anymore. As he started down from the 16 foot high stand, he fell again and hit the ground hard. Mike said it was a dangerous fall (obviously) and if Mark hadn't been in such good shape, it could have really done some damage. Joseph should have been in that stand, and said he probably would have broken something if he'd had that fall.

One game Mark and his friends in the neighborhood liked playing was "Fireball Run." Two people would stand opposite of each other on the ground at the sides of the trampoline. Then, they would throw whatever balls they could find at the person on the trampoline. Once the person got hit (or didn't catch a touched ball), he was off on the ground to throw at the next person up on the tramp.

Mark and his buddies would play this game for hours. When they finally got bored with it, they'd push the trampoline close to the house and jump from the roof. There were very few limits to the games they could play or invent as their days and nights wore on. Later, when Mark and I were roommates, (I was working and he was a student at the University of Alabama) we'd reminisce about our younger days and wonder how we ever survived, or at least avoided more broken bones..

From a very early age, Mark was a natural athlete. In our yard, he played all the tackle football he could, as well as plenty of basketball in our driveway, and wiffle ball with his brothers and his friends in the neighborhood. During his elementary school years, he played on numerous basketball and baseball teams. His biggest strength when he was little was his ability to run fast—he was a speedster. He was also a very good baseball pitcher, but didn't enjoy it. So, he normally played second base or short stop.

When Mark was in fourth grade, he went skiing with his friend Scott Hughes at Keystone in Colorado. I was jealous because he got to fly and I had never been on an airplane. After rolling down his first hill, he was skiing blacks by the end of the first day, and loved skiing "Last Hoot". He was determined to master that slope and felt he did before the trip was over. It's an example of how he turned his "Hammer Head[8]" to his favor. He was so determined to be the best he could be, he wouldn't quit until he satisfied himself that he'd done the absolute best he could.

Joseph, Patsy and I went skiing with him in 2007 and he was still hitting the blacks—after a 15 year break. The rest of us cramped his style in those days. Regardless, that was definitely one of the most fun times I've ever had. We skied and tubed and made a lot of noise doing it. I cannot believe we didn't break some bones after all the falling we did.

Dad often took us fishing at our grandmother's pond while growing up. This went right along with Mark's love for the outdoors. Mounted on my wall is his first big catch. It's a 6 lb. 10 oz. bass he caught May 29, 1996. Two years later, he caught a 10 lb. 4 oz. bass from another pond and after that one, the owner of the pond told him he couldn't come back.

---

[8]   Dad's nick-name for Mark because of his stubbornness.

We didn't know it at the time, but money was tight when we were little. Regardless, we never wanted. We had a swing set, rope swing, tire swing, and plenty to eat. When dad pushed us in the tire swing, we felt like we were higher than the house. Mark was the luckiest of us because he had three older brothers who were big enough to push him high, but never as high as dad could.

Mark grew up watching Teenage Mutant Ninja Turtles (TMNT), Fraggle Rock, He-Man, GI-Joe, Thundercats, and Smurfs. He watched the first two TMNT movies *many* times. I was surprised to see Fraggle Rock on TV recently. I only ever watched it when he did. So of course, even as a grown man, I had to watch it a little because it reminded me of my little brother.

His favorite (and mine), though, was certainly the Smurfs. For several Halloweens he dressed as one. We have a picture of little Mark in front of his Smurf birthday cake when he turned two. His blonde hair, twinkling eyes and heart-melting smile make the picture glow. He really loved Smurfs

Mark with a Smurf cake on his 2nd birthday.

and many times, we took friends in the woods to find their village. We often visualized it near an old mattress we'd seen. We knew it wasn't really true, but still convinced ourselves it was possible. Plus, our oldest brother, David, told us it was true and we believed anything he said.

When you see this picture of his blonde hair, and hear stories of his love of his hair as an adult, it's not too surprising that he went crazy during his first haircut as a kid. I remember being there with him and he started screaming his head off when those clippers touched his head. Fortunately the barber had his own office and shut the door to prevent everyone else from having to endure his screams. And yes, that vein was popping out in his neck. Even 2 1/2 years after Mark's death, one of his teammates at Cobra told me, "He had glorious hair and he loved talking about it."

Growing up we all liked and watched many of the same movies; Rocky, Rambo, Conan the Destroyer, True Lies, Police Academy, Red Sonja, Pee Wee's Big Adventure (for some weird reason), and many others. Mom also watched a lot of these with us, over and over. Rated 'R' movies were not allowed, except that we could watch some of the movies with Arnold Schwarzenegger and Sylvester Stallone. We must have gotten away with it because mom and Terri liked these actors too.

"Embrace integrity as you would someone you love."
– Ray Forester

CHAPTER 3

The Unwelcome Homecoming

Two terms are used to describe the somber flights that return our fallen service members to their families. The Pentagon calls the first step *Dignified Transfer,* where the fallen is brought back to American soil. *Dignified Arrival* is the trip that returns the fallen to his or her family. But most often, the flights are called *Angel Flights* by those who participate in the solemn process.

Mark's last trip home took him from Shah Mashad Village to Tarin Kowt Air Base, then to the base at Kandahar, off to Ramstein Air Base in Germany, and finally across the Atlantic to Dover AFB in Delaware. The Air Force offered to cover the costs to have three members of our family on hand to meet the C-17 when it landed stateside.

The night of Mark's death, Barry and Sascha went straight to work organizing our flight to Dover for Mark's arrival the next day. At the same time, a family friend, Bo Knight, was working on his own plans. He arranged to have mom, dad and me fly from the Haleyville airport (only a few miles from our home) to Dover on a friend's private plane. This was a life-saver because we didn't have to endure the usual inconveniences of commercial flight. This also allowed Joseph to take advantage of the Air Force's offer. He flew from San Antonio and met us at Dover.

It was raining heavily when we arrived, adding to the dreary and somber spirit that hung over the entire scene and everyone there. Quickly, we connected with Joseph and then met up with Chris Shultz of USAF

Mortuary Affairs to discuss arrangements for Mark's body, media at the transfer, pick out his casket, and several other details.

We got to Dover well before the Angel Flight arrived. It was a long, surreal wait. Almost immediately after our arrival, Joseph leaned in and said to me, "This rain won't last. It'll break before he gets here." It just seemed right; I accepted it and watched for the break to come. It never did. We joked about that later.

Even after the plane landed, we still had a long wait. Before long though, Mark's best friend, Bobby Bonello, found us. He'd been on the flight and had deplaned to meet up with us ahead of the ceremony. Seeing Bobby was comforting because we knew him. He'd been in our home, he was Mark's friend and roommate, and we knew he cared deeply for Mark. He looked worn, sad, exhausted and shocked.[9] One of the first things mom said to Bobby was, "Mark was supposed to be invincible." Later, Bobby's thought was, "He is now."

We specifically asked Bobby if he saw Mark's wounds and he said he had. When we asked for more details, he looked at Col. Armfield for permission. The Colonel nodded for him to proceed. Bobby told us Mark had a wound on his left forearm and hole in his upper left chest. This seemed to confirm Mark had his rifle raised and was moving forward to confront the enemy. Here is what Bobby had to share:

I was in Eastern Afghanistan at my forward operating base (FOB). We were doing a base training exercise because our base got hit a week prior so we wanted to be better prepared. As the exercise started, my job was to hop on one of the HMWV's (a gun truck), but I actually messed this up and went inside to the operations center (OPCEN) where we have the secure computers, phones and radios.

> (As related in Chapter 1, Bobby stepped inside the OPCEN where he heard the TIC report.) After about 30 seconds of hearing the radio traffic, I noticed it was Mark's team because I recognized their call sign. Shortly after that, I heard the call come over

---

[9]   On a side note, Bobby met Will Lyle's replacement when the Angel Flight stopped in Germany. Will was one of Mark's SF teammates (Captain) and he lost his legs to an IED not long before the battle at Shah Mashad. I can only imagine how this captain felt, in-bound to replace a severely wounded officer and seeing two of that officer's former teammates heading home dead. Bobby said the captain was clearly concerned.

the radio reporting the JTAC and the Medic were KIA. Of course, at first I was in denial because this could have been a mistake. I then got on the secure phone and called the STOC (Special Tactics Operation Center) at Bagram. Amy Osborne answered the phone. I could tell

Bobby with Mark at Kandahar

that she had been crying. I remember saying, "Tell me it's not Mark…" and her response was kind of a lost, "Tell me what I can do." She couldn't contain her emotions.

I was overwhelmed with anger and threw the phone down. My other teammates in the room knew what was going on. I left the room in disbelief. About 10 minutes later, after I'd collected myself a little, I went back in the OPCEN and called Amy again. She picked up and again asked, "What can I do?" I told her to get me a flight out of my FOB.

As I left the OPCEN, I noticed that a few of the guys on my team had tears in their eyes. They didn't even know Mark, but they could see in my actions just how much I cared for Mark and it was enough to choke them up. I left the OPCEN and went to my room to pack my stuff. My team leader came to my room and said I had a flight that night.

When the time came to leave the weather was very bad. The Helicopters shouldn't have been flying, but ignoring this, a MEDEVAC helo came to pick me up anyway, because they knew the circumstances. From my FOB the flight took me to an airfield somewhere I didn't recognize to catch a fixed wing plane to Kandahar. I just barely made it in time.

I showed up and immediately asked to see Mark. They uncovered his body, and I could see that it was indeed Mark. A sensation hit me that is impossible to describe. Except for the wounds to his arm and chest, he looked just like the Mark I knew, even though I hadn't seen him in 5 months. I could clearly see the wound on the side of his left chest. I knew that the round must have come at him at an angle and just missed his armor and hit his heart. I stood there for about five minutes with my thoughts and emotions, then left. The Mortuary Affairs team then got him ready to transport and off we went on this huge C-17 with only three American bodies and the three of us escorts.

It's hard to remember all the details now, but I recall only seeing one other family waiting there that evening. (Bobby remembers only three fallen warriors on the flight, a Marine, Cal, and Mark.) We acknowledged each other (which must have been the Marine's family), but never spoke. I guess we all preferred to keep our grief to ourselves, or maybe we just didn't have the strength to talk with strangers about a tragedy that was still too fresh to comprehend. Unfortunately, Calvin Harrison's family couldn't be there. At the time, we didn't know of his connection to Mark, but I wish we had. We would have paid him and his escort extra attention.

Mark's body carefully taken from the plane at Dover. The rain never let up.

When it was time to go on the tarmac for the ceremony, I specifically remember the man in charge telling the families in what order the bodies would be taken off the plane. He sounded the first and last name for

Cal and the Marine, then looked at us saying, "And Mark will be last." Somehow, this small thing stood out.

After the short ceremony, we were rushed back to the Mortuary Affairs building, and then were put on our plane back to Haleyville. During the time we watched the transfer cases being removed from the plane, our friends Bo and Sylvia Knight were back at the office talking to members of the Air Force who had come that night to meet the families. One man in particular was Maj. Gen. Edward Bolton, Jr. from the Pentagon. He told Bo that was the first time he had come to Dover to be with families meeting their fallen loved ones. We don't know why this flight was an exception for him.

We arrived back in Haleyville late that night and found members of our family, including Rozlynn, still at the house up and waiting on us. They had been answering phone calls from all over and accepting food, gifts and expressions of sympathy.

We were very appreciative of Mike Bailey who piloted the plane for us that day. He said the guys at Dover had never seen a private jet land there, so they were confused when preparing him for landing, refueling and taking off. Someone higher up in the Air Force must have pulled some strings to make that happen.

That Saturday, many of our family and friends gathered at the house to watch the Alabama/Florida game. We hooked up a big TV on the carport and had a good time. We were told the pre-game flyover would be dedicated to Mark, though I don't think they announced it at the stadium. We did hear Eli Gold, radio voice for Crimson Tide football, recognize Mark and his sacrifice during the pre-game. I remember seeing tears in dad's eyes when he heard this on the radio. Fortunately, Alabama won because I didn't need any more disappointment at this time.

Earlier that day, I contacted the Patriot Guard Riders (PRG)[10] and asked them to watch over Mark's services. (They will not show up without an invitation from the family.) We also got word that day that Mark would be arriving in Haleyville on Tuesday, 5 October 2010. Since our brother Joseph is a doctor in the AF, he was able to fly back to Dover and escort

---

[10] From the Patriot Guard Riders' mission statement: *The Patriot Guard Riders is a diverse amalgamation of riders from across the nation. We have one thing in common besides motorcycles, [it is] an unwavering respect for those who risk their very lives for America's freedom and security.* (http://www.patriotguard.org)

Mark on his last leg home. Joseph said this was a peaceful, special time with Mark during that last leg of the Angel Flight.

It was a special ceremony on that cold morning. We arrived at the Haleyville Airport (Posey Field) and discovered a number of somber supporters outside. Some of the Patriot Guard Riders were on hand too. There were even two or three people on their golf carts watching from the nearby golf course. Before landing, Joseph asked the pilot to do a fly-by over the airport and city. He also flew over the school.

Upon landing, the jet taxied in and came to a stop near the assembled party. When everything with the plane was ready, with deliberate, emotional dignity, members of the 21 STS (Mark's unit) carried his flag-draped casket from the plane and out to the waiting hearse. Once loaded, the PGR lead the way from Posey Field, followed by the hearse which was closely shadowed in solemn procession by police, family, and a number of close friends, all headed to Pinkard Funeral Home.

All along the way, the streets were lined with people holding flags, signs, and hands over hearts. The supporters were everywhere: in front of the hospital, outside Wal-Mart, Burger King, etc. We were touched at the respect the people in our great town showed to Mark.

At the funeral home we had our first chance to look at Mark's body. Tim Pinkard asked my brothers and me back first, he wanted to make sure everything looked okay before our parents and Terri saw him. The scene is a little vague in my mind. What I remember clearly was not being impressed about the way his hair was parted—it just wasn't his look. Also, even though I knew that was my brother, it just wasn't really *him*. And not only was the essence not there, but physically, he didn't look the same. I understand this is normal, muscles relax and color fades. In any case, it really confuses the mind on some deep level.

Despite our misgivings, we didn't have it in us to make a fuss; we said he was okay and called for mom and dad. They came to the back and we spent some time together as a family, along with a few of Mark's friends in the squadron. Mom was not happy about his hair, so Mark's teammate, Ish Villegas, put his own red beret on Mark in the casket. It was an improvement and made us feel better. On the downside, though, to this day, Terri does not like seeing pictures of Mark in his red beret because all she can think of is him wearing one in the casket.

One of the 21 STS members there was Chief Calvin Markham. He was one of the men who bore the news to mom and dad. Terri loved him from the start because of his unique bearing. His very presence inspired massive respect, yet he demonstrated extraordinary tenderness.

During those quiet, reverent moments, Chief Markham told us he often admonished other members of the squadron to "Be like Mark" because he was such a vivid example of what a Combat Controller should be and how each should perform. Chief was saying this long before Mark was killed, so it was not just some bit of rose-colored eulogizing. Dad loved it and through his grief, he visibly swelled with pride. Later, we had bracelets made with that phrase imprinted on them to remind and encourage us and others to follow the Chief's advice.

Two of the gel bracelets with Chief's encouraging advice

"Believe it will happen and it will."
– Ray Forester

CHAPTER 4

Mark the Miracle Baby, "Mom's Story"

As this book has progressed, our mom took time to write down her reflections on Mark and the family our parents brought him home to. I know she did it while struggling with a mix of strong emotions. Others who have read the early drafts of this book tell me they can sense the deep joy and devotion she feels toward her family. There is also a glimpse of the loss that is unique to a Gold Star Mother.

The first gift Ray bought for me after we were married was a *Better Homes & Gardens* Baby Book. We had been married for about two and half months when Ray had to go on a two-week business trip to Atlanta for an IBM school. When he got home, he said he had something for me. Reaching into his suitcase, he handed that book to me. I looked at him and asked, "Is this a hint?" He said, "I'm ready for a baby whenever you are." That's all it took because all I had ever wanted was to be married, be a homemaker, and have lots of babies.

Ray and I decided to get married after dating a little over two months. I was 18 and he was 24. Ray sold his horse, horse trailer and boat to get enough for a down payment on having us a 12' x 60' mobile home built. It only took two weeks and it was in place waiting on us. As soon as it was ready, we went to the courthouse in Jasper, AL and got married on December 17,

1964. I thought that mobile home was the most beautiful thing in this world. I loved it with all my heart and to this very day, I can't think about it without getting teary eyed. It was there that Ray and I began our family. In fact, we lived there eight years and had three children.

As much as I loved it, though, we had outgrown it. Ray bought a second house, except I didn't want to leave our mobile home, even though we were getting cramped in it, and the new house had a dishwasher. Finally, one day while Ray was at work, I called and told him not to come to the mobile home; I had gotten a couple of men to move us to the new house up town. Ray still talks about how happy he was that he didn't have to do anything to move us. I have to admit, we couldn't bear to sell the mobile home so we rented it out for over 20 years before we finally decided to let it go.

Since we had only dated a little over two months before getting married, there was so much we didn't know about each other. We had never even talked about having children or how many we wanted. I was brought up in The Church of Jesus Christ of Latter-day Saints (Mormon). My mother and daddy had divorced when I was about 10 years old, and from that experience I knew what it was like not having the mother in the home. I learned the value of a strong family and it has always been the most important thing to me. More than anything, I wanted to have children, stay at home with them, and see after their every need. Ray felt the same way and nothing has brought me more happiness than being a wife and mother.

Pregnancy was not an easy thing for me though. About six months after Ray bought me the baby book, I became pregnant, but we were terribly disappointed when I miscarried just a few weeks later. Then, I got pregnant again and I was horribly sick almost the entire pregnancy. I could hardly keep anything down and mostly survived on glucose for the first five months. My stomach finally settled down about a month before the baby was born, June 1966. We had a beautiful little girl. I named her Terri and Ray named her Suzanne, after the movie star Suzanne Pleshette. I was grateful to have an easy delivery after such a long, hard pregnancy. The doctor told me I was made for having children and that I should have a dozen. That suited me just fine, but it wasn't meant to be.

From the very start, I could hardly bring myself to put Terri down. When I did let her nap in her bed, I checked on her constantly, and if she slept too long I would go lay down in the baby bed with her just to be next to her. I don't know how that same baby bed made it through all my children but it did. Maybe it's because the bed didn't really get that much use, I needed to keep my babies close to me, so they most often slept with us.

When Terri was about three years old, I miscarried again. This was very upsetting, I couldn't understand why I miscarried since the doctor told me I was built for having children. Then, a year later we had our first son, David Raymond, born July 1970. But this wasn't the easy delivery like my first; I had to have an emergency caesarian because the placenta was coming first. It was a rough few days, and I hated not being able to get up and take care of myself right away.

When I got home, all I wanted to do was hold the baby, but David had a big sister who also wanted to hold him. She was a little loving mother from then on. Even though she was just four, taking care of children was completely natural to her. She was so much help to me in caring for my babies. It is no surprise that she has a large family of six sweet children of her own.

David was such a quiet and easy child but he didn't want to be rocked or to sleep with us. It killed me not holding and cuddling him, but he preferred to be put in his baby bed where he would go right to sleep. As he grew to be a toddler, he always wanted things in his room kept in their place. If he left his room for a while, before rentering, he'd stand in the doorway and take a survey to make sure everything was just as it was supposed to be. He wouldn't even tolerate a piece of lint on his carpet. He is still the same today as a father of four. He prefers everything neat, but accepts the realities of living with children.

Three years later, we had our second son, Joseph Patrick, born July 1973. Talk about having an easy baby. He was the best little baby any mother could ask for. He never cried. He was always so pleasant. I could rock him and love on him; and he always smiled. He hardly ever got mad. As he grew, he always had a plan and he used his ingenuity as a child to make money to get the things he wanted. He was friendly and a hard worker, and he's still that way as a husband and father of five children.

In four years, we were blessed with another son, Thad Jarrett, born January 1977. Ray named him after an Alabama football player. Alabama was playing in a Bowl Game when they introduced a football player named Thad. It may seem strange to some, but Ray said, "Look what a clean cut boy that is, let's name the baby Thad if it's a boy." Ray doesn't remember anything about how he played; just that he was a clean cut boy.

When Thad was born, Terri was 11 years old and she treated Thad almost like her own. However, Thad wasn't an easy baby to take care of. He had colic for eight months and cried a lot. I tried everything I could think of, I even quit nursing and put him on soymilk, but it didn't help. Finally, he seemed to outgrow it when he was about eight months old. He quit crying and from then on he had a wide smile for everyone. Thad was the friendliest and the cutest little fellow. He loved to get dressed up, especially in a little suit for church. And yes, he is still the same today. (Thad and his wife just had their first child, Jackson Mark Forester, born February 4, 2013.)

Thad was two when I found out I was pregnant again. Unfortunately, about five weeks along I miscarried again. I was discouraged by this time and didn't know if I wanted to try for more children. I hated being so helpless and sick during pregnancy, followed by recovery from a caesarian section. So, I put the thought of another baby out of my mind for a while.

For Ray and me, the deciding factor about whether we would have another child was the feeling I'd get that someone was missing. It happened with little things like getting ready to go somewhere and I'd keep looking around to make sure I had everyone. Or, when I went to the store and found myself searching around like someone was missing. That feeling started again after about a year and I talked to Ray about it. He said whatever I wanted to do was alright with him. He said, "But, you know how hard pregnancy is on you, so only you can decide to go through it again."

I don't think spiritual experiences should be talked about with just anyone. They are for our personal benefit, so telling this is very uncomfortable for me, but it is the biggest part of Mark's story. I wanted another baby but I didn't want to go through another pregnancy. I was thirty-four and felt like I was at the end of the best years for having children. I had prayed fervently for about two months to know what the Lord would have me do. It was after one of these prayers in my closet one day when I had a very spiritual experience.

As I was praying this particular day, I saw, in my mind, myself holding a baby. It reminded me of pictures you see of Mary holding baby Jesus and I saw the love on her face for her precious little child. I knew it was the answer to my prayer—I was to have another baby. Without this experience, I probably wouldn't have had my precious Mark. However, he was meant to be born and I was meant to be his momma. Despite this, I fought against it for a while. I just wasn't ready to be pregnant again. I finally told Ray that I knew we should have another baby and he was all for it.

Anyone who is familiar with football in the South and the local rivalries between teams knows what a big deal is made about some of these games. That's the way it is with the rivalry between Haleyville High School and Hamilton High School football. Our family lives in Haleyville, but at the time we had to travel to Hamilton to attend church. I taught a weekly scripture study class for students in the ninth through twelfth grades. Over the course of four years, each school day, we studied all the scriptures. About half of the students were from Haleyville, and the other half were from Hamilton. The students had planned a big party at my house after the ballgame on a Friday night.

They decided that whichever team lost, the ones from the winning school would get to put cream pies in the losers' faces. Haleyville lost—again! The party started and we were having a big time. The Hamilton kids were really bragging about another win and then the pie throwing started. I thought it was only supposed to be between the students, but one of the boys from Hamilton started after me with a pie, so I started running from him. I ran around the outside of the house and then ran inside.

Ray was there. He stopped me and asked if I thought I should be running like that. He reminded me that I might be pregnant and that I needed to be very careful. With my miscarriage history, I knew that my most dangerous time was during the first few weeks. I told Ray that I would be fine and not to worry. He wasn't at all happy. When I went back outside I couldn't avoid finally getting a pie in my face but I was a good sport about it.

Later, at about 2:00 a.m. that night, I woke up in a pool of blood. I had never seen so much blood and I knew it had to be a miscarriage, even though I didn't know that I was pregnant. I was horrified because I kept thinking of what Ray had said and I was searching my heart and mind, telling myself that I must not have really wanted to be pregnant so I had been careless. I knew from my miscarriage history that if I ever saw a spot of blood, that I would miscarry. And this was blood that almost covered my side of the bed. I was depressed and full of sorrow. I had received an answer to my prayers and I knew I was supposed to have another child, yet, I really didn't want to go through it. I prayed to be forgiven and that the Lord would bless me even though I thought it was too late.

The next morning, Ray took a urine specimen to the hospital to be tested to see if I was pregnant. I called my doctor, the same one I'd had for all my pregnancies, and he told me that knowing my history, he didn't think there was any way in this world that I could have a viable pregnancy at this point. The test came back positive with a question mark. The doctor called and told me to stay in bed, even though he really didn't think I would keep the baby. I shed many, many tears and prayed so hard to keep the baby. The next morning, Ray took another specimen to the hospital and again it came back positive with a question mark.

After three specimens, the doctor told me that I was definitely pregnant even though he didn't think it would be a successful pregnancy and certainly didn't know how it could be after so much blood loss. But, I knew how it was possible. This baby was meant to come to Earth. It was a special and determined little spirit who was fighting to take its place here and in our home. I was to be its mother.

I stayed on bed rest for the next few days, hoping and praying. It was truly a miracle that the bleeding stopped. I was soon released from bed rest and everything progressed pretty much as it had with my earlier babies. I was sick a lot, but I had some good help from Terri and the boys.

After three boys in a row, I just knew I would have a little girl this time. I had everything decorated in pink. Terri wanted a sister so badly, even though she was almost 15 years old. Two weeks before the baby was due, I had an ultra-sound to see if everything was all right. I had never had an ultra sound before and it showed I was having a little boy. I was disappointed but I knew Terri would be more disappointed. When she found out she was having another brother, I told her that I would let her name him. She thought about it for a few days and then decided on naming him Mark. I asked her why she wanted that name and she said she just liked the sound of it. I didn't care for it much but I made a deal with her so it was set. On May 15, 1981, Mark Andrew Forester was born into this world.

Having another caesarian, I wasn't able to do much for myself, so when they brought Mark to me, I asked Terri to take care of him for me. In fact, while I was still in the hospital, Ray snuck her in to help me with Mark there.[11] She loved every minute of it and from then on, she treated Mark like he was her baby too. Terri would take care of him every afternoon while I was cooking supper and she would ride him around in the car until he went to sleep. Mark slept with Ray and me, but after he nursed, Terri would come get him and take him in the bed with her. He had the biggest, bluest eyes and the blondest hair. When he wanted to nurse again she would bring him back to me. I guess the Lord knew that I needed a girl first to help me with my boys. I only got Mark to myself when Terri went off to college; I guess having another brother wasn't so bad for her after all.

Some of the meanings of the name "Mark" are "warlike" or "smashing hammer." As Mark became a toddler, his daddy

---

[11] This played out exactly the same again on Feb 4, 2013 when my son was born by emergency C-section. Terri happened to be in town, she stayed and took great care of Roz and baby Jack. She was a life-saver.

gave him the nickname, "Hammerhead." Mark was a stubborn, hardheaded little fellow. He was a cutie, but he loved to get into things. His brothers, David (10) and Joseph (8), didn't play with him a lot when he was little because of the age difference. Thad was four years old when Mark was born, so he and Mark were buddies.

Mark thought he was as big as all his brothers and any other boy over at our house playing. The boys didn't take it easy on him but Mark would never let them get the best of him. That's where his hardhead prepared him for life. He wouldn't give up. If he believed in something, it was as good as done. I always told Ray that if Mark did anything wrong it would be because he wanted to and not because anyone talked him into it. Mark wasn't led around by anyone else.

Each brother had a special part of preparing him for life. David was such an outdoorsman, he loved to go out in the woods and be in nature. He had his special places in the woods behind our house where he would go camp out by himself when he was 12 years old. These places were his secret and Mark was the only one of his brothers he would take. He showed Mark how to start a fire without matches, set traps, and build tree houses. Mark loved the outdoors so much that several times he took himself on hikes into the woods when he was still very young. He scared me to death too many times as we would all have to go out looking for him.

Joseph is the brother that taught Mark the love of hunting and fishing. Mark had a nearly photographic memory, so if he ever read or saw anything, he didn't forget it. He knew a lot about many things and soaked up all the information he could. We all asked his opinions about things and Mark always had one, which was usually right. He and Joseph especially loved to talk about guns, knives, fishing tackle, etc. Joseph, Thad and even Ray usually picked Mark's brain before buying a car or a gun or anything because Mark nearly always knew all the particulars.

Joseph was the arm wrestling champion in our family and Mark always wanted to arm wrestle with him. Joseph showed no mercy and I was afraid he would hurt him. However, Mark refused to quit even though Joseph always put him down. By the time Mark was serious competition, Joseph "retired" at the top so he could hold his title as champion.

Thad and Mark, Mark and Thad. I've said that combination of names so many times, it is still hard to separate them. We have countless pictures of those two boys. What buddies they were and continued to be throughout adolescence and into adulthood. Thad wasn't a hunter, fisher or outdoorsman, but he loved to have friends over, boys and girls, and Mark was right there with them. The girls always took good care of Mark and made him feel special. I think Thad would have taken off someone's head if they had ever been mean to Mark.

Mark had a special ability that very few people have. He wasn't a judgmental person but, if he thought you were doing something that wasn't right, he could tell you without making you mad at him. He could say what was on his mind and you would not just respect him, but you wouldn't want to let him down.

Our children worked after school and during the summers to earn their own gas and spending money. We taught them to pay tithing on their gross wages. Mark had a big truck and it used a lot of gas, but he never asked us for money. He always worked and saved his money so he could buy his hunting and fishing gear. How he was able to save as much money as he did was one of the fascinating things about Mark; such a good saver, but he never did without the things he really wanted. Even more, he was the most unselfish person you could meet. He was quick to share, and if he knew one of his brothers or sisters or nieces or nephews needed something, he would get it for them or give me the money to get it.

I think the Lord blessed Mark with this ability to save money because of his charity toward others and his love of the Lord. Instead of paying a 10% tithing on his gross earnings, Mark would pay more. Before leaving for Afghanistan, he gave his checkbook to Ray and told him to pay his tithing for him while he was gone. Mark told him how much to pay and to keep check on his bank statement every month. Ray could see by Mark's bank statement that Mark had been paying over the 10% tithing on his gross earnings and mentioned it to Mark. He said he knew and to keep paying that amount. He said he didn't need it and it was the Lord's money anyway. As it turned out, he really didn't need the money. We can't take material things with us when we die. We only take our faith, character, the knowledge we've gained, and our love for others when we leave this life. Mark had all his priorities in order and never for one minute was afraid to die.

I've always said that I feel like I had lived a fairy tale life. I've had everything that ever meant anything to me. The most important of any of this is my family. I've had the most wonderful husband and children. It's hard to comprehend just how much love one heart can hold. I've thought my heart would burst open with so much love at times. I have a firm testimony of my faith and the teachings of my church. I know without a doubt that families are meant to be together forever. However, I haven't escaped my trials and sorrows. Losing Mark is the hardest thing on this earth I've had to go through.

If you have ever read stories of people's near-death experiences, I've noticed they all have one thing in common; the inability to explain with words we use in our language the things they saw and felt when their spirit left their body. That's what it's like now for me. How can I find words to explain my broken heart, my sadness, my emptiness, my longing to hear Mark say "momma" and see his handsome face with that captivating smile of his. I don't have words for my sorrow as I try to add this to a book about my baby boy who gave his life for his country and his fellow brothers in arms. It's impossible, so I'm not going to try.

My purpose is to let it be known to the world that despite great odds against him, Mark was meant to be born. He had a purpose to fulfill. He was truly a miracle! I am honored to be his momma. I didn't know he would be here for such a short time but we will be together forever someday. I loved him so much and he knows that I love him and I know he loves me. I would have done anything possible for him and he knew that too. We had a very special bond between a mother and her baby boy that death cannot break. Mark came to this earth and gained his earthly body. He honored himself and his family and country and never faltered in his faith. He fulfilled his life with greatness and returned to our Heavenly Father with HONOR. Now, if I can only do the same.

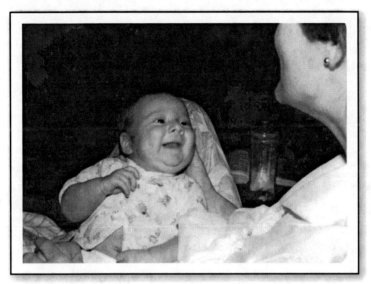

What mother looks at her baby and says, "My baby boy will be killed fighting a war in a foreign land."?

"Most people are about as happy as they make up their minds to be."
– Ray Forester

CHAPTER 5

Honors

Our parent's home (and all of Haleyville, it seemed) was in a great commotion, like a disturbed bee's nest. Countless folks called and visited expressing their sympathies. In the middle of the raw emotion, bewildering disbelief and frenzied activity, we had to plan Mark's funeral.

Not really thinking about it, we expected to hold the services at Pinkard Funeral Home. However, the owner, Tim Pinkard, knew his place would be inadequate if we opted for a public service. Before mentioning it to us, Tim took the initiative to huddle with the mayor and Haleyville High School's principal, Roger Satcher, to see if the gym could be used. It is the only place in town that could hold all the expected mourners.

Planning any funeral is complicated, I'm sure. Even though we knew losing Mark was *possible*, almost nothing was done to prepare. Looking back on it all, only Mark gave any real thought or preparation to the possibility. The day after returning from Dover, we went to Winston Memorial Cemetery to get Mark's burial plot. We found a nice open row, so we purchased five plots – Mark's, mom's, dad's, then mine (next to Mark) and Rozlynn's. There was so much involved, plus we had the added ceremonies of full military honors. Thankfully, Barry and Sascha handled most of it from the military side. The funeral was scheduled for Thursday, October 7, 2010 at 2 p.m. This meant students at the high school had to be let out of school early.

Some teachers asked our family if we would talk to the high school student body on Wednesday so the kids understood why their day would be cut short. Joseph and I agreed and we threw together a slide show and some notes. We also asked some of Mark's teammates from the 21 STS to attend with us, and invited Chief Calvin Markham to speak as well. Like so many of Mark's teammates we've met, he naturally and quietly commands deep respect. No need for him to demand it or make a show, people instinctively know he is different in important ways. When he stood to speak, dressed in his ABUs (Airman Battle Uniform), he had the full attention of everyone in the assembly.

It was a beautiful, early fall day and just a little cool. The breeze was light and the blue skies above were dotted with an occasional white cloud. As we arrived for the presentation, the entire elementary school—students and staff—lined both sides of the street holding flags. (This alone probably accounts for the complete lack of flags in any of the local stores.) We were at least 10 minutes behind schedule, so they had been out there for a while. Despite this, they could not have been more respectful and proper. Their show of support and sympathy was very touching. I don't remember the looks on the kids' faces so much, but I know some waved.

The teachers and staff were different. I clearly remember the pained and sad looks on their faces. Many had either taught Mark and my siblings, or they grew up with us.

In the assembly, we wanted everyone to know that Mark had walked the same halls and sat through the same classes they did. We wanted them to know that he was not much different than themselves, and that if he could accomplish his goals, the only thing holding them back was their own commitment. We hoped his example would inspire them to stay true to their standards. Looking back, I don't know how Joseph and I had the time or mental focus to put this together, but we did it quickly.

After our presentations, the assembly concluded and the students filed out with a quiet murmur. A few lingered, however, talking quietly and watching the Airmen. They froze in place when next, the members of Mark's squadron fell-in, forming a perfect line while the ranking member called out the steps for a ritual that is, as far as I can tell, unique to the Combat Control community: Memorial Pushups.

I wanted to understand their significance, but no one could tell me very much. "It's just what we do," is what I heard most. Finally, Ish Villegas suggested I contact Wayne Norrad. He joined the Air Force in 1966, and still serves the USAF as a civilian employee at Hurlburt Field. He clearly remembers the first time he did Memorial Pushups, though it's not what they called it.

Technical Sergeant David A. Atkinson had been an active-duty CCT who had transitioned to reserve status, attached to 123rd Tactical Airlift Wing Combat Control Team of the Kentucky Air National Guard. On the evening of 22 July 1991 he was participating in a "high-opening" jump (from about 12,500 feet) training exercise at Hurlburt Field near Fort Walton Beach, Florida.

His parachute failed to deploy properly and he impacted the ground at high speed. At first, all his team and instructors knew was that he was missing. Wayne Norrad and others set out in the dark to locate TSgt Atkinson. After locating his body, investigators were called in to gather evidence. When they completed their work, another team respectfully lifted David from the field and left the scene.

Wayne and several others stood there in a numb and awkward silence. Finally, wanting to both break the tension and do something in honor of TSgt Atkinson, he called out the command for the men to line up for pushups in honor of their fallen comrade. They repeated this in their dress blues at David's memorial service, and it seems the ritual took root.

We don't know if this is *the first* occurrence of Memorial Pushups, but at minimum, it was a spontaneous response to tragic loss in the CCT community. And if it was not the original event, it at least contributed significantly to establishing this rite as an enduring part of the Combat Controller's lives. I have participated in them several times since Mark died, and will never miss an opportunity as long as I can physically do them.

That evening we arrived at the funeral home to spend more time in the parlor as a family with Mark. Before we split up to go in the chapel for the viewing, our family gathered around to say a prayer. Before we did, dad asked our paw-paw (mom's dad) if he wanted to say anything since he was the patriarch of the family. In his old, somewhat weak voice he said, "Well, the Lord giveth, and the Lord taketh away." (Job 1:21). What I took away from it was Mark left earth when it was his time and God was fully involved. He may not have caused Mark to be killed, but He was aware of him and allowed events to take their course according to Mark's appointed time.

Hundreds and hundreds attended the viewing. We were given strength from above to stand there for hours greeting and hugging people. Mom and dad, especially, were given strength—they stood right by the casket and I don't think they shed a tear during those grueling but uplifting hours. I specifically remember looking at mom as she spoke with one visitor after another and being amazed she was even standing, especially for so long. They were strong and inspiring.[12]

Later, we learned the city had planned their support carefully. Everyone knew their roles and executed them perfectly. Parking at Pinkard's is limited, so police and volunteers directed cars to alternate sites, including behind McDonald's, at the old elementary school, and other places. They also had a van to shuttle people to the viewing and back to their cars. I was repeatedly told later on how well organized it was.

The fire and police departments not only controlled traffic, parking and the crowds, but they were also on alert for any protestors or disturbances. They stood all around the outside of the funeral home. And not just city employees, but the PGR were there too. They stayed until the very last family member left, which was me at about 10:30 pm.

Our mayor, Ken Sunseri, is a retired U.S. Army Colonel and no one was more committed to preventing a disruption than he was. He said that by law, any protesters had to be given a permit, but he could decide *where* that would be—and it wouldn't be anywhere near the memorial events. Later my wife and I met with Dave and Cheryl Haines, who were in charge of Mark's services for the PGR and they told us they were very well received in Haleyville and to this day they love riding their bikes to Haleyville just to visit. When they do, they stop by the fire station and have coffee with the men there.

As I said in Chapter 2, Haleyville epitomizes all the best of small-town, red-white-and blue America. I can think of no other time where these values were more powerfully displayed than during the repeated shows of support for Mark, our family, and all those in the service.

---

[12] Recalling these days, mom later said that she had to be strong, for dad, Mark and the family. Her time to feel the full force of her grieving, broken heart would come later.

"Why should I let him decide how I'm going to act?"
– Ray Forester

CHAPTER 6

At the Edge of Manhood

Of everything Mark experienced growing up, I am certain our home life had the greatest effect. He enjoyed a carefree childhood that too few kids experience today. We had dinner together as a family most every night. Our stay-at-home, full-time mom was there when we got off the school bus, and all through every holiday and summer break. She was there, setting a good example for how we should behave, and making *sure* we were following her example.

As Mark got older, our play together more and more revolved around sports; basketball on the driveway and football anywhere that was open enough to throw and run. I remember when I couldn't tackle Joseph because he was so much bigger than I was. The same thing played out for Mark and me. And just like Joseph had done, I sometimes played on my knees to give him a chance, but only when we played in the house. I stayed on my feet in the yard.

We'd play football in the house which was crazy, I'm amazed mom let us get away with it. For many years, the picture frames hanging on the wall down our long hallway had no glass because we broke it all, and the air conditioning vent at the end of the hall was permanently dented from our roughness. Even though he was four years younger, and significantly smaller, I never *let* him win at anything, I seldom even gave him a break. I wasn't trying to be mean, I just felt that if he didn't earn it, he shouldn't win, even if (or maybe because) he was the little brother.

I suppose I was kind of hard on him in the way big brothers often are, and I have to admit regretting this now. When I was a senior, Mark was in eighth grade, and I was a teacher's aide for one period. One day I thought it would be funny to call to Mark's class over the intercom and tell his teacher, "little Mark Forester needs to come to the office." When I said this, I could hear several kids in his class laughing. Mark wasn't happy with me—especially since there wasn't a reason for him to even come to the office, only that I wanted to pick at him a little. I know I was just being a brother, and I like to think it helped build his determination and drive, which is clearly some of what made him so exceptional as an adult and warrior. We've heard the scriptures that mention "brotherly love". I know what that means because I could treat Mark how I wanted, but others couldn't. In the end, Mark was fixed with a determination to conquer his enemies (and ours) as a Combat Controller.

When he turned 16, Mark got his first real summer job. It was expected that all of us Forester kids would start making our own money by the time we were 16 years old. He worked at R&R Supply as a warehouse laborer/ delivery man. The business supplied the mobile home plants in the area with crown molding, tile, and insulation. When he made deliveries in the company pickup, some customers would question his age. Honestly, even though he was 16, he could have passed for 12 or 13 years old. Because of this, he was a magnet for good-natured teasing from the folks he worked with.

One incident that is kind of funny (though it bothers me too) happened when his co-workers convinced him to get on the forks of the lift and check for something on the top rack in the warehouse. When they got him up there, they lowered the forks and he was stuck. Remember, this was summer time in Alabama. If the temperature outside was in the 90's, 20 feet up inside that warehouse, it had to be at least 110°F. I think they left him there through lunch. He took it in stride, and never complained, but I have to think he was not very happy about it.

The guys were not mean spirited, they were just playing. I know, because the following summer, 1998, I had just completed my missionary service and took a job there with Mark and all those guys. I didn't see him have much difficulty with our co-workers. I like to think they didn't bother him because I was very protective[13] of him. When I left for college, I asked

---

[13] Long before this, I wouldn't be mean to other kids at school because I didn't want people being mean to Mark. I guess I learned empathy for kids who got picked on by realizing how I'd feel if Mark was treated that way.

one guy in particular to watch out for him. He said there would not be any problems. There weren't any and R&R still stands out as my best part-time job ever.

I still felt this need to protect Mark when I left on my two-year mission. I asked a good friend of mine to watch after Mark while I was gone. They had lots in common, both loved to hunt, fish, swim and play basketball. I felt better knowing he, in fact, did spend time with Mark, even checked him out of school at times for some outdoor activities.

Even though I was protective of Mark, I don't feel I was as close to him at that time as I should have been—or as I now wish I had. I was busy and focused on my own things. When I got home from my mission, Mark was almost 17. I went to school down in Tuscaloosa, only 1 ½ hours away. I saw him and our folks regularly, but I still didn't take as much interest in his life at this time as I now wish I had.

Mark's summers at R&R Supply didn't last, because of an industry slowdown. Next, he began pouring concrete with our cousin Mike. This forced him to work extremely hard in the summer heat, though he could take a break when it rained. On the days he didn't work, he devoted much of his time to a weird computer game called *"Return of the Shadow."* It was a *Lord of the Rings*-type game he was introduced to in a high school computer programming class. I was amazed how he could waste so much time on it. If there was a good thing about it, though, it helped him learn to type incredibly fast, but that was not a benefit I considered worth so much of his time and effort.

Now, the Mark most people remember was a guy determined to excel at everything he did, and if he couldn't be the absolute best, then he'd drive himself to at least perform to his utmost ability. As a missionary, in sports, and in the Air Force, this was certainly so. In school, though, he didn't really push himself, but he didn't have to. His great memory made school pretty easy for him. All he had to do was show up for classes and do his assignments. After graduating high school, his grades were good enough that he was awarded a partial academic scholarship to Northwest-Shoals Community College. And then he lost it.

I am certain that *Return of the Shadow* game was a big reason why. In light of how Mark was raised, and the man he became, it's a little hard to believe he was basically addicted to a computer role-playing game. It really wasn't his personality, but then again, he was incredibly good at it; just like he was very good a few years later with Halo and the Call of Duty series on Xbox. (His teammates later told us how unbeatable he was, especially at Call of Duty. He'd maneuver himself into the JTAC or Combat Controller role and just wipeout his opponents—like he did on the real-life battlefield.)

Another thing about Mark, in high school he was far from the big, powerful guy he eventually became. He played sports all the time he grew up, but despite his natural athleticism, he was small and physically too immature to compete in some high school sports. Even though he eventually got to be 6' 3" (around age 23), he was only about 5' 9" when he graduated.

So, by the time he was in 9th or 10th grade, he was tired of most organized sports. I'm sure it didn't help that in the 9th grade he was cut from the basketball team by the self-proclaimed "professional" coach—even though he'd played basketball non-stop for years. He was good, just not tall and that put him at a disadvantage some didn't think he could overcome.

I'm sure this played with Mark's psyche, but if it affected him, Joseph and I agree that it only made him work that much harder in areas where he could make a difference. Also, I'm certain it prepared him emotionally and helped him build the determination he needed in order to succeed about 12 years later when facing some of the most rigorous and demanding training known to man. Despite (or maybe because of) the basketball experience, he stuck with tennis and became the number one seed on the team his senior year and finished with the Best Record in 1999.

One of Mark's close friends at this time was Amos (Mo) Bryant. He lived almost a rocks-throw through the woods. They took their trucks mudding, cruised around town, rode 4-wheelers, and talked on their CB's. They also loved playing paintball. They had a little group of friends who would get together to hunt and pelt each other with paintballs.

In December of 1999, I had a small bachelor party for two friends in Tuscaloosa who were getting married that month. Several of us went to Haleyville to get away because mom and dad's house was a great place to retreat, with good food, lots to do, and plenty of room since the basement had been finished.

Mark owned two pairs of 14 oz. boxing gloves, which he introduced to my friends. We used to love boxing when we were younger, but we never had actual gloves; we made them by taping throw pillows around our fists—

you can imagine how our mom loved that. When the gloves came out, Krager Vaughn wanted to take on Mark. Krager outweighed Mark by at least 50 lbs. and had at least 4-5 inches on him. Krager got at least one good pop on Mark's beak, but Mark kept going back for more. He did not like losing, no matter the pain. I remember feeling protective and on-edge seeing Mark get hit, even though I knew it was all in fun and he enjoyed it.

About this same time, Mark and Joseph were at a store. Mark was about 18 and Joseph was 26. A guy helping them at the store asked Joseph if Mark was his son. You can imagine that didn't make Mark feel good about himself. I wish I'd been more aware of his trials during that time in his life. Of course, he may not have viewed them as trials.

As mentioned earlier, missionaries often visited our home while growing up. This was partly because our dad was the leader of the local congregation of The Church of Jesus Christ of Latter-day Saints, called the Branch President. Additionally, it was natural for those young men to spend time with us because we had several boys and our home was a welcoming place to relax a little and have some fun in their very limited free time.

Although we met countless Elders (the title the Mormon missionaries are called by) through the years, a couple stand out. One of those is Elder Kevin Moore. The first time Elder Moore met Mark, he heard Mark's old Dodge Ram pickup well before seeing the truck or Mark. It didn't have the best exhaust system, so it roared as he came up the driveway. Mom had invited Kevin (Elder Moore) and his missionary companion, Elder Jones, for lunch. Mark was 16 years old at the time, and home for lunch too. Before long, the conversation turned to hunting, a topic Mark and the missionaries were passionate about.

At one point, Kevin's companion got excited and uttered something a little off-color that bothered Mark. Now, he didn't use a really terrible phrase. Kevin remembers thinking that it wasn't the best thing to say as a missionary, but he kept quiet. Mark, on the other hand, walked over to this missionary (who was at least three years older), looked him in the eye, and with great conviction said, "Elder, I don't know how they talk in Utah or Idaho or wherever it is you're from, but we choose not to use that word and I would ask that you do the same." The missionary had a stunned look as if Mark had suddenly slapped him across the face! Then, breaking the tension, Mark gave him a slug in the shoulder, put his arm around him and said, "I think Momma has some dessert waiting."

Funny how the remark set him off, Mark was only 16, but he would not hesitate to stand up for what he thought was right. More than that, though, is that he was not condemning or judgmental. It was just as important for Mark to let that missionary know his standards as it was to show him love and acceptance. Mark and those two Elders became good friends in the days and weeks after this encounter. (Kevin now has three young sons of his own. All have heard about Mark, and his example for how they ought to be, and that includes being careful of the words they use.)

Also, with Mark being the youngest, and last at home during these years, the missionaries he met set a good example for him as well. I'm sure he noted their love of the Lord, determination, and willingness to sacrifice to help others.

A little after their first lunch together, Elder Moore and his missionary companion attended a Haleyville High School football game on a Friday evening. As they entered the stadium seating, they were greeted with a loud welcome from Mark, who called them over to sit with him and his friends. Kevin (formerly Elder Moore) recalls being impressed and wondering whether he would have been so open and vocal in front of his peers about knowing the Mormon Missionaries when he was 16.

They all sat there together, enjoying the game, until just before half time. That's when some annoying teenager noticed the missionaries' white shirts, ties and name tags (hard to miss). He immediately called them out and started heckling them.

It started slowly, but as time passed, it became a constant verbal berating. They ignored it for a while, but as the kid's comments become more abusive, Kevin could tell Mark was having his fill. Kevin and Mark would look at each other and exchange smiles, strengthening each other to hold their composure for a few minutes longer.

They tolerated the insults until only a few minutes were left in the game. Then, the little punk cranked up his abuse and became very personal in his attacks against the missionaries. Mark was at a boiling point, but before he reacted, the kid muttered something like, "I need to get a drink. My mouth is dry from yelling at these Mormons!"

He got up to make his way down the bleachers. Kevin leaned over to Mark and whispered, "I wish someone could knock him down and shut him up." The moment he uttered those words, the kid slipped and landed hard on his rear. Shocked, Mark and Kevin gaped wide-eyed at each other and Mark, slapping Kevin on the knee, loudly exclaimed, "Giddy-up!" Kevin busted out laughing.

The kid's fall and Mark's "giddy-up" made it impossible for Kevin and the other missionary to hold back the laughter. The punk pulled himself back up, with a sore rear end, bruised pride and embarrassment so bad he never returned from getting his drink. Mark's use of the phrase "giddy-up" is common among the Forester men. We attribute it to Kramer from *Seinfeld*, and all who knew Mark, heard him deliver it at well-timed moments just like at that football game.

I'm still proud of him for not being ashamed of hanging out with the missionaries in front of his classmates. Mormon missionaries aren't often considered the coolest people to hang with, especially in a small southern town. But then again, Mark was most committed to doing the right thing. And he seemed to have a gift for making the right thing to do, the cool thing to do.

"It matters not how a man dies, but how he lives."
– Samuel Johnson

CHAPTER 7

The Joke's On Us

It was eight days between learning the awful news, and being ready to hold the funeral. Those days were a blur of activity as we were consumed by the blizzard of tasks, decisions and people.

I ate and slept very little and was so busy when awake that I kind of settled into a numb, auto-pilot state. I was awake, busy and conscious, but I was not fully engaged. Moving from one task to the next—and there was always something next—I had no time, or even energy, to really think or feel. I just did.

Ever since Mark's death, I'd had zero alone time. This wasn't a big deal until after Mark's body arrived on Tuesday. Then, we were surrounded by many supporters whenever we were at the funeral home. When I woke up early the day of the funeral, I called Tim Pinkard and asked to spend some time alone with Mark. I knew Tim was up early and would be accommodating to my request. When I arrived at the funeral home, about 6:00 am, Tim had a chair in the parlor for me to sit next to Mark and his casket. I was eager for some alone time with him and I finally got it. My quite time with my brother that morning was special. It was what I needed. One topic on my mind was what I should say at his funeral later that day. I left his side that morning calmer than I'd been the previous eight days.

Later on that morning, we assembled at Pinkard's with close family and friends. David and Joseph (my brothers), Max Sadler (nephew),

Mike Forester (cousin), Brad Knight (old friend), and I were designated to be Mark's pallbearers. Someone offered a sweet prayer. Through the consuming sadness that bore down upon us, we were touched and strengthened by the Spirit.

The other pallbearers and I then took up our burden and carried the casket out to the hearse. As we left the reverent shelter of the funeral home, there seemed consolation in the mildness of the day itself. It was as though nature tried telling us that this was not a day of dread and mourning, but of remembrance and gratitude. It was very pleasant. Even with the breeze, the temperature was mild and a scattering of white clouds drifted through a calm blue sky.

Waiting outside, a huge group had already assembled for the procession, including TV crews covering the event for the news. We followed behind the police escort and nearly 100 Patriot Guard Riders on our way to the high school for the funeral. I don't know how many others took up positions in our trail. (Sometime later we were told around 1,400 people had attended the services.) All along the way, people lined the streets, holding flags, saluting, placing their hands over their hearts. We were so moved by this outpouring of caring and patriotism.

Joseph never told anyone until we were preparing the funeral, but well before Mark died, the feeling came over him that if anything ever happened to Mark, he would give the eulogy. He even outlined the whole thing in his mind. It took him maybe 10 or 15 minutes to sketch it out on paper, once he knew he would need it.

Joseph was not alone, I had similar impressions, only that I knew I should be the closing speaker for the service. When the time came, we both were ready to play our part in remembering our brother, commemorating his life, and using the opportunity to bear witness of our faith—and Mark's—in the Gospel.

Like everything else since that knock at our door a few days earlier, much of the experience is a blur, but a few things still stand out from the comments and talks given at the funeral. Brigadier General Otis G. Mannon of USAF Special Operations Command spoke, giving an account of Mark's service in the Air Force. He started by describing Mark as an exceptional man "who lived as he was raised, with virtue and integrity and a moral compass that others in the unit admired and [were] inspired to develop [themselves]."

Major Edmond Loughran was acting Commander of the 21 STS while Lt Col Hughes was deployed. He commented that Mark chose to live in the dorms. He was older and a college graduate, so Major Loughran offered to sign some forms that would have let him live off base. Mark replied, "It's hard to get in trouble living in the dorms. The food's not so bad, and there might be someone there who could use my help." It was typical of Mark's commitment to sacrificing of himself for the good of others.

Major Loughran recounted that as Mark quickly advanced through his Combat Controller training, his exceptional skill and professionalism stood out. This led directly to the decision of his commanders to assign Mark, along with another, senior, CCT, to one of the "most dangerous, and therefore, most coveted areas in Afghanistan." It was a place where a Combat Controller was certain to apply his skills almost any time he went off base. As they considered this recommendation, the unit commanders questioned Mark's instructors and team leaders, "'Are you *sure*?' The response back was a resounding, 'Affirmative. Sir, he's *that* good.'"

Major Loughran assured everyone listening that the confidence of Mark's leaders was very well placed. He "executed his training with skill and precision that devastated the enemy and won him the respect of special operators and combat aviators alike."

Major Loughran told of a closed-door discussion he had with the deployed squadron commander, Lt Col Parks Hughes, during the summer of 2010. Lt Col Hughes said, "Ed, Forester may be the best young Combat Controller the career field has seen in a long time." This assessment was repeatedly backed up by reports from everyone Mark worked with, from his Green Beret team, to the combat aviators and artillery units who Mark coordinated with to hurt the enemy and protect his team. They repeatedly noted how ready he was to expose himself to danger, if it meant safeguarding his comrades.

Mark never ceased to manifest the same concern for those around him that he demonstrated repeatedly throughout his life. Only this time, "it was face-to-face with a well-trained and well-armed enemy." Major Loughran paid Mark a great complement in comparing him to the sheepdog described by LTC Dave Grossman as one "who stands silent and alone in the night to get between the flock he loves so much and the wolves that are bent on their destruction."

"Without being told or having to ask, Mark understood what the Shepherd asked of him for the sake of his flock. And to that duty, he relentlessly strove."

Speaking for himself and Mark's other close friends, Bobby Bonello, Mark's friend and teammate through most of their CCT training, let everyone know what it was like to be Mark's friend. For several months, they lived, ate, traveled, slept, studied, commuted, trained, worked-out, barbequed, and sometimes even went to church together.

Bobby noted what an exceptionally hard trainer Mark was. He'd work at a task until he *mastered* it. Also, Mark seemed to know the answer to everything. "Whether it was nutrition, finance, music, computers, sports, guns or whatever, Mark knew it all." And if he didn't know it, he'd act so much like he did that Bobby wouldn't even question it.

He told how Mark got his nickname. Mark always had a thing about his hair. He had great hair, he knew it, and he worked to keep it that way. One time, he came back to the schoolhouse after getting a cut that was tight on the sides, and flat on top. It reminded his teammates of Dolph Lundgren's cut in Rocky IV, so after that, they called him Dolph.

Bobby and Mark deployed at the same time, and were scheduled to rotate home at the same time as well. Not long before Mark died, he and Bobby were discussing plans for a trip after they got home. Knowing how much Mark liked to hunt, Bobby suggested an Alaskan hunting expedition he'd heard about. A little surprisingly, Mark said, "Bobby, I think I've had enough of shooting at things for a while. Let's go to Hawaii…."

Bobby lost his best friend when Mark died. His only regret is that he couldn't be there in the last five minutes, either to help, or to at least be with him. Bobby's perspective is great, though. He said that although he lost his best friend, he gained a whole new family. A lot of the time, men and women in the service end up with two families: the one like the rest of us have, and their family in the service. Usually, there is not much cross-over between the two, but since his death, we have made every effort to welcome Mark's military family, and they have welcomed us too. We all know that's how Mark wants it.

David took a few moments to share his thoughts and memories of Mark. He said that while most people thought of Mark as the hero—and he was—David remembers him as the little brother who needed his advice. Mark was the brother he never fought with, or became angry with. Mark was the little brother who was always eager to go for a hike in the woods. He was the little brother who was always willing to watch ridiculous "B" movies and British sitcoms with him. I remember them often quoting lines from Monty Python's *Life of Brian*.

David remembered Mark was the uncle who always wrestled with his nieces and nephews. He was the one who David's kids always asked, "When is Mark coming home?" I suppose the answer now is that Mark is "home," but his influence still runs through all our lives. A few months after Mark's death, David and his wife had a baby boy and they named him Andrew, after Mark's middle name.

In the weeks and months before Mark's death, I noticed him telling me more often than usual that he loved and appreciated our family and me. Others in the family noticed this too. We heard numerous reports of how effective Mark was on the battlefield. We'd heard that he was, "always looking for a fight." I was worried that he was feeling invincible, and I talked to him about it once. He said, "Brother, believe me. I am reminded every day that I am not [invincible]." Regardless of that, he was going to do his job, whatever the outcome.

Mom, dad and Terri were simply too overcome to speak at the service, so they left it to us, Mark's brothers, to represent our family. I remember feeling very calm during the service, and that when my turn came, I stood without fear or nervousness. I felt lifted up by the Holy Spirit, and inspired as to what words I should say to reiterate the faith Mark lived by all his life.

He possessed a firm belief in our Shepherd, Jesus Christ, and in following His example. I know that it was for Mark as it was with prophets of old, *"I have fought a good fight, I have finished my course, I have kept the faith." (2 Timothy 4:7) "For behold, this life is the time for men to prepare to meet God; yea, behold the day of this life is the day for men to perform their labors." (Alma 34:32)* I know Mark completed his mission here on Earth, that he fought the good fight, and that he performed his labors well.

I also know Mark had faith in the continuance of life after we pass, that *"... the spirits of those who are righteous are received into a state of happiness, which is called paradise, a state of rest, a state of peace, where they shall rest from all their troubles and from all care, and sorrow." (Alma 40:12)*

What may be most inspiring of all, though, is that I watched my brother truly live up to so many high standards. We were taught as children and had to memorize: *"We believe in being honest, true, chaste, benevolent, virtuous, and in doing good to all men; indeed, we may say that we follow the admonition of Paul--We believe all things, we hope all things, we have endured many things, and hope to be able to endure all things. If there is anything virtuous, lovely, or of good report or praiseworthy, we seek after these things." (Article of Faith #13)* I quoted it in my talk at the funeral—still from memory—because that is how Mark lived. He was ready to meet his God.

We closed the meeting with a recording of the Mormon Tabernacle Choir singing, *"The Battle Hymn of the Republic."* This was mom's choice. Rozlynn's mother sent that CD to us before the funeral and mom played that disk many times on her kitchen stereo; it seemed fitting. Then we left the gym for the cemetery where the burial service was held.

The precision of the military funeral with its rituals, reverence and respect was more moving than I can describe. I think everyone has some idea of the process: the 21-gun salute, the ritual folding of the flag that covered his casket. Nothing I can write or say could ever capture the powerful feelings that swelled within me as the men and women in uniform passed the sacred article from one to another; then finally, standing witness to the heartbreaking presentation of that flag to our mother as token gratitude of our nation to the woman bereft of her dear, youngest child. Then there was the playing of taps. To this day, I do not like hearing that tune.

Then, the rumble of four F-16 jets from Maxwell AFB punctuated the moment as they flew low overhead, and performed the missing man formation where one breaks from the group and shoots skyward until the plane is completely out of sight. It seemed to symbolize Mark's ascent to a better place, leaving us earth-bound, gazing up after him. I can't help thinking that the roar of jet engines like those we heard that day (many call it the sound of freedom) was probably one of the last sounds Mark heard.

The shock, the broken hearts, the unfulfilled promises of a productive, love-filled life, of adventures never taken, a sister-in-law, nieces, nephews and grandchildren we'll never meet, are all soothed by the faith we hold that Mark passed at his appointed time. We know that God is aware of him, and that his days were known and not numbered less. Especially that in the eternal perspective, Mark will ultimately enjoy all of God's blessings, in His due time. So, in a way, the joke is on us because Mark is happy, busy, and still serving in what only briefly seems as the most foreign of lands, *home*. Our original home where we will rejoice in seeing him again, and see the fulfillment of all we saw in him.

After the funeral service, the crowds surrounding us slowly began to disperse to their own homes and reflections on the day. We who remained, Mark's family and closest friends and members of the military, shared dinner at Haleyville Middle School, delicious BBQ cooked by Bud Wilson. The gathering was permeated by a peculiar mix of laughter, celebration and very tender feelings. Naturally, the meal concluded with memorial pushups in the hallway adjacent to the cafeteria.

Late that evening, we returned to the cemetery to dedicate the grave. Maybe the best explanation of this ceremony is the one posted on the LDS Church's website:

Dedication of Graves[14]

Graves should be dedicated by a Melchizedek Priesthood holder, as authorized by the priesthood officer who conducts the service. To dedicate a grave, he:

1. *Addresses Heavenly Father.*
2. *States that he is acting by the authority of the Melchizedek Priesthood.*
3. *Dedicates and consecrates the burial plot as the resting place for the body of the deceased.*
4. *(Where appropriate) prays that the place may be hallowed and protected until the Resurrection.*
5. *Asks the Lord to comfort the family and expresses thoughts as the Spirit directs.*
6. *Closes in the name of Jesus Christ.*

It was dusk when we arrived and quickly growing dark. As we got out of the car and approached the gravesite, we noticed a man in the shadows a little way off. We didn't recognize him in the dim light, but he waved and we waved back. He then approached respectfully. I didn't know him, but I did notice he was armed.

Dad recognized he had gone to school with the man, but hadn't seen him in many years. He told us he was standing watch over Mark to be sure there would be no trouble with vandals or protesters. He told us there were

[14] http://www.lds.org/handbook/handbook-2-administering-the-church/priesthood-ordinances-and-blessings/20.9#209

others who had eagerly volunteered to stand watch, and each would take his turn through the night. We had not asked for this. We had not even thought of it. It's amazing that so many people were so inspired to reach out and freely share of themselves.

After our brief exchange, he faded back into the shadows and left us to perform this last rite of the funeral service. It was brief and to the point. When completed, we turned and somberly walked back to the car. We said very little on the ride home, leaving each of us alone with our thoughts and heavy burden of sadness.

Even though the funeral was over, we had another ceremony to attend. Later that night, after squeezing in some basketball in the driveway, we boarded two *Senators Coaches* VIP buses and headed for Pope AFB, in North Carolina where Mark's squadron held a special memorial on Friday, Oct 9. Once again, good friends got together behind the scenes to arrange the easiest travel possible because they knew we had slept very little the last eight days. We even had a police escort the entire way, except through Georgia, but even then, law enforcement was made aware of us. Originally, we were all going to ride in one bus, but some other good folks realized we needed a second bus. (We have a big family.) I suspect the people at *Senators Coaches* insisted we take the second bus free of charge. This was a life saver because one coach was mostly a sleeper and the other was set up for entertainment. Most of the adults slept nearly the entire way in one bus, while the kids stayed occupied in the other. It was the first good sleep I'd had the entire week.

We toured the 21 STS, went to Mark's cage (where he kept all his gear) and saw it just as he left it before deploying, and then attended the memorial service. Honestly, it was a little hard to get emotional because I was still running on autopilot. I was fully functional, but not feeling a whole lot. We met a lot of people who knew and worked with Mark, met his bishop from the congregation he attended while at Pope, and witnessed many tears shed. It was a touching service. Later that evening, we boarded the same buses and headed back to Haleyville. We returned home sometime early Saturday morning.

Thinking back on this experience, it is clear that there was no way we could have driven ourselves the 12 hours to Fayetteville, NC for the service—especially having to be there the day after the funeral. We can't thank our friends and others enough who donated the buses for us, as well as *Senators Coaches*. Everyone's generosity truly lightened our burden at the time. There were even friends who came from out of state to help. They ran errands, cleaned the house, answered the phones and I don't know what else. We deeply appreciated their efforts; it made a difference.

In the months and years that have followed, Mark's passing has understandably weighed most heavily on our mom. Fortunately, she's mostly stayed very busy, teaching the youth at church, helping my sister Terri, since she now lives near mom and dad, spoiling her many grandchildren, and looking after dad. She and our family have also attended numerous ceremonies and events which have honored Mark's sacrifice and commitment. She appreciates the attention and support, but it is also a heavy burden. At the same time the honors and attention lift her up, it also brings all the pain of a mother's loss to the surface. I know Dad's feelings are just as tender; he just doesn't verbalize them as much.

Once life settled back to something like it had been before that knock at our door, there were moments when it was a little hard to grasp the change. It almost seemed as if life was normal again. Mark had been gone so much before his deployment that on the surface, having him *gone* was not so different. However, these were only brief respites between the deep sadness and tears as my mind wrestled with what I had lost. To cope, I just stayed busy and worked at moving on.

Then the parcels started showing up. Some were delivered by couriers, others by Mark's military buddies, Ish and Bobby. Slowly, Mark's personal items that were scattered from his home in North Carolina, to the 21 STS at Pope to FOB Cobra were returned to us. I had gone home to help mom and dad, and as dad and I were carrying the packages from the carport to the basement, he asked me, "Thad, what are we gonna do with all this stuff?" I had no response except that we would just carry it down to the basement and leave it untouched until the entire family could go through it together. It was only a few weeks later, during the Thanksgiving holiday, that we were all together. This was the day of the Iron Bowl. Mark, Joseph and I had planned to be at that game together. But now, the game wasn't that important. We were together again, gathered in the basement, with the stack on one end of the pool table and all around it on the ground. One by one, we opened the packages, set the items on the pool table, and divided up the stuff Mark left behind. That's a weird act to go through.

"Forget yourself and go to work."
– Ray Forester, quoting a letter written to Gordon B. Hinckley
by his father when he was a missionary

CHAPTER 8

No Joy in Mediocrity

Even people who know almost nothing about Mormons will often recognize the missionaries. The suits, bikes, white shirts and black nametags are hard to miss. These young men are volunteers who dedicate two years of their early adulthood to full-time teaching and service work in communities far from their homes. They leave behind their families, friends, and most everything their peers are doing, and put school, training and plans for their future on hold.[15]

After watching each of his older brothers volunteer, it's probably not too surprising that Mark submitted his application to serve as soon as he had met the requirements. Some of these included being at least 19 years old, having the means to support himself for the two years, and having spiritually prepared himself for the work. That means he'd sought a spiritual confirmation that a mission was part of Heavenly Father's plan for him.

---

[15] I have to mention that in the LDS church, young women and older couples also serve as missionaries, though they may be less visible. The requirements for women are similar to the young men, with the primary differences of being a year older and serving 18 months rather than 24. Senior couples serve in a wide range of capacities ranging from medical care to genealogical work to filling leadership roles in the church and community, and countless other services. For the purpose of this book, my comments focus on the young men.

Mark had most of a year to wait between his graduation from Haleyville High School and being old enough to apply. He spent most of that year at the local community college taking classes, working, and playing that stupid computer game I mentioned earlier. Somewhere in there, though, he started to seriously prepare. It had always been his plan, but this was the time to make it a reality. Based upon the reports from his missionary companions and leaders, he was definitely ready to put all else on hold and dedicate himself to fulfilling the duty he felt he owed to his Heavenly Father.

Mormon missionaries don't choose their area of service; instead they leave it to God to inspire church leaders as to where each can do the most good for the mission, and himself. Mark was called to serve in the Oakland, CA mission and he departed for the Missionary Training Center (MTC)[16] in Provo, UT on 30 August 2000. He was excited about it because he didn't want to go foreign and had never been to California. At the MTC, he joined up with other missionaries who were called to the same area, and together they learned the basics for about three weeks before traveling to their assigned location. I know he was eager to leave the MTC and get to work and eat some better food. (It seems the MTC cafeteria holds to a time-honored tradition of providing meals that encourage missionaries to look forward to *leaving*.)

He left as a 19 year old boy not knowing what he was getting in to, only he knew it was the right thing. Mark started his mission strong, but still had plenty of growing to do, physically, mentally and spiritually. Since graduation, he'd grown to just over six feet, but he still looked very young. (Two years later, he was even taller, weighed 230 lbs., but still had that baby face.)

To be honest, we were a little worried about Mark stepping up to the rigors of missionary life because before he left, he would not get up in the mornings without a fight. I can still hear mom, or me, or another family member, yelling at Mark to get out of the bed. He would lie there forever, making the rest of us late many times. He was a procrastinator.

---

[16]   The MTC is like a college campus, only with full-time missionaries and part-time instructors. Many of the missionaries are learning a new language. Each day consists of class work, study and eating. There is designated time for exercise in the MTC, but it is limited. The missionaries are mostly young men and some young women who have left behind all normal life: no TV, radio, dating, hanging out, etc. From this point on through the next 1.5-2 years, they will eat, drink, and breathe missionary work. It is a very unique place.

And because my brothers and I had served missions ourselves, we knew what he was in for: up by 6:30 every morning and drive hard working all day, every day. No one was there to babysit; it was his responsibility to not waste his time and money or the Lord's time. Later, we learned we had no need to worry. By all accounts, he was ready to work and serve from his first day.

After three weeks in the MTC, he was sent to Oakland and met his mission president, Richard DeVries, from Michigan. He and his wife were responsible for about 200 young missionaries from all over the world assigned to the Oakland mission, which included areas as far as Concord, Union City, Berkeley and Brentwood. This is where he really became a man—tall in stature and even taller in spirit.

This is how his mission president, **Rick DeVries** and his family, remember him:

> For the last while I have searched my records for everything related to Elder Forester, and have interviewed family members in that regard. It was a sweet, sacred experience to spend time remembering this great man and all he became while in mortality.
>
> Dyana (my wife) and I remember Mark as the tall, pure looking young man with a smile that radiated love and a warmth that could melt ice. He had an unconquerable spirit and was up to every challenge given him. He was polite and courteous to a fault.
>
> On one occasion, Sister DeVries told Mark that he didn't have to say, "Yes Ma'am" whenever she asked him a question. Mark's quick response was that he didn't have a choice because that was what his Momma had taught him and that he would get a whoopin' if he didn't live up to those standards! He had a twinkle in his eye and a chuckle in his voice as he said it, and it became clear over time that he was a self-admitted Momma's boy, who, like the sons of Helaman, remembered the words that their mothers had taught them.[17] His love for, and admiration of his mom, dad and siblings were always a central part of who Mark was.
>
> Mark was also like the sons of Helaman in his exact obedience. It never mattered what was asked of him, he was one of those

---

missionaries who would go the extra mile to do whatever the Lord required of him. In the words of Mormon, he was *"Exceedingly valiant for courage, and also for strength and activity; but behold, this was not all-they were men who were true at all times in whatsoever thing they were entrusted. Yea, they were men of truth and soberness, for they had been taught to keep the commandments of God and to walk uprightly before him."*[18]

Mark, like the Sons of Helaman, had a strong sense of duty and loyalty, and was always ready to step up to the plate to defend others and to defend the truth. I suspect that his strong desire to be a soldier came—at least in part—from this sense of duty and desire to defend others from those who would take away their freedom and liberty.

Mark's exact obedience, valiant service, and perfect love made him a powerful force in the mission field. He was given the privilege of working with missionaries who were struggling, of moving into areas that had experienced little or no success, and of serving as one of the Assistants to the President.

As our assistant,[19] Mark became a part of our family. He ate many meals with us, played with our children, knelt in prayer with our family, and he shared in our joys and our sorrows. When asked about Mark, our son Jon, who knew him best, said the following: "When I think about Elder Forester, I don't think about any single attribute—rather, I think about the remarkable man that he was. Whenever I was with him I wanted to become like him - I wanted to be a missionary and a man like him."

Mark used to talk to Jon about hunting, and one day presented him with a beautiful hunting knife, telling Jon that he should save it for his first skinning! Well, just a few months ago Jon took up hunting, went on his first expedition, and skinned a rabbit with that knife. He said it was a sweet experience, remembering that conversation and thinking about Mark.

---

[18] Book of Mormon, Book of Alma 53:20-21

[19] The president of a mission will typically have two missionaries spend a portion of their mission serving as his assistants, mostly focusing on supporting and directing other missionaries.

Mark had a wonderful appetite and loved to eat—and Sister DeVries loved cooking for him. Every bite was received with gratitude and spending time with him at the dinner table was always a treat for us.

Mark taught and testified with great power and authority. He could do so because he walked the talk. His teaching was reflected in his life, and he lived his testimony every day. I can honestly say that in the two years we served with him, I cannot ever remember a moment of disobedience or discouragement. He was always where he was supposed to be, doing what he was supposed to be doing.

While going through my records I came across one of the weekly letters that Elder Forester sent to me. In one of the comments he made he said, "I have great hopes for this area. There's not much going on now, but that will change." This is so illustrative of his attitude towards life. If something needed to be done, he had the faith to do it. Later in the letter, he mentioned his concern for his companion[20] who was struggling and feeling somewhat discouraged. He was always concerned about those around him.

What I want you to know is that Mark was as valiant a missionary as ever walked this earth. He was truly a modern day Captain Moroni.[21] I have no doubt but that his faith, because of his valiant, obedient service, allowed him to ask Heavenly Father in confidence for those things he needed. I am sure that he was so brave and bold as a missionary because he understood this principle. I am likewise confident that everything he did in life, including serving our country and giving his own life, was based on that same truth—that he could go forward in any assignment with confidence because he served a valiant mission.

I know that he served a valiant mission because I witnessed it. I met with him knee to knee every six weeks in an interview. I

---

[20] Missionaries are assigned by their mission president to work in pairs for a period of time. As such they are referred to as a "companionship", so Mark's "companion" was the fellow missionary who he worked with at the time.

[21] Book of Mormon, Book of Alma 48:11-14. The excerpt at the beginning of Chapter 1 describes both Mark and Captain Moroni.

spent endless hours with him while he served as my assistant. I felt the Spirit as he taught and bore testimony of the restoration of the gospel and of the divinity of Jesus Christ as the Savior of the world.

He lived valiantly and he ended his mortal sojourn valiantly, and we all give thanks to Heavenly Father for what we learned from him and for the joy we had because of him. We are likewise grateful for the goodly parents and siblings who raised him to become such a great man.

Mark's journey and mission are far from over. We do not know exactly what he is doing now, but one thing we do know; he is doing it faithfully, valiantly and well. We all look forward to our reunion with him and will strive more to become like the Savior because of him.

He was first assigned to serve with **Elder Ammon Matsuda**, a fellow missionary who was in the final few months of his 24-month missionary service. Ammon was his trainer, responsible for really teaching Mark the mission rules, introducing him to local church members and leaders, and helping him develop effective teaching techniques. Ammon remembers:

Mark and I served in the Livermore 2nd Ward together, and I could not have asked for a better, more faithful companion. He and I worked hard and had wonderful missionary experiences together, but perhaps most important, we enjoyed the friendship we shared. We laughed, rode our bikes in the rain, studied, prayed and taught. I truly enjoyed the few months we spent together.

I have fond memories of hearing him repeatedly sing the chorus to "I Am the Walrus" by The Beatles, or say "What's the dill, pickle?" I remember his fun-loving, friendly Alabama accent. In fact, I remember to this day the very first door we knocked on together where he took the lead. Poor Elder Forester was heartbroken after getting up his nerve to introduce us, only to find that the California native who answered our knock couldn't understand what he'd said.

I have to admit, though, Mark struggled with mornings. At that time in our apartment of four missionaries, our companionship had second shift on showers, so the standard routine was to have personal scripture study right after getting up at 6 a.m. This was tough for Mark; he dozed off the first few days in the field.

So we switched around our morning schedule so that at 6 am we had companionship study and planning. This way he had no choice but to stay awake because we'd have to talk and think aloud together. It worked!

Growing up in a military community, perhaps I absorbed some drill sergeant tendencies. I remember helping Mark memorize the key scriptures for each discussion. We'd work on these throughout the day, including lunch and upon returning home for the night. Most often, he sat himself in the middle of our ugly yellow couch and I'd pace the room in front of him going through the verses. Sometimes I took to throwing a mini soccer ball at him whenever he missed a word. Fortunately for him (and me, he was much taller and larger than I was), he had good reflexes, so aside from a few gut shots we avoided injury. That's how I remember Mark: always good-natured, wanting to be great at missionary work, being a good friend.

I remember hearing Mark talk about how much he loved his mom's cooking and how dismayed he was when he discovered we didn't have a jar of bacon grease sitting on the stove to flavor the meals we made. But he quickly got used to doing his own cooking and laundry, although we both enjoyed being well cared for in the food department by our congregation. One night at a member's home the food was particularly good, and Mark ate multiple helpings (maybe 3?). He was so full, he could barely get on his bike and pedal. But I think he learned a lesson there because that never seemed to be an issue again.

If I remember correctly, he and I served together for 12 weeks in that area (two transfer cycles). We did not see any baptisms together, but we taught a lot of people. I remember being frustrated at not knowing what the fruits of our labor would be, but that never seemed to bother Mark. He trusted that we were doing the right things, and that everything would work out, whatever form that took.

Some other random details that I'll always remember about Mark: one of his suits was a dark olive green, which I always

73

thought suited him given the family name. He rode a gray Trek mountain bike (with red shocks I think). He loved to show pictures of his family and friends, and was always proud to talk of his parents and brothers. I never quite figured out where his college football allegiance rested, since I think the family rooted for Crimson but there was a brother at Auburn? There was another Japanese missionary in our apartment and Mark never tired of trying to say our names in a Japanese-sounding way (funnier than anything). He was just fun to be around.

Serving a mission is a culture shock for anyone, but Mark probably had more to adjust to than most. He had only lived in a small town in Alabama. Then suddenly, he was dropped into one of the largest cities in California, surrounded everyday by people from all over the world. To give an idea of how much he needed to learn, every year the seniors from Haleyville High School go on a Senior Trip to Washington, DC and New York City. While in New York City, Mark moseyed right across a street and was almost run over. Cars started honking. One of his teachers asked why he didn't pay attention to the "DON'T WALK" sign. He said he'd never seen one. Got to learn sometime, right?

Another fellow missionary, **Elder Bryan Radcliffe**, said he always felt he had to raise the bar when he was with Mark. He always kept him on his toes and Bryan respected him for that. "He followed the spirit, never gave up, and had an amazing sense of humor; but knew when to be serious." Bryan served in the Spanish speaking program (Mark was English), but Mark always wanted to go tracting (door-to-door proselyting) with Bryan because he wanted to learn the Spanish language. When Mark returned from his two-year mission, he was very familiar with Spanish. He couldn't necessarily carry on a conversation, but could understand most statements.

Mark's last missionary companion, **Elder Cody Anderson**, told me that Mark didn't have a fearful bone in his body. "He opened his mouth to declare the gospel to anyone who would listen, and sometimes, even to those who wouldn't. He was a brilliant teacher and had a way of personalizing the message so each individual could understand." Cody thinks Mark was such an effective teacher because of his love for the Lord and for the people he was teaching. He loved serving in the Oakland area.

He said one time they went several weeks without a day off because of so many mission assignments from President DeVries. They were tired, had no food in their apartment, and probably didn't have the best smelling clothes, but Mark never complained and his smile didn't falter. Knowing Mark, I am sure he locked-on to the mindset that this was just part of what he'd agreed to, and nothing was going to distract him from accomplishing what his mission president asked of him. This is similar to the mindset he had while fighting terrorists in Afghanistan.

Cody said he still ties his tie like he learned from Mark. He always measured the large portion by the length of his arm. The other missionaries living with him used to give him a hard time, but Mark would smile and say, "It works. You should try it". Cody eventually gave in, tried it, and never went back to his old method. I remember Mark measuring his ties like this, and that he usually had his tongue barely sticking out while he tied his tie. I never asked him about it, though, and now that I can't, I really wish I'd paid more attention to details like this.

I'm not sure how many companions Mark had, but a normal missionary will live and work with about 8 to 10 companions during his two years of service. Because Mark was committed and a good example, he was called upon to train a few new missionaries (like Ammon did for Mark). One "greenie" he trained was **Elder Garn Blackburn**, who remembers:

> Mark was a great companion and I was very fortunate to have served a mission with him. He was my mission trainer in Brentwood, CA where we had a lot of great experiences and he taught me many things that I needed to learn. He loved the outdoors as much as I do, and Mark helped me stay on my mission when things were getting rough... He helped me to understand how important the work we were doing out there was, even if we didn't see much success.
>
> Although we did not have any baptisms while we were companions, I know that he was able to touch the lives of many that we spoke with and taught. As far as stories go, here's one I remember that might make you laugh: While in Brentwood, I complained that I missed hunting. So Mark and I made some blow guns with McDonald's straws, some plastic Q-tips and small nails melted in them. We never got anything, but we scared a lot of pigeons.

These comments are only a small sample of the reports we heard of Mark's time in California. Many came when he was still there. Clearly, Mark was dedicated and hardworking, but there were days that really challenged him. Becoming discouraged is very easy to do because, often, missionaries don't see immediate results from their efforts. Imagine being in sales, only your job is every day from 6:30 am to 9:30 pm, with only one partial day off each week. It can be easy to become burnt out and discouraged, especially when you can't do much to ease your tensions and stress, such as work out, go on long drive, watch TV, be alone, etc. Mark was human and did have his hard times.

He reflected on one of those times a few years later when he dated a sweet girl while at The University of Alabama. They had many lengthy conversations about everything young men and women discuss, and, probably more than most, about faith and religion and being true to God. Megan recalls the time:

> I was trying to understand where Mark was coming from so I told him about my relationship with God, the journey I had gone through to really come to know Him and how I surrendered my life to Him. I asked Mark if he had ever experienced something similar.
>
> He told me that when he was on his mission, he had gotten home late one night and was just hurt from the day. People were being rude and closing doors in his face. He said when he got to his room that night he knelt on the floor beside his bed and started praying. He was just talking to God and asking Him that if this were real, if this was what he was supposed to be doing, that if all of that were so, would God just give him a hug. Mark said he felt such a presence and could feel His arms wrapped around him and he had peace. He said he was able to sleep that night and he never had to look back or ever question what he was doing. Regardless of whether we agreed on everything or not, I know I became stronger from knowing Mark.

Mark would tell you that his mission prepared him for the rest of his life, including his time in the military. He gained experience leading other missionaries while at the same time being their peer. He learned about setting goals and doing what it took to achieve them. He learned how to deal with rejection. Believe me, rejection and persecution are daily experiences. He learned how to live and work with others from various backgrounds toward a common goal. He gained experience in planning and prioritizing his days. In two years, he gained many years' worth of experience by meeting and talking to complete strangers. And most importantly, he developed self-confidence and increased his faith in God.

Before Mark left on his mission, I gave him a list of suggestions, based on what I'd learned on my mission. Some of them were: *work on your temper, do what your mission president says, forget yourself and go to work, love the people whom you serve.* I know he followed these suggestions and more. I am certain he was an effective and excellent missionary. Regarding his mission, Mark never asked what he could get, but rather what he could give. He gave two years of full, selfless service; which is exactly what was asked of him.

President and Sister DeVries had a set of traditions for departing missionaries. It started the morning of a missionary's last full day when he would arrive at the mission office in the morning along with a few others who were also finishing their missions. President DeVries held a last interview with each missionary, "one on one, knee to knee" to discuss experiences, lessons learned, and the future. The president says it was "always a sacred time."

Later, they had lunch together as a group, followed by a walk across the street for a last service in the Oakland Temple. Then back to the mission home for dinner, followed by a testimony meeting.

President DeVries continues, "We then walked across the parking lot of the mission home to a path along the hillside, from which you could see the Oakland Temple lit up at night. We would all stand silently and just reflect on the times that the missionaries had experienced during their years of service. Again, this was a sacred time. After our walk to the hill, we would return to the mission home, where we filmed each missionary sharing their thoughts and advice to incoming missionaries. In typical fashion, Elder Forester counseled the missionaries, 'Always do your best and never settle for anything less—*there is no joy in mediocrity.*'"

Giddy-up!
– Mark Forester

CHAPTER 9

Friends, 'Bama, USAF CCT

Mark served an "honorable mission," as we call it in our faith. When he landed in Birmingham on his way back to Haleyville, his shoes were worn out, most of his suits were ready for retirement, and he was physically tired. These are all signs of a good missionary. There is also a term used in the mission field of "sprinting to the end". It means he worked hard and remained focused on his calling right up to the very end of his service. I'm sure he joked about going home with other missionaries, but he didn't let it affect his work. He sprinted to the end, and certainly earned the great sense of satisfaction and accomplishment for the years he'd served.

Even though he loved his mission and hated to leave the people of Oakland, he was relieved to be home. Mark was set on attending The University of Alabama. So after returning from his mission on 16 October 2002, he moved in with me in Tuscaloosa. I hope I helped Mark adjust to life after being a full-time missionary. All returned missionaries need a little time to re-adjust to "normal life."

Over the previous two years, he had grown a few inches and gained some weight (he was about 235 lbs.), but he still had that baby face. He also talked funny. I guess two years in California changed his accent some. I heard the same thing when I returned from my mission in Salt Lake City, UT. Some of us in the family told Mark he needed to change the voicemail message on his cell phone because he just didn't sound like himself.

After settling in with me in Tuscaloosa, he quickly made friends even before starting school in January. He first became friends with my friends then started making friends with some new students who I didn't know well because I was already out of school and working full time. I was very excited to have my brother live with me, and I know mom was very excited. It seemed to bring her comfort to have her two youngest, un-married boys living together. Plus, she could visit us both at the same time.

We lived at the Palisades apartments and I remember being frustrated many days when I'd come home from work and Mark would be lying on the couch watching TV, pretty much as he was when I left that morning. He was lazy and inactive. He was a little pudgy and still hadn't really filled out. We didn't fight or argue much, but when we did, it was mostly over some chore that he had neglected. Looking back on it now, I think that although he was physically sedentary during this time, his mind was in high gear, working out his next steps.

The 9/11 attacks happened when Mark was about half way through his mission. As the world around him reacted, he received his next "calling" in life: he would be that sheepdog[22] Major Loughran talked about during the funeral. He didn't know exactly how he'd do it, but there was no doubt in his mind that he was obliged to defend his country, his family and friends, and their right to worship as they felt they should.

Looking back, I remember us watching the news coverage of the Fall of Bagdad together, and being amazed at the history taking place then. Of course, I had no idea that only seven years later, Mark would also be in that part of the world fighting, and that he would die there.

Mark considered military service since high school. Mo Bryant, one of his best friends in those days, says they talked about the different special operations teams like SEALs and PJs (USAF Pararescue Jumpers) and Green Berets and what it would be like to be one. I know it was on his mind when he left for Oakland, and although he was committed to completing a college degree, the military service was high on his list. The terrorist attacks of that clear Tuesday morning sealed the deal.

---

[22] http://www.youtube.com/watch?v=U_TsxjGbhuk; http://www.killology.com/sheep_dog.htm;
http://www.killology.com/art_buckeye.htm

Mark and I not only got along well, but we genuinely enjoyed being together. Often times when we'd be driving together, we would quiz each other on what county a vehicle in front of us was from. In Alabama, the first digits of the license plate represent the county where the vehicle is registered. I think I enjoyed this game more than he did, but he was the one who was usually asking, "Which county is that?" I kept a card in my truck I could refer to when we didn't know the answer. We'd talk about lots of random things. Once, we were driving someplace and started talking about movies and actors we liked. Then we moved to discussing which actor we'd want to have play us if we were ever the subject of a movie. Mark wanted Christian Bale to play him. He loved the role Christian played in *Batman Begins*. This was well before Mark joined the military. Little things like this had entertained us since we were kids.

Another example is Mark passionately telling me how amazed he was when he saw self-checkout lanes at a Wal-Mart Neighborhood Market. This was about 2004, before he or I had seen them anywhere. I always think about him when I use this option in any store now.

Two other activities we did a lot were tennis and throwing the football back and forth. Mark had been a good tennis player in high school but he hadn't played in a couple years because of his mission. I remember him having such a temper on the court. To be honest, it's easy to get mad while playing tennis. He'd get mad about the game, and then I'd get mad at him. I know he broke at least one of his rackets by smashing it on the court. I suppose I didn't help matters, because I also had a bad temper when I played tennis, and am certain it rubbed off on him.

Regardless of his flashes of temper, he had a heart of gold. I worked in Mississippi for a year and during that time he roomed with our friend Doug Cole. When Doug got engaged, he moved out to his own place so Mark had to get a one-bedroom apartment. Shortly after this, I moved back to Tuscaloosa and, naturally, we planned to room together again. When I arrived, we couldn't get the new apartment for a week so I stayed in Mark's small place. He insisted on me sleeping in his bed while he took the couch that week. I didn't ask it of him, he just offered. And since I was the older brother, I took him up on it. Looking back, I wish I'd been quicker to follow his selfless example.

One Saturday we played tennis with Jay and Mary Stubbs at the university courts. After playing, we had a race across the three side by side courts. I blew him away and he was so mad. He hated losing at anything. I didn't hold my advantage long though, because he soon began working out hard and I could never come close to keeping up with him in any sport, except tennis. And believe me, we raced many times since and I was amazed how much faster than me he was.

His attitude on strength and personal discipline reminds me of a particular quote: *"Now if you are going to win any battle you have to do one thing. You have to make the mind run the body. Never let the body tell the mind what to do. The body will always give up. It is always tired morning, noon, and night. But the body is never tired if the mind is not tired."* – George S. Patton, U.S. Army General and 1912 Olympian

I don't know if he ever heard Patton's quote, but it certainly fit him. He loved knowing he had full control over his body. One time he decided he would not pee the entire trip from Tuscaloosa to San Antonio to see Joseph. We were driving with mom and dad and it was a 14.5 hour trip. He did it somehow. We even stopped to eat once or twice. Also, when we visited Joseph in Colorado, he loved to hold his breath through the Eisenhower Tunnel. He could do it too. It's over 1.5 miles long. He did this when we'd be going and coming from snow skiing.

We loved throwing the football in the front of our house, either in the yard or in the street. We did this as brothers when we'd get together in Haleyville too. Mark's throwing motion (right or left handed) was such that his lower body didn't move much, mostly just his upper (reminded me of Danny Wuerffel, 1996 Heisman Trophy winner). He could still throw a long ways. When David and Joseph were there, we'd throw the Frisbee too.

Mark always said he had "fairy shoulders,"[23] so he finally had surgery on his right shoulder. This was to help him prepare for the Air Force. After his surgery, he started throwing the football left handed, so his right could heal. He got good at it too. I recall the Sunday at church after his surgery, a man from the congregation patted Mark on the shoulder and asked him how he was doing and what was wrong. Apparently the sling didn't say "don't touch" loud enough. It hurt Mark and ticked both of us off. I'm not sure if the guy was clueless, or felt like being a jerk that day.

---

[23] Mark used the word 'Fairy' to mean "wimpy" or "weak." Sometimes we called each other fairies when one of us was being a baby about something. His shoulders gave him problems and were weaker than normal. It must be inherited because my shoulders have given me problems too and I've consulted the same doctor who operated on Mark.

Mark was also lactose intolerant and had to take medicine regularly as an adult, or at least before he ate/drank dairy. He, and we, called that pill his "fairy pill." Referring to dairy products, he'd jokingly say, "I can't tolerate it." He put at least one in every vehicle he might be in, his truck, my truck, mom's and dad's. Mine still has his "fairy pills" in the console and I don't plan to remove them.

In 2003, he got a part time job at a doctor's office at the DCH Medical Tower, called Tuscaloosa Lung and Sleep. The office was full of women and, predictably, there was lots of drama. The women loved him and he became friends with many, especially Dana Brewer. She thought of him as a younger brother and invited him to eat at her home many times.

I often heard Mark speak of Dana and her daughter Meagon. Dana loved Mark so much that she nick-named him "Marky-doodle". This was a name she called her cousin before he died years before. Apparently, this name caught on quick in the office. He knew about some struggles she was having and always made himself available for her to vent and talk it out. Dana also says that Mark was a great mentor to Meagon, like a big brother. Meagon talked to him about the jerk boys she knew. He never failed to make her feel better, even if he knew she was infatuated[24] with him.

He started classes in January and we attended the same church. It was a family congregation, but there were a lot of students too. Not surprisingly, because he was confident (sometimes a little cocky), out-going, up-beat and funny, he made friends easily. Even before he started working out and sculpting his body, he was a good-looking kid and never lacked attention from young women. He dated and had a couple sort-of girlfriends through college. The relationships went only so far, though.

My friends and I often felt frustrated by the lack of eligible young women, and it was no different for Mark. There was no shortage of very pretty girls around, but Mark was interested in a committed, life-long relationship, not just hangin' out. And Mark's expectations were pretty high. I know he wanted a wife who not only shared his values and commitment to live by them, but who could challenge him to always strive to be better. That takes more than a pretty face and nice build.

---

[24] Whenever Meagon saw Mark, she virtually beamed. I specifically made sure she was comfortable with me using this word to describe her reaction to Mark. I suppose there is absolutely no shame in a girl taking a fancy to someone like Mark: honorable, productive, and a physical specimen—how could she help herself??

I guess one up-side of this situation was the "male bonding" opportunities it provided. There were five of us guys who were pretty much in the same boat: single, active, in school (or just out, in my case), and not really involved with anyone. We all shared an ironic sense of humor that was heavily laced with quotes and references to movies and TV shows like *Seinfeld*. We sarcastically called ourselves "The Fab Five." I was not the oldest, but had lived in Tuscaloosa a long time, so I was #1, #2 was Michael Shiffler, Drew Richetto was #3, Aaron Huff was #4, last to "join" and youngest was Mark. It didn't matter whether we were going out for good food, playing video games, or watching *Terry Tate: Office Linebacker* commercials, we always had a good time together.

I bought a house in 2005 and of course Mark moved in with me. We were known in the neighborhood as the guys with trucks and 4-wheelers. We had great neighbors, whom we quickly got to know. One told me that she always felt better knowing Mark was home during the day (since he had a non-standard schedule) when she was at work and her kids were home alone at times. Later, in early 2012, my wife and I finally moved from this home to take a job in the Birmingham area. It wasn't easy for me to let that house go since Mark and I had shared so many good memories there. Before Rozlynn and I left, we wrote these words on the inside of the air vent of his old bedroom: "Bedroom of American Hero Mark Forester."

We saw a lot of **Michael Shiffler.** In addition to our fun times, he came over every Sunday afternoon to do his laundry at our house. Looking back on it, I suppose some people would get annoyed with the same guy coming over to use their place every week, but it just became part of our routine. Mark and I thought nothing of it, but Michael says he really appreciated it then, and it's a big deal to him still.

During those days, Michael was also teaching biology and Mark took the class. He was a good student and easily earned an "A," but clearly, he didn't struggle much. Sometimes, though, he wouldn't get a concept right off, and he was not shy about asking for clarification. With a little help he got it and didn't forget.

Michael says the thing that stands out most about Mark was his readiness to help anybody, anytime. "He never said, 'no'." In Michael's case, one day he had to move from one apartment to another, but couldn't find anybody to help him. Finally, he called Mark and soon after, Mark appeared with his pickup. Just the two of them moved all of Michael's stuff to the new apartment. While moving, Mark seemed as content doing this job (that most others loath and avoid) as he would have been doing anything else. Afterward, they went to (Mark's *favorite*) Chick-fil-A to recharge. Michael says Mark never even hinted that he might "owe him one."

Michael also let me know just how much video game playing went on while I was at work or sleeping. He and Mark would set up on separate TVs in our house (instead of playing split-screen in the same room), and could easily kill six hours on a Saturday. Michael figures it's no exaggeration to say that Mark dedicated *thousands* of hours to the games, "maybe even a whole year's worth!" It's no wonder he crushed his buddies at Cobra playing video games.

I have to wonder if this was not good training for him. Those games require exceptional coordination and dexterity, and not just hand-eye. To be that good, players have to coordinate numerous variables—near simultaneously—and react very quickly to changes on the field. Also, they were not just playing against the machine, but playing against other humans via the internet. It sounds a lot like how a combat controller has to work.

As my brother progressed through school—and then on to the Air Force—he met lots of people and had many experiences that I couldn't share with him. To fill in some of these times, many of his friends and teammates have generously shared their memories.

Drew Richetto:

> One of the most memorable and noble things I recall Mark doing was an enormous favor for my little sister, Victoria, who was still in high school. I was in California going to school when she called me in tears. I could feel the sense of panic and sorrow in her voice as she explained to me that she just found out that the kid who was supposed to be her prom date was backing out.
>
> For most of us, prom is the single most profound and important event that can make or break your entire year. After a long discussion with my sister, I told her things will work out and it will be her best prom ever.
>
> Next, I spoke with my parents and we all decided the best solution would be to find a knight in shining armor to rescue Victoria from certain humiliation. The discussion about who could qualify was pretty short. And my parents and I almost

immediately agreed that the only man we knew who could (and probably would) step in at the last second and undo all the wrong heaped upon Victoria.

When he answered my call, the first thing out of my mouth was, "Mark, something bad has happened to Victoria, and I need ya buddy!" True to his reputation, Mark immediately rose to the occasion, and graciously escorted Victoria to her Senior Prom.

It was the best possible outcome. If Victoria had known she could have had Mark as her original date, she would have never given her first prospect a second thought. She was always very fond of Mark. Small wonder too, Mark was always caring and sincere in any situation.

Now, it's important to note that this was 2004 and Mark was almost 23 years old—going to a high school prom. He wasn't thrilled to hang out with high schoolers on their prom night, but he was glad to help out Victoria and put her brother and family at ease. He had a good time bowling with them later that night too. I chalk it up to another example of Mark putting loyalty to his friends ahead of his own comfort.

Doug Cole roomed with Mark after I left Tuscaloosa to work in Mississippi for a year. They were already good friends, having entered Alabama during the same semester and actually had a class together. Doug remembers:

It was an English Literature class that we both loathed. The teacher was alright, though, and allowed Mark and me to cut up every once in a while. Mark was not shy and would ask questions when he did not understand things. It would crack the teacher up too, because we would be reading some Old English stuff (Chaucer or Milton?) and Mark would interject mid-sentence and say, "wait a minute ...*now what was that?*" The whole class would snicker because they were thinking the same thing; he just had the guts to say something about it."

As roommates, we had some house rules. To be honest, we both had a lot of rules because many things would annoy us. If a guest would violate a rule, he or she would have to receive a yardstick lashing. This got a little ridiculous because people would purposely break rules to provoke us and see if we would follow through. We *always* followed through, and it was usually hilarious.

Rooming with Mark was very entertaining, because you never knew what you would get from him day to day--he was passionately opinionated. Something would get him riled up at school, like campus preachers or handicap parking slots taken by able-bodied people, and he would rant for a while. I loved the rants because they were so ridiculous, but so important to Mark.

If I could have put off my marriage and continued to room with Mark, I would have. We would talk about everything, and I mean everything. We spent hours discussing girls, relationships, computers, what businesses we could start, school, sports, careers, the gospel, and many, many more topics.

I will always regard Mark as one of the most influential people in my life. He had grown up with the family of the girl I was dating, Sarah Tinker. His intimate perspective on her life and family was key to encouraging me to ask her to marry me.

By Mark's second year at Alabama, he was very serious about going into the military after graduation. Part of his preparation was to work out and train seriously. He and Joseph had always been close, but with Joseph being in the Air Force, they talked about the military a lot. Joseph had hoped that Mark would get married before graduation, and that would point him away from the clearly dangerous jobs he usually talked about, like Special Forces, or the Navy SEALs. However, with less than a year and a half to go, and no clear prospects

Our Family 2004

for a wife, Joseph focused on steering Mark toward a job that would give him some marketable skills after military separation, and maybe keep him out of harm's way.

Being an Air Force doctor, Joseph had heard plenty about people in the other services getting hurt. So on one of Mark's visits when Patsy and

Joseph were in San Antonio, TX, Joseph took him on base and they checked out the PJs as they worked out. Mark listened and watched closely, then someone mentioned some Combat Controllers who were also training nearby. Mark went over and met with some of those guys. He came back with his mind made up; he wanted to be a Combat Controller. Joseph had never heard of CCTs, and certainly had never heard of any of them dying.

Only Mark seemed to have a clear idea about what being a CCT meant. Joseph figured that with them being so highly trained—and valuable—they would be less likely to out in the very front. If Mark didn't actually encourage the misperceptions of everyone in the family, he certainly didn't discourage any of them. "It was more dangerous for me on my mission in Oakland," he'd say. For the next two years, as he finished his degree, he focused on getting ready for Combat Control.

He had always been athletically skilled, and now that he had caught up to his peers in stature, he was serious competition. Mark and his friends enjoyed a number of intramural sports, but flag football was a particular favorite.

This story from **Anthony Bassett** highlights how Mark and his friends blended good humor and inside jokes:

> The football team was called the Mullet Militia. We wore black t-shirts with a white skull on the front center. Mark was our most-used quarterback. He had a good arm, so it made sense. He was also pretty fast and tall, so he was an advantage to have as a receiver too. Michael Shiffler was the coach and came up with most of our offensive plays. This particular year we made it to the semi-finals of the playoffs. We were undefeated until we lost in the championship game.
>
> During our first intramural game, Mark threw a pass to me for a two point conversion. It was a beautiful play. When we got back to the sideline, he walked over to me and Rochelle. Mark looked at her and said, referring to me sarcastically, "He's sexual, athletic and without a trace of self-consciousness." I laughed hysterically because it was obviously a reference to Kramer from *Seinfeld* modeling for Calvin Klein.
>
> As Mark turned to walk away, I shot back, "Don't forget—my buttocks are sublime!"

He laughed and responded, "Of course, your pectorals could use some work. I suppose we could get you to the weight room…."

Rochelle looked at us with a more than slight confusion on her face.

Exchanges like this happened all the time; mixtures of sarcastic mockery and quotes from shows always peppered our good, honest fun.

Around this same time, Mark, one of his friends and I, were discussing how bad the punter at Alabama was. Mark knew he could punt better than that guy could. He had arranged with a friend of ours, Tyler Knight, to set up a small try-out. Tyler was a trainer and thought he could make it happen. Mark was on board, along with his friend Chase Layton. Mark wasn't interested in a scholarship; he just wanted to prove that he was better than the starting punter. He wanted to be one of those guys that not only could kick, but also wasn't afraid to lay a lick on someone. I'm not sure why, but this try-out never happened. It's really too bad, but I guess it was a long shot anyway.

Later, Anthony shared a couple other stories with me:

In 2004, shortly after Hurricane Ivan, Mark and I were part of a clean-up team that went down to the Gulf Coast. On one particularly hot day, Mark and I worked for hours trying to move an enormous tree off the main road that ran in front of this particular neighborhood. After about three hours of struggling and fighting, Mark finally began to make some progress with a chainsaw.

As Mark cut the branches away, I would carry them off and load them in a nearby truck. Our system was working out quite well. Mark got to be so fast at clearing off the branches that I couldn't keep up with him. So, as he would cut them, he'd then just throw them off to the side. I guess that he had gotten into such a rhythm that he did not see me behind him. Out of nowhere, a rather sizeable log landed on my foot. I shouted, "Geez, man, I think you broke my toe." Mark, in an attempt to make me laugh, responded, "If you didn't want your foot broken, you shouldn't have put it there." We kept working without incident through the rest of that day and without a word spoken about my injured foot. On our way back home to Tuscaloosa, Mark stopped and bought me Chick-fil-A for dinner. He said that it was his way of apologizing for "mangling" my foot. That was the ultimate apology coming from Mark because, in his words, "I don't buy this stuff for just anyone."

The year following Hurricane Ivan, Katrina slammed the gulf and we found ourselves in Hattiesburg, MS helping with the cleanup. At one house, some limbs needed to be removed that were about 20 feet up over the house. Mark was the only one who volunteered (and probably the only one brave enough) to climb the tree, anchored by a rope, and remove the limbs. Most everyone helping that day was standing around watching Mark in action.

Anthony continues: I had a number of opportunities to perform service with Mark. It seemed like Mark was close by every time I got a call from the local church leadership. We would regularly take the Sacrament to members of the church that were unable to attend Sunday meetings. Mark's immaculately cleaned truck was also helpful when people needed large pieces of furniture moved across town. In all of those services opportunities, I never once heard Mark complain.

One time, Mark and I went to the Birmingham LDS Temple with a group of the youth from church. After the youth had finished, we decided to stay behind and do some additional temple work. When we came out of the temple, it was rather late and Mark had told me that he needed to get home to study. As we got out to the parking lot, we noticed an older gentleman trying to change a flat tire. Mark immediately went over to see if he could help out in any way. Mark did not really ask if he could help. Instead, he just walked over and started taking the flat tire off the car. There he was in his white shirt and tie, changing a flat tire.

Mark tried to convince me that the two greatest songs ever were *"You're the Best Around"* from *"The Karate Kid"* soundtrack and *"There's No Easy Way Out"* from one of the Rocky films.

One day, a mutual friend introduced us to a website that contained links to various humorous videos and sound clips. Mark was especially impressed with one of the links on the site that contained a library of sound clips from various Arnold Schwarzenegger movies. The idea was that you could string a number of these clips together to use for prank phone calls.

Mark loved this idea and immediately wanted to use this newly found website to prank some of our friends. Of course, most people knew that it was a joke when we called them, but that did not derail Mark's efforts to keep calling. In fact, Mark even used this website during one of our last phone conversations together. His favorite line came from the movie "Kindergarten Cop." In this film, Arnold asks the question, "Who is your daddy and what does he do?"

I can still hear Mark and his friends playing this audio clip over and over. As juvenile as it was, it was hilarious.

One last story Anthony shared has to do with Mark's frustration with not finding the love of his life while he was in college. This brought about some juvenile behaviors that have to make you laugh. Anthony says:

> During our days at Alabama, the guys from our Tuscaloosa Young Single Adult (YSA) group would get together and spend countless hours playing "Halo" and various other games. After one of these "Halo" sessions, a few of the guys stuck around and the topic somehow turned to the dating difficulties many of us were having. Being the ridiculous college-aged men that we were, we decided that it would be a "good" idea to type a list of grievances that we had with the girls in our YSA group. All of us, including Mark, made contributions to this list. The items listed were pretty absurd and basically the result of our own dating weaknesses. Mark did not hold any punches. His main complaint was, and I quote, "The girls do not know how to flirt, and do not attempt to learn." It is hard to tell if he was being completely serious or not, but that line was delivered in a typical Mark style.

In the summer of 2006, Mark and I took a trip to Utah to see a few friends. At some point, we went to a Dick's Sporting Goods that had a very high climbing wall and Mark decided to climb it. As he was getting hooked up, Mark's friend and I started acting like Mark had never climbed before and that he stood no chance getting up, because he'd chosen the hardest path up the wall.

There was a man and his son standing there with us and he asked if Mark had climbed before and for some reason, we told him "no" even though Mark had done a fair bit of rock climbing. The guy gave us a smirk and said, "There's no way he'd make it to the top." At that moment, Mark was just starting up and I yelled, "Hey Mark, this guy says you don't have a chance of getting to the top." He looked over his shoulder and said very calmly, "Alright, then I will get to the top."

Mark looked great going up that wall, like a machine. I loved seeing the look on that guy's face when Mark was almost at the top and realized this wasn't Mark first rodeo. He was very close to the top when he had to quit. Not because he was tired, but because the wall was missing pegs that made it impossible to go any higher.

Another story from that trip shows how we fed off each other: We were leaving Temple Square in downtown Salt Lake City when we noticed a protestor just outside the north gate. He was holding a sign, giving away some kind of handout, and heckling unassuming visitors as they passed near the gate. (This is common around Temple Square.) I said to myself, "I can't let this go today."[25] So we walked over and tried talking with him, but it really wasn't a conversation because he immediately launched into an angry tirade against the LDS church. Mark and I never once got mad but we did joke around with him because nothing he said made much sense.

The more worked up he got, the more fun we had talking to him. I noticed some of the sister missionaries started checking out what we were doing. I'm sure they thought we were causing trouble. Actually, we weren't much interested in taunting him, we just wanted him to pack up and go home. It didn't take long before he got mad and started pointing his finger in our faces, that's when we noticed his index finger was half missing. Mark instantly asked him about it which derailed him mid-rant. Let's just say we didn't take his preaching seriously. Finally, we wished him well and as we walked across the street to our car, he shot a sarcastic, "Have a nice day!" after us. Mark replied, "Don't say that when you really want us to get hit by a car."

As we left the parking lot, we saw him gather his stuff and stomp off. I asked Mark if we handled it right. He said, "Thad, he packed up and left. Yes, it worked." Maybe he left because of us or maybe because his shift was over. We didn't know, but we preferred to think it was us. It may not be right, but I have to confess some satisfaction about the encounter. One thing is certain and that is I sure loved hanging out with Mark.

---

[25] When I was a missionary, I dealt with these kinds of people all the time, but was limited in how I could respond. This time, I wasn't a missionary and could engage them on my terms.

By June of 2008, Joseph and his family had moved to Colorado. Mark made one of his visits and had plans for a day of rafting on the Arkansas River. While gathered around the raft for the safety briefing, Joseph and Mark were acting several years less than their age, making jokes and not paying much attention, which is still typical when we brothers are together. One thing Joseph did catch is that if two or more people were thrown from the boat, they should swim toward each other and hang onto the same paddle so they could stay together as they rode the rapids down to smooth water.

They all got underway with Joseph and Mark in the same boat, continuing their joking around. They hit a couple small rapids and my brothers teased the guide, "Is this all ya got??" It wasn't, and with the first big rapid, Mark's corner got sucked in a little and instantly swept him out of the boat. Joseph says, "We came up and Mark wasn't there! I leaned forward looking for him when the next bump hit and I went flying through the air and landed right on top of Mark, who'd just barely gotten his head above the churning water."

Then it got scary. The current seemed to hold him underwater for a long time. The water was just deep enough that Joseph could feel the bottom in places with his toes, but he couldn't kick off of it to get a breath. He said he was down long enough to start wondering if this was going to be "it" and that if today was his day, then drowning wasn't quite as bad as he'd thought it would be. Finally, the river smoothed, the life jacket did its job and Joseph popped up, gasping and sputtering. He glanced around in time to see Mark's head pop up. "Are you alright?" Mark was fine, but he was just as disoriented as Joseph. Remembering the safety lecture, he called out, "Mark, give me your paddle!" "What?" Joseph yelled it again, "Give me your paddle." Mark raised it out of the water, tossed it toward Joseph, then started swimming to shore. Joseph had his own paddle in one hand, had to grab Mark's with his other, and then struggle to get himself to shore with both paddles.

Once on the river bank, Joseph (between coughing up river water) asked, "Why did you throw your paddle at me?" Mark said, "You said you wanted it—I didn't know why." Clearly, he hadn't paid attention to the safety briefing. As they discussed the situation, Mark had had the same trouble of feeling trapped between the surface and bottom. He'd also begun to worry whether he'd get above water again before it was too late.

The rest of the trip was fun and gratefully uneventful, but there was still another near-death experience for them to share that weekend. The next day, Patsy went off to do some shopping, leaving the guys with the kids. Joseph had just grilled some tri-tip steaks. The end of one was a little burnt, so he cut a piece off that end and popped it in his mouth.

It started down the wrong way making him cough and choke a little. Mark joked, "Do ya need me to give you the Heimlich??" Joseph coughed slightly, caught his breath, and then took a drink from his soda. That made it worse, sending the meat back down the wrong way, even deeper this time. Soda fizzed up in his mouth and nose and Joseph was in real trouble now, grabbing his throat in the universal choking gesture. Mark knew what to do and made good on his offer, getting behind Joseph and giving him a strong heave. It didn't come right away, so, "Mark just started whalin' on me." Finally it came up, Joseph was gagging, leaning over the kitchen sink, struggling to suppress the urge to vomit. Eventually, he caught his breath enough to wheeze, "Hey buddy, I owe ya one." All of their kids were very small then. "If Mark hadn't been there, I would have been in real trouble." Some say trouble comes in threes, and after these two events, Joseph was on alert for the third one. Fortunately it seems fate had toyed with them enough for that weekend.

Brad Knight, an old friend from Haleyville who was at UA at the same time as Mark, wrote to mom and dad after Mark's death:

> No matter what story I tell you, Mark made that story better for everyone around him. He always made things better. If we were playing paintball, football, or even wrestling as kids, Mark made it more fun. If we were sitting in church or in Sunday School, Mark made it more interesting.
>
> Our last year or so in Tuscaloosa together, after Mark had made up his mind that he was going into the Air Force, we were doing some pretty intense workouts—he made them harder.

Hayden Hill is a friend who Mark and I both knew while in Tuscaloosa. She dated a mutual friend of ours, and is responsible for introducing me to Rozlynn, so she's got a special spot with us.

> I distinctly remember the conversation I had with Mark when he decided to join the Air Force. We were hanging with a friend in his living room on a typical, ridiculously hot Alabama day and I asked him—somewhat perplexed—why he decided to enlist. "You graduated from college, Mark! Why would you enlist??"

Of course, he told me that he wanted to be the guy on the ground, in the action, pulling the trigger.

Then he said, in his characteristically no-nonsense way, that he wanted to be the person standing between me and the people who would want to hurt me. Absolutely incredible! "Greater love hath no man than this, that a man lay down his life for his friends."

Jason Stanley, another college buddy who, like Mark, planned on a career in the military after graduation.

I first met Mark in our SCUBA diving class at UA. He was the assistant instructor, and my buddies, John McDow, William Hopper and I, were pretty much the Three Amigos/class clowns. Fortunately, Mark didn't hold it against us and we all began to pal around, making the Three Amigos the "Whatever You Want to Call It" Four.

First, we all had an interest in the military. I was in the military and ROTC, John was pursuing a Marine Corps Commission, and Mark told us he was planning to join the military. I tried persuading him to join the Army and John argued that he should be a Marine. I think Mark had already made up his mind about the Air Force, but he never let on about it.

Our days consisted of classes, homework, and plenty of clowning around; in the evenings we usually got together and watched *Seinfeld* (a lot), and of course *Anchorman*. For whatever reason, whenever we all got around each other, our voices would instantly become like Ron Burgundy and we would put our fingers on top of our lips making a mustache. To call us a silly bunch was an understatement. Entire conversations would be quotes from *Seinfeld* or *Anchorman*, and yet they would make perfect sense, to us anyway! The only times I remember us being serious is when we were in the gym.

I remember a big change in Mark. It all started after we went to the opening of the movie, "300." From then on, we thought we were Spartans. John's strength and endurance already made him a freak of nature, but I could hold my own physically. I had not known Mark very long at that point, so I had no idea what he was really made of. Boy did I get educated.

I think by this time Mark had settled on being a Combat Controller, and he was eager to get ready for it. I saw a thrill on his face and knew something good was happening for him. That's when he began the transformation I told you about in the past—all the kettle bells, running, pull-ups and "Spartanization" that we used to call it.

Over the following weeks, we watched as Mark went from the quiet, somewhat skinny guy, to a freaking *WARRIOR*. It seemed that whenever we saw him, he was just about to go workout, had just finished working out, or he was thinking of ways to "Spartanize" himself. I was impressed.

For whatever reason—I have no idea why—whenever a group of military men get together, we start pounding our chests about how awesome or strong we are, and we follow it up with a "homo" comment. It's beyond me why, but that is the way it goes sometimes.

This tendency played out in a very comical way once. Mark and I were doings pull-ups in the gym, I was knocking out a set and Mark was there to give me a spot for the last couple reps. I can still remember him saying it like it was five minutes ago: "Jason, you know there is not a gay thing about me in the WORLD, but I have to tell you that you have the nicest calves of anyone I have ever seen." I busted out laughing hard because it was obvious that Mark was uncomfortable saying this to another guy. I was laughing and then he started laughing. Finally, I composed myself enough to say, "Thanks Mark.....ya homo!"

Then we got back to our workout and he proceeded to crush me in upper body strength exercises.

Whenever Mark set his mind to something, NOTHING could stand in his way. But of all the things I admire about him, his determination and dedication to his values stand out most. Mark was different. He was an example of what *right* looks like. He was the model Christian Soldier (or Airman, in his case).

One time, I asked him why the Air Force and not the Army (or Marines). I remember him vaguely telling me that Joseph was in the Air Force and that he was an officer, but nothing really more than just that. When I really started to get to know him, he had mentioned something about CCT, and I, having not really known much about the Air Force, just kind of passed it off as some pretend high speed job. Boy was I off base!

Mark wanted to be in the best type of Air Force unit because that meant he would be able to fight the much tougher and more determined enemy with more firepower and combat skill than any other joker in the Air Force. Any tater could fly a plane and drop bombs, but Mark....no way, he wanted to be where the metal met the meat and personally see to the destruction of the nasty, nasty people who wanted to do harm to his teammates and America. He knew EXACTLY where he wanted to put that bomb and silence the enemy for good.

Although I never heard him say it, I heard later about "God told me to" and I fully believe it. I also like to think there is a spin on it that says that Mark had so much desire and commitment to his job because God telling him to kill terrorists was in line with destroying an enemy that was intent on doing bad things to America. I only saw Mark get excited about a couple things: America and Chick-fil-A. Don't come in between him and either one of those things. You might not get your hand back.

Finally, although Mark was absolutely rock solid in his faith, he never made himself out to be better than the rest because of it. He was never rude or condescending; he never thought less of anyone because they did things that he wouldn't do.

He was the real deal, even willing to give his life to help someone else, as he proved. I wish I could have known him longer, but I am thankful for the times that we shared.

As long as heroes like Mark walk the Earth, we will have stories to tell our sons of what they should aspire to be.

Another standout memory from our great Tuscaloosa days is from Thanksgiving Day 2009, when Mark was home for a few days. He and I played with some friends and several people from church in a Turkey Bowl (flag football) game. Not only did Mark and I plan to be on the same team, but we plotted our first play. I would be the QB. He would run a fly route and I'd bomb him one because he's so fast and tall, he'd be hard to stop.

Well, when we started picking teams, someone immediately said, "Mark and Thad can't be on the same team." I'm really not sure why they said that, maybe because we were just about the tallest players, or they knew how competitive we could get. Anyway, it turned out we didn't even play against each other. There were 4 teams, so we were on different fields for both games played. Mark still dominated. In fact, someone said after we were done, "Mark is a beast!" He often ran farther than the QB could throw. I remember he was wearing his five-finger shoes the whole time too. I really wish I could have played with him that day.

Mark stayed on with the scuba class as an assistant to the instructor even after his buddies, the "Three Amigos," completed the course. In researching this book, I learned that Mark was present when a tragedy took place in that class:

On April 17, 2007, the class took part in a "doff and don" drill, removing their equipment, descending to the bottom of the 18-foot, Olympic-sized pool, recovering their gear and staying at depth breathing from regulators until everyone finished the drill. According to the civil lawsuit, [the class instructor] was not in the pool during the training exercise. Instead, she was giving a private lesson to [someone who was] not enrolled in the class, at the opposite end of the pool. She appointed her two assistants, Mark Forester and Henry McIntyre, to oversee the drill, but both were only certified as open-water divers and had no instructor qualifications.

Zachary M., [one of the students in the class], ascended after taking off his gear but was found floating face-down on the surface. An autopsy revealed he had inhaled the compressed air while descending but didn't exhale while swimming to the surface... Forester and McIntyre removed [the student] from the pool and called 911. [He] was rushed to the hospital, where he was pronounced dead from a lung overexpansion injury and an arterial gas embolism.[26]

Mark told me about it, but never in much detail. One of his friends remembers discussing it and Mark said he and Henry McIntyre were able to help calm down the shaken instructor and address this situation. Although we don't have a lot of detail about Mark's role, I am certain he acted without delay when it was clear that Moore was in trouble.

---

[26] http://www.undercurrent.org/UCnow/dive_magazine/2008/ DiveInstructor200809.html – Used with permission of *Undercurrent* 3020 Bridgeway, Suite 102, Sausalito, CA 94965

Rozlynn Forester – Mark's Sister-in-Law, my wife:

The first time I met Mark was after a 12-hour journey with my big sister, Brooke. We had driven from Washington, D.C. to Alabama, prior to my marrying Thad. We planned to meet Mark and Thad at a *Regions Bank* location in Tuscaloosa. They would then escort us the rest of the way to make sure we didn't get lost on the rest of the trip to my new home.

I remember waiting there in front of *Regions* when the green Toyota Tundra I'd been watching for pulled up next to us. Mark jumped out and greeted us warmly. I have to say, it was sorta weird because here I was engaged to his brother, but it was impossible to ignore how tall and handsome he was. And my happily married, mom-of-three sister was awestruck by Mark as if he were a male model or movie star.

Brooke stayed with me at Thad's house and helped me get settled into my new city for a few days. During that time, we were able to spend some time with Mark.

The second day we were in Alabama, Mark was a gentleman and paid for us to go to the University pool. I remember the three of us laying there; Brooke and I were pointing out girls and asking Mark if he thought they were cute. He would either praise or critique each girl. There was a really cute girl who clearly caught Mark's eye. Brooke and I pressed him to go talk to her and I swear he almost did.

That day, we floated around the lazy river, swam and soaked up the sun some more. All while teasing Mark, talking about girls, and doing my usual "over shares." He was such a good sport and took it all with smiles and some chuckling. I'm sure he had to be thinking, "Who *is* this girl?" I remember coming away from that day thinking that although he was tall, big and strong, that deep down he was a big teddy bear. I liked that combo.

Other things about Mark that I remember are whether he was at our house, or at Pat and Ray's, he'd lean up against the counter with his legs crossed whenever he was in the kitchen. I am not sure why that sticks in my head but it does, maybe because he was just so comfortable with himself and what he was doing.

Also, whenever he was at Pat and Ray's, Mark could often be found stretched out on the green couch, scrolling through his iPhone or watching something on the Discovery Channel. He often stayed with Thad and me and since we didn't have a big green couch, he'd roost in our old armchair, tucked in the corner of the room. Knowing how much he loved that chair, I joked that I would sell it to him for $50.

Despite Mark's many accomplishments, it was clear he looked up to Thad and loved him. They were tight. I can still hear him saying to Thad "come on bro" with his Mark tone. Even after he'd moved out of Thad's house and was in the Air Force, he could not have been more at home when he visited. I'd often find Chick-fil-A leftovers on the counter.

Mark would often talk about meeting girls or wanting to meet girls. I remember when he met Megan and him telling Thad that he had met this girl with the cutest voice and accent ever. He was smitten.

I so wish I had more memories and experiences with Mark. He is and was my handsome and strong brother-in-law. I didn't know the younger, smaller Mark, I knew Mark the tough Combat Controller. He and Thad loved each other very much. They were each other's' best friend.

When Mark came to visit us, he'd pull his big green truck up and park on the front lawn. It used to drive me crazy, but now what I wouldn't give to have him park on the lawn again.

As much of a straight-shooter as Mark was, he could be impulsive. This almost cost him his shot at becoming a Combat Controller, or even joining the military at all:

Mark Forester
Tuscaloosa, AL 35406

To whom it may concern,

On the afternoon of July 2, 2003, I was headed to the beach when I made a very regrettable decision that has plagued me since. I was traveling in a group of vehicles when we passed a Florala city policeman. In my rearview mirror I saw him turn around and started heading in our direction. I made the unfortunate decision to turn off of the road into a neighborhood. After seeing him go past the road I was now driving down, I realized that my decision was not appropriate and was unlawful, so I made the decision to go back to the main road that I was originally headed down and head in the direction I last saw the policeman and try to rectify the problem. The officer saw me turn back on the road and made a quick turnaround. Upon seeing this I quickly pulled over and waited for him to approach the vehicle. He then proceeded to give me a ticket for attempting to allude.

I have tried to live my life in a manner free from any vices or evils that would bring my character into question. Unfortunately, On July 2, 2003 I made an unwise decision that has done just that. That decision has caused my character to be questioned in other ways, and it is something that will never be repeated. I felt terrible about that decision at the time I made it, and I still feel just as terrible now as I am writing this letter of appeal. For the past few years my main desire has been to serve my country in the greatest Air Force in the world. Given the opportunity, I will serve in a manner that will continue to bring integrity, justice, and honor to my fellow airmen and leaders, and also to my country.

Sincerely,
Mark Forester

This was an isolated incident and honestly, we actually got a good laugh out of it. Regardless, it wasn't the right decision; therefore his license was suspended for a few months. Mark had to get rides from everyone. Many times mom came down and drove him to class. He would walk to work after class. In fact, one day we were under a tornado warning, and a tornado was near the hospital where Mark worked. His luck was bad that day because it was right when he was walking to work. He later told me how bad the wind and lightning was on that walk. He ran most of the way. I think it was a little scary, but it was funny to hear him tell about it.

There are many other stories, and there is no way to capture them all. Mostly, I wanted to share an idea of what it was like to live with and be Mark's friend. Reflecting on his friendship with Mark, **Scott Bradberry** wrote:

> I have to acknowledge the wrenching in my gut that has come *every* time I attempt to sit down and write about Mark. I'm sure that this pain belongs to you and all of the Forester family (that I love so dearly) each waking moment that his face comes to mind. You have my sympathies and my love.

Mark and I became interested in rock climbing during my junior year of high school and the obsession grew over time. Whenever Mark was in Haleyville he would come to the house and we would unload our heavy equipment from his truck and carry it the short distance to the place we climbed. There just happened to be a beautiful spot in the bluffs behind our barn that was very good for climbing. We lovingly referred to this rock as, *The Face*.

There were great places for foot holds and hand holds. There were places that required our greatest reach to grab hold, while praying that we could hold on for just a second more. My personal favorite was a spot near the top that required one to leap, with all of the body leaving the rock for a split second, to a ledge several feet up *The Face*.

In reflection, I'm not sure what the biggest attraction was for Mark. It might have been the workout that climbing the rock provided. Was it the rush that came with not knowing whether you would be hanging on one second or falling through space the next? It may have been the challenge the rock presented to us every day: Get over the top.

It was a manly activity. During the summer months, you could bet we would have our shirts off and the camera on, filming our incredible climbing skills. Maybe one day some fine honeys might see our videos and be impressed. Yeah, right.

We tried for months to climb some fifty feet to the ledge and make it over. Five feet from the top was a massive overhang in the rock which required the climber to use only his arms to pull himself up and over the edge. After climbing the distance to the overhang, we were always too tired to get over the edge. Each time I watched Mark go up I just knew it was going to be the time that his body would slither from view over the edge. The moment never came. We got tired. We got scared. Whatever it was, it kept us from our goal: Get over the top.

The person on belay (holding the rope at the bottom) would always provide some type of encouragement to the climber. When I was on belay, I said things like, "You climb like my grandmother" and, quoting Mark, "You make me sick!" In reply,

I would hear Mark Forester of the Channel 4 News team, *"Hello, my name is Mark Forester. I enjoy a bowl of ice cream and a nice pair of slacks. Years from now a doctor will tell me I have an I.Q. of 47 and am, what some people call, mentally retarded."* All I could do was laugh.

Whenever Mark was belaying me, I would complain about my arms being tired, and how far away the top was. All Mark would say was, "If that helps you get over the top..." When I wanted to give up, he wouldn't release the belay so that I could float back to the ground. He would tell me, "Scott, you are going to rest up there. You will get blood back in your fingers and you will continue to climb. When I would come to that impossible ledge though, Mark's words would change. Almost pleadingly he would say, "You're right there! Just go over the top."

Soon after another failed day of climbing, I went out to climb with another friend of mine. That day I did something that I will never forget, and something that I will regret forever. I went over the top. Mark was not there. At the time, I was so proud to tell him that I made it, and that I couldn't wait until he could come back and do it himself. So the very next time that Mark came to town he came over. We unpacked the gear, he tied the knots as he always did, and we walked the same path to the bottom as we always had. The only thing different was Mark. His first climb that day he exploded up The Face. His long body making holds I had never seen him perform. There was a spot below the overhang that was especially tough for Mark because of his size. He grunted a little in pain and fatigue, his muscles tensed, he slipped once or twice but hung on. Finally, with a scream like a mad-man, he threw himself forward and up the overhang. His body disappeared a few seconds later. Then his feet reappeared as he dangled them over the edge at me in victory. He never gave up.

When Mark went away, he left me all of the equipment so that I could climb whenever I wished. I haven't climbed since the 29th of September 2010. I don't know that I will ever climb again.

I asked Scott about this recently. On 29 October 2012 he wrote:

I used to climb with a lot of different people in the same spot, with the same equipment that Mark and I used. It was different though. I think because Mark and I started it, everybody else just kind of fell in and fell out, but Mark was always ready for a climb.

I'm not sure how to explain why I haven't climbed since Mark was killed. The best way I know to say it is that it just wouldn't feel right. If I went now, I think I would feel like I was telling a secret that I promised somebody I wouldn't ever tell, or betraying somebody who trusted me.

Like I said, I'm not sure how to describe it other than that.

"If it was easy anybody could do it."
– Ray Forester

CHAPTER 10

The Schoolhouse

In the Combat Control community, they affectionately refer to their extensive training program as *"The Schoolhouse"* and *"The Pipeline."* Every CCT, from lowest enlisted man (like Mark was) to academy graduates, must master the same skills and endure the same rigors and hardships. The following is directly from the USAF Fact Sheet. Not only is it the most concise explanation of a profession that receives very little attention, but at some point—very early on—Mark had to have read these same words and thought, *"That's what I'm going to do."*

U.S. Air Force Fact Sheet: COMBAT CONTROLLERS

Mission
Air Force Special Operations Command's combat controllers, or CCT, are Battlefield Airmen assigned to special tactics squadrons. The CCT mission is to deploy undetected into combat and hostile environments to establish assault zones or airfields, while simultaneously conducting air traffic control, fire support, command and control, direct action, counter-terrorism, foreign internal defense, humanitarian assistance and special reconnaissance.

Motto
Their motto, "First There," reaffirms the combat controller's commitment to undertaking the most dangerous missions behind enemy lines by leading the way for other forces to follow.

Training

Combat controllers are among the most highly trained special operations force in the U.S. military. They maintain their core skill as air traffic controllers throughout their career in addition to other unique skills. They are trained in infiltration methods including static-line and freefall parachuting, scuba, rubber raiding craft, all-terrain vehicles, rappelling and fast rope methods. Most qualify and maintain currency as joint terminal attack controllers.

The initial 35-weeks of training and unique mission skills earn them their initial certification and the right to wear the distinctive scarlet red beret. An additional 11-12 months of advanced skills training takes place at the Special Tactics Training Squadron, Hurlburt Field, Fla., before they can be assigned to an operational special tactics squadron and considered combat ready

Combat Control Screening Course, Lackland Air Force Base, Texas *This 10-day screening course focuses on physical fitness with classes in sports physiology, nutrition, basic exercises, CCT history and fundamentals.*

Combat Control Operator Course, Keesler AFB, Miss. *This 15 and a half-week course teaches aircraft recognition and performance, air navigation aids, weather, airport traffic control, flight assistance service, communication procedures, conventional approach control, radar procedures and air traffic rules. This is the same course that all Air Force air traffic controllers attend and is the core skill of a combat controller's job.*

U.S. Army Airborne School, Fort Benning, Ga. *Trainees learn the basic parachuting skills required to infiltrate an objective area by static line airdrop in a three-week course.*

U.S. Air Force Basic Survival School, Fairchild AFB, Wash. *This two- and a half-week course teaches basic survival techniques for remote areas. Instruction includes principles, procedures, equipment and techniques, which enable individuals to survive, regardless of climatic conditions or unfriendly environments and return home.*

Combat Control School, Pope AFB, N.C. *This 13-week course provides final combat controller qualifications. Training includes physical training, small unit tactics, land navigation, communications, assault zones, demolitions, fire support and field operations including parachuting. At the completion of this course, each graduate is awarded the 3-skill level (journeymen), scarlet beret and CCT flash.*

Special Tactics Advanced Skills Training, Hurlburt Field, Fla. *Advanced skills training is a 12-to-15-month program for newly assigned combat controller operators. AST produces mission-ready operators for the Air Force and U.S. Special Operations Command. The AST schedule is broken down into four phases: water, ground, employment and full mission profile. The course tests the trainee's personal limits through demanding mental and physical training. Combat controllers also attend the following schools during AST:*

> ***U.S. Army Military Free Fall Parachutist School, Fort Bragg, N.C., and Yuma Proving Grounds, Ariz.*** *This course instructs free fall parachuting procedures. The five-week course provides wind tunnel training, in-air instruction focusing on student stability, aerial maneuvers, air sense, parachute opening procedures and parachute canopy control.*

> ***U.S. Air Force Combat Diver School[27], Panama City, Fla.*** *Trainees become combat divers, learning to use scuba and closed circuit diving equipment to covertly infiltrate denied areas. The six-week course provides training to depths of 130 feet, stressing development of maximum underwater mobility under various operating conditions.[28]*

History

Army pathfinders originated in 1943 out of need for accurate airdrops during airborne campaigns of World War II. These pathfinders preceded main assault forces into objective areas to provide weather information and visual guidance to inbound aircraft through the use of high-powered lights, flares and smoke pots.

---

[27] Later, Mark said everyday he wondered whether he was going to survive this school.

[28] http://www.af.mil/information/factsheets/factsheet_print.asp?fsID=174&page=1

> *When the Air Force became a separate service, Air Force pathfinders, later called combat control teams, were activated in 1953 to provide navigational aids and air traffic control for a growing Air Force. In the Vietnam War, combat controllers helped assure mission safety and expedited air traffic flow during countless airlifts. Combat controllers also flew as forward air guides in support of indigenous forces in Laos and Cambodia.*
>
> *Combat controllers continue to be the "First There" when they are called upon to participate in international emergencies and humanitarian relief efforts.*

Once Mark decided to enlist in the Air Force, we knew the day of his departure would come. It was 24 June 2007 and it arrived sooner than any of us wished it would have. That was his day to report to Basic Military Training at Maxwell Air Force Base in Montgomery, then on to Lackland AFB. The weekend before, Terri, her family, and I gathered at Mom and Dad's for Mark's farewell. Others wanted to be there, but Mark had recently visited Joseph, David and their families. With Joseph living in Colorado and David in Florida, they couldn't make it.

The farewell consisted of swimming, wrestling with the nephews (particularly Nick), riding the golf cart, and cooking out. Mom bought some patriotic t-shirts from Wal-Mart that had the American flag and a picture of a fighter jet. We all wore them that Saturday. The next day, as usual, we went to church. Afterwards, we had Sunday dinner and spent time together as Mark prepared to leave. As soon as he pulled out of the driveway in the Tahoe with mom and dad, I immediately went to my bedroom at mom and dad's and cried my eyes out. I didn't show any emotion while he was there, but I was extremely sad to see him leave, and I knew he'd be going to war. I didn't know what he'd be doing, but I knew it would be dangerous, and thinking of it left me with a gnawing sense of foreboding. It had shadowed me since he enlisted, but it hit hard the day he left for basic.

When I returned to my house in Tuscaloosa, it was empty. I remember that first night I was home alone I had trouble sleeping, and then all the sudden the paper shredder turned on for a few seconds for no particular reason. It was a long night as I thought about Mark, our times together and how I already missed him. Also, I thought about how I didn't like living alone. (Little did I know that within one year I would meet my future wife and have the honor of never living alone again.)

Mark and I had lived together for the last five years in Tuscaloosa. Not only was I concerned about him going off to war, but plain and simple, I was going to miss him. We sat together at church, we ate Sunday dinners together, we threw the football in our front yard and street, we rode 4-wheelers, traveled to see our other brothers and sister, and countless other things best friends and brothers do. When we'd go out to eat, I'd laugh as he complained that we got a dude as our waiter instead of one of the cute girls. It always seemed to happen this way with us, especially to Mark. During our entire life, Mark was my little brother and never afraid to ask me what words meant or just to ask me for advice. During our last few months together, I had the strong feeling that he was really grown up and didn't need his big brother as much anymore. Truth is, he knew more about everything than I did.

Mark entered USAF Basic Military Training as a 26 year old man with a Bachelor's degree in Business Finance from The University of Alabama, and had served a full time mission for his church. He was well-prepared for his new life, and in keeping with unofficial military tradition, he was immediately called "Pop" by many of his younger teammates. He said at one point they were all gathered around and were asked by Sgt Shanty, "Why did you join the Air Force?" Responses from the young trainees typically include statements like: "I wanted money for college." "The Air Force is a tradition in my family." "To help me figure out what to do with my future." And so on.

When it was Mark's turn, he matter-of-factly stated, "Because God wants me to kill bad people." He said it like it was about the most normal thing ever, but everyone was taken back. Even the Trainee Instructors didn't really have a response to it and moved on to the next recruit. Regardless, it was exactly how Mark felt. His calling at this point in his life was to help rid the world of terrorism. He had prepared the best he could before entering basic training, and was now ready to move on and excel at all challenges placed before him while in the service. His eyes were now set on becoming a Combat Controller, even though he had to get through basic first.

While in basic, Joseph sent him a short letter that reads: "Mom tells me you are getting quite the workout with all the punitive flutter kicks and push-ups. Element Leader…impressive. I kind of figured that they would pick you. I'm sure they saw your leadership skills and potential and it had nothing to do with you being taller and older than everyone else… I know that physically it is not a challenge to you and that your biggest challenge is dealing with the other stuff that comes with being in basic training…"

Basic Military Training graduation was 10 August 2007 at Lackland Air Force Base. Mom, Dad, Joseph, and I were there. We stood with excitement, and some anxiety, waiting for his team to come running by. When I saw his skinny body and shaved head, I was proud and almost broke down. It was emotional for me to see my little brother out there. And once we got to see him, I'll never forget how bad he smelled. I think they all smelled bad. He told me not to make fun of him when he had to sit bolt upright at attention while some Air Force dude spoke to the crowd[29]. Of course, being the good brothers we are, Joseph and I laughed at him anyway.

One thing Mark loved about that day happened when we met his Training Instructor, Sgt Shanty: She stood at attention when she met Joseph because he was a Captain in the USAF at that time and was in uniform. After spending some time with his group, I could tell Sgt Shanty liked and respected Mark. I'm sure he was always respectful and not only met, but exceeded expectations in Basic Military Training.

While we were in San Antonio for graduation, the new Airmen were allowed to leave base to attend the WNBA game at the SBC Center (now AT&T Center), if they wanted. They could get in free if they wore their uniform. Even though we aren't WNBA fans, we gladly went. Mark would have taken any offer to leave base for a little while. We had a great time there. I don't know the name of the San Antonio team, and I have no idea who they played, but we brothers loved being together and even implemented the "high-five posse" for a short period. Mom and dad enjoyed themselves while there too, but I think they mostly loved seeing their boys having fun together.

After completing basic, it was time for Mark to start his specialized training at Lackland AFB. The whole CCT training pipeline takes a solid two years, and they kept Mark very busy. Long before he died, we heard from people who'd worked with him about how well he progressed. After he passed, there were more people than I can even guess who shared their memories and experiences of working, training and living with him. The following is a collection of comments and remembrances from teammates, instructors and leaders. However, in no way is it everything people shared

---

[29] I vividly remember this. It was my first encounter with the respect level of those ranked higher that you.

with us. Clearly, Mark touched many people and he left a lasting—and positive—impression.

Sean Gleffe - Commandant of Combat Control School

Mark and I crossed paths at the Combat Control School (CCS). I was the one running the school and the reason for all of Marks "motivation" to get through. I enforced all the curriculum, physical training and corrective actions for the students. I remember Mark vividly because he was always in good spirits no matter what the cadre (instructors) was running them through. I can't recall a time when he was unmotivated or not focused on earning his beret.

The last time I saw Mark was at the annual Will Jefferson poker tournament hosted by his squadron. He was there with Bobby to show support and relax a little before shipping overseas the very next day. I remember telling both of them to have a good trip and to keep their heads on a swivel. I remember seeing confidence and excitement in both of them as they were getting ready to go and do everything they had trained to do.

He was true to his faith and accepted by all of his teammates. He wasn't the top performer or the weakest, but most importantly, he wasn't the grey man. He performed to the best of his ability, was a good teammate and exceeded the high standards of the school. I'm not just saying this because of the surrounding circumstances (i.e. this is not a eulogy), it's the way it was and is.

Jordan Fuller – roommate in Basic Military Training (BMT), USAF

He was a cut above the rest. Mark carried himself in such a unique way. It was almost as if when he entered the room everyone felt his presence no matter what they were doing. He always had this level head on his shoulders even when everybody else was stressed out and going crazy.

One of my favorite memories of Mark is when we were in basic training and everybody would be stressed out trying to shine their shoes or make sure their uniforms where good for the next inspection, Mark would pull out a script from the movie *Anchorman*. I think your mom mailed it to him or something. He would sit there and read everybody the script as if he were actually in the movie. It put a huge smile on everyone's face. It was almost as if, for that brief moment, everything was OK and back to normal. Mark was great at making people feel safe and secure.

Joseph (rather than mom) actually sent the quotes to Mark. As I read through them now, it brings back so many great memories of Mark quoting Ron Burgundy. I'd give anything to hear him declare, "By the beard of Zeus!" either jokingly or when he was a little frustrated and it was his way to make light of the situation.

Bryan Floyd – Pipeline teammate, friend

I had the privilege to spend nearly two years with Mark as we trudged our way through the growling Combat Control Pipeline. Mark was always in a good mood and naturally lifted others up. That's probably why so many people wanted to be around him. At first, I saw Mark as a brother in my faith, another good Latter-day Saint (Mormon) and the kind of guy I could comfortably spend my free time with. No cursing. No drinking. And we attended Church when we could.

We were at Keesler AFB learning Air Traffic Control, but because we were on different teams, we could only spend time together on the weekends. One thing we did on a regular basis was go out to Waffle House on Saturday nights. Usually with Jeremy Schlaubach or Brian Hunt and for some reason, the *All Star Breakfast* was the only thing we ever ordered.

John Blake (pseudonym) was a young 19 year old at the time who hadn't found fashion yet. Mark took it upon himself to fix him up, kind of like Bobby had done for Mark. In just a few short weeks of being around Mark, John was looking sharp, pushing out of his shell and exhibiting real confidence. He's now a great operator *and* happily married. I like to think Mark had a little something to do with both!

Finally, when we got to Combat Control School at Hurlburt Field in Florida, our two teams combined and I really got to know Mark. My lasting impression is that he just always had it together. I don't know how else to describe it. He knew exactly what he wanted, from some fancy cereal (Kashi) to the kind of girl he wanted to marry. Mark and I talked about that a lot. I will never forget when he told me that he wanted to marry a good LDS girl who had a hint of irreverence. I thought that to be a wonderful combination and was impressed by how much he knew he wanted.

During Tactics Week at CCS (Combat Control School), Mark made sure that he would be the point man in formation. He WANTED to be the first one in the fight. He said that his eye surgery[30] put him at the top of the list anyway. So our TL (Team Leader) agreed and Mark got what he wanted.

I was the Communications guy and had to make all the radio transmissions for the TL which left me jealous of Mark. While I was the TL's appointed secretary, Mark got to stalk around with the new NVGs (Night Vision Goggles) and lead the patrol through the woods. I have to admit, though, he was great at it. On one patrol, Mark stopped and pointed his fingers at two Army Special Forces Trainees hiding under a bush.

It turned out the Army guys were also doing a Recon Mission on the same building. Later that night, when our patrol split up, Mark and a few others ran into those guys. Each guy raised his barrel thinking the other soldier was the "bad guy." A quick discussion ensued, "Who are you?" "No, who are you?" Mark replied that we were Air Force. Those guys were all confused and wondered what we were doing there. Amazingly, no shots were fired and the patrolling instructors never found either team.

After CCS graduation, we went to Florida for Advanced Skills Training (AST). It would take a long time to recount every memory and event with Mark I had there. AST was a bit different for me compared to the other guys because I was already married. So I moved my family down to Florida and, of course, my limited time off was dedicated to them.

Mark shared a place with a few of the other guys and built very strong friendships with them. That said, AST is AST and I'm

---

[30] Mark had worn glasses and contacts since he was a young teenager. He had PRK surgery for his eyes in preparation for joining the Air Force. This surgery improved his eye sight significantly and the Air Force accepted it (they don't accept all vision correction procedures).

sure I spent more time training with the Team than I spent with my family; and I have hundreds of great memories there.

The main thing I saw in Mark during AST was a happy guy. He had a great sense of humor and consistently positive attitude. He once said to me, only slightly joking, "Floyd, I thrive on positivity." His tone of voice and Alabama accent makes it impossible to forget that line. It's still crystal clear in my head, and I've repeated it to others as if they were my own words. I've seen it affect behavior, especially toward the end of a deployment when all you hear from guys are complaints. That simple statement can turn off the griping.

In all of our Tactics Training, Mark always wanted to be the "Point Man" in the formation, first to be seen, first to the danger, first to shoot back. I have a video of Mark leading a three-man formation on an assault of a building. Mark runs from cover in a dead sprint to a ditch and jumps in to return fire so his teammates can advance. It is exactly where Mark wanted to be, the guy closest to danger, the brave one, the go-to guy. Even though he was not the highest-ranking guy on the team, he was a leader.

Fast forward to the end of AST, during our final Field Training Exercises (FTX). I remember assaulting a building. We had two gun trucks approach the front of the building while two circled around to the back to keep guys from escaping out of the back door. Mark got to be the JTAC that day. He was the only one actually playing a CCT role. The rest of us were just shooters.

My role was to run from the truck to the front door and secure it for the team that would breach. The Team breached and entered. You could hear the "bad guys" shouting, then a few shots (blank rounds). I pulled security by the front door.

I remember looking back towards the trucks and noticing Mark standing there next to the instructor, Mark was talking into the radio—a lot. Then I realized the instructor was pointing out targets for Mark to engage with aircraft. At this point, no one had received any JTAC training, only Call For Fires[31]. I wondered

---

[31] They were only practicing to direct indirect fire from artillery and/or mortars, which is a commonly practiced skill among soldiers. The JTAC role, one of the key responsibilities of a Combat Controller, is coordinating fire from aircraft.

how Mark did since it looked like he was being challenged pretty good. No surprise to anyone, the instructor told Mark that he did pretty well, even for having just been kicked into the deep end without any real training!

During a longer weekend, a bunch of us took a trip to Gold Coast Sky Divers in Mississippi to jump for a day. All of our jumps so far had been with the military, work jumps. Going to Gold Coast was to have some *fun*!

During one jump, Mark and I were jump buddies. Our plan was to exit the aircraft holding onto each other hoping that we would level out still connected. We really didn't know what we were doing, but we had a plan. Mark would get ready to exit first, facing the aircraft. I would hold on to his chest strap and perform a dive exit right behind him.

Well, somewhere right after we left the plane, we started to spin rapidly. Again, we didn't know how to jump in this fashion. I think we completed two full rotations as we hurtled toward earth. As Mark jumped, I pushed off slightly harder than I should have and sent him spinning like crazy.

That guy (wearing a bright red jump suit) tumbled 4,000 feet before finally leveling off! At that point, we still had some time to goof-off, so we did a few mirror drills, pretty much a game of copycat. At six thousand feet above the ground, we stopped the horseplay and tracked away from each other. I remember watching him streak across the sky faster than I'd ever seen.

Now, it has to be understood that his pride was at stake here. When Combat Controllers jump out of airplanes, we all know: *never get caught tumbling*. Even though it was my fault that he tumbled, he didn't have to do it for four thousand feet.

Once we got back on the ground, we did as all jumpers do, we talked about the jump and threw down a high five. Before I could say anything about the four thousand feet of whatever you want to call it, he leaned in, and with that strong southern accent said, "Did you see how fast I tracked across that sky?! I was like a red missile up there!"

That was Mark, rarely made a mistake; and when he did, he was quick to highlight the better parts to distract you. It was a part of what made him seem larger than life. We later laughed about that jump—though never when the other guys were around.

Mark and I spoke a lot about marriage. More than anything else in life, he wanted to find that special girl to settle down with and start a family. When the guys would go out for the night, I would usually turn down their offer to go along because I had a family at home that needed my attention. I would always apologize in some way, but Mark was quick to correct me on the spot. "You're living the dream brother," he said to me more than once. I asked once, "What do you mean?" "You're married; you have a wife and kids, that's way better than anything else." I think that's the only thing Mark wanted more than to be in combat.

The bottom line is Mark was larger than life, even when we were just trainees. He was a friend and a leader who demanded to be at the front. He was committed and faithful to his core beliefs. He was true. That's the best way for me to describe Mark. He was *true*—always.

Mark and Bobby Bonello went through the CCT training pipeline in the same group. That's where they became good friends, but it didn't happen right off. At different stages of the training, graduation ceremonies are held for those who complete another grueling step toward becoming a Combat Controller.

Family members often attend these ceremonies. Sometime early in Mark's trip through the pipeline, Bobby's dad, Tony, was at one of these ceremonies to show his support and pride in Bobby. As the crowd mingled afterward, Mark came up to Tony and briefly introduced himself. He left such a strong impression in this brief encounter than Tony asked Bobby, "Hey, are you friends with that Forester kid?" Bobby said he knew Mark, being in the same group, but not really well yet. Tony then told his son, "You stay close to Forester. He's genuine and will always have your back." And he did. Bobby admits to benefitting from Mark's "older, wiser" presence.

Later on, Mark's team merged with another that included Johnnie Yellock II. They were destined to be great friends. For starters, the two of them were the oldest in the group and naturally took on big-brother duties: looking out for the younger guys, making sure they didn't get into trouble,

These photos were taken about the time Mark and Johnnie became friends. They were hamming for the camera, and Johnnie told him, "You're doing it wrong! As you fold your arms, you've got to use your hand to boost your arm so your biceps look huge."

drink and drive, or miss getting back to base on time. We got to know Johnnie during this time too. There were several holidays and weekend trips when he'd come up to Tuscaloosa and Haleyville with Mark.

Johnnie was in the group just ahead of Mark. However, their teams were eventually combined as fewer CCT candidates progressed through the demanding training program. They also got to be roommates at some of the different schools they attended including HALO, SOTAC, and Dive School.

Both of Johnnie's parents, Johnnie Sr. and Reagan, spent their careers in the Air Force. His dad worked in Specialty Aircraft Maintenance and later, Acquisition Logistics. His Mom fulfilled various USAF media roles. In 1984, the Air Force opened a radio and TV station at Soesterberg Air Base in The Netherlands. Reagan was selected to be the first broadcaster there, and she happened to be 7 ½ months pregnant with Johnnie II when she reported for duty. Johnnie II was born at the Dutch Military Hospital in Utrecht and lived in The Netherlands until moving to Texas in 1987, where Johnnie II[32] grew up.

He says, "I went to college for my parents, but I didn't really have my heart in it. I wanted to do something important, something that would make a tangible difference. So when I finished school, I found out about CCT, and went for it."

---

[32] Just to keep things straight, from now on, whenever Johnnie is mentioned, it's Johnnie II.

I suppose it was easy for Mark and Johnnie to become very good friends, they had more in common than most of the guys in the pipeline. Both were older than their teammates. Both had college degrees, but didn't want to be officers. They shared similar standards for their personal conduct. He didn't party or carouse, he's a devout Christian and the two of them found extensive common ground between them. Johnnie says that whenever he thinks of Mark, *faith* is the first thing that comes to mind. And not just faith in God, but faith in other people. "Mark had a unique way of recognizing the good in people, and dealing with them on that basis. Maybe that's part of why people liked being around him, and why he had such a strong influence. He wasn't judgmental at all." The other thing Johnnie remembers is how Mark's attitude made it easy to "Embrace the Suck" as they ground through training. But it didn't all suck and they had plenty of good times too.

One day, they wanted to check out a gun store in Panama City they'd heard about. Out in Johnnie's Mustang, they cruised around looking for it without luck. Finally, they settled for Chick-fil-A, and then planned to head back for the base. As they were about to leave, the scene was perfect: a gorgeous day, a good car, a great buddy and a wide, empty lot. Perfect for an impromptu donut. With a jab of the throttle and crank of the wheel, the car spun around—engine roaring, tires shrieking, Mark and Johnnie whooping and hollering—for a second. When he straightened it out and looked ahead, about 200 meters, he spotted the Florida State Trooper he'd missed at first.

Johnnie paused a moment, then seeing the trooper heading toward them, he shut off his car and got ready. The officer didn't get out, but instead pulled up alongside and asked what they were up to. Sheepishly, Mark mentioned the gun store. The officer said, "It's just over here. I'll show you guys." When they arrived, Mark and the officer struck up a great conversation about guns, and dive school, etc. Johnnie was grateful they made a new friend, rather than getting a ticket.

Mark had the ability to make friends quickly. This reminds me when he and I were riding 4-wheelers out in the country near our home in Tuscaloosa. Apparently we were on private hunting land. When we drove by the land owners/leasers, they stopped us and kindly asked us not to ride there. Mark started talking to them about hunting, since they were working on their green fields for the upcoming season. Within a few minutes, the guy told us we could come back any time. And he gave us his name to use in case someone questioned us.

Later, while still at dive school near Panama City, the instructors gave the guys a break from the usual routine and turned them loose in kayaks. They were to paddle across the bay and back. It wasn't supposed to be a race, but these guys are all CCT candidates, and competitiveness is just part of their character. The Cadre doesn't need to stoke it much. As they ran for the boats, Johnnie noticed they were all one-man, except for one two-holer. Mark ran for it and called for Johnnie to join him. Johnnie had never been in a kayak, and figured the safe bet was to go with Mark who exuded confidence, as usual. Also, with two guys paddling, Johnnie figured they should be the fastest boat in the group.

Well, they got out on the bay, it was windy and kind of choppy, and Johnnie and Mark didn't coordinate well. They started falling behind. Finally, Johnnie shouted, "I thought you knew what you were doing!" Mark shouted back, "Heck no! This is my first time in a kayak!"

Between the wind, the waves, their lack of coordination, and some frustration at falling farther and farther behind, it didn't take long before Johnnie and Mark capsized the boat, sending them both in the water. Now, without any prior instruction, they had to figure out how to get going again. First, one could climb in with the other holding the boat steady, but then they found it nearly impossible for the guy in the boat to hold it steady enough for the other one to climb in from the water. Back in the bay they both went again and again. Johnnie remembers seeing the other boats fading away to the far side of the bay. Then, as he and Mark laughed and struggled to get out of their fix, Johnnie noticed the other boats turn around and start heading back. Finally, Mark and Johnnie were both back in their boat (by climbing in over the pointed end, rather than the side), and they joined the rest of their team as they all paddled back to base.

Johnnie remembers an interesting incident that highlights Mark's character:

> We were in the pool again, doing our dive training when one of the instructors called out a student for wearing swim shorts with a hole in them. Without thinking, the guy blurted out, "Well, Forester ran them through the drier."

> Mark hadn't done that, but he didn't contradict his teammate, either. Later, the guy came up to Mark and apologized. He said he didn't know why he did it. It wasn't a big deal, it just came out. Mark was cool about it. I suppose he understood about impulsiveness, like when he dodged the cop back in his college days....

Another of Mark's teammates through the pipeline, **Ted Hofknecht**, shared this story with us Easter 2011 in Haleyville:

> Mark was a true leader on and off the battlefield. On one occasion, he and our team were eating dinner at Mellow Mushroom. There were about 16 of us, and we had all gone through rigorous training together, so we had grown close.
>
> While eating, one teammate in particular was getting rowdy and using rather harsh language. Mark was bothered because there were families and children all around. Finally, he stood up, pointed to this teammate, called him by name, and said in a loud voice, "You need to be quiet. There are families all around."
>
> Not only did his teammates hear him, but most everyone in the restaurant did. Mark was one of the lowest ranking members of our team but no one said anything to him for that. The teammate took it well. He knew he was in the wrong.

Chivalry at its best. That was Mark, consistent in his behavior and they respected him for that. He wasn't preachy; he wasn't stiff, but he knew what was going on was inappropriate. He wasn't afraid to stand up for what was right—just as he had always been.

Many times, long before Mark was in the pipeline or in Afghanistan, I would be dealing with situations at work or other places and I'd ask myself, "How would Mark handle this?" or "What would Mark do?" I may be the big brother, but Mark gave me plenty of reasons to look up to him too. Stories expressed here are good reasons why.

Dave – SSgt, 21 STS Blue Team

> In the spring of 2009, I had just been promoted to Staff Sergeant, and I was waiting to receive the first Airman I would supervise at the 21 STS. The first troop[33] I was responsible for was Mark Forester. As someone new to the NCO corps, this was a huge blessing. Mark was the easiest Airman to supervise that I've ever seen: never late, always prepared, very smart, looked sharp, and always, always ready to train and be the best. When I think of Mark Forester, I think of two things: determined and committed.

---

[33] "Troop" is often used in the same way an Army NCO would use "soldier". That is the case here, and others in the book do the same. I suppose it's a little handier than saying "airman" all the time.

Mark's commitment to being the best at everything he did was only outdone by his commitment to his faith. Mark was one of the most determined people I've ever met. When he arrived at the 21 STS, along with Bobby Bonello, not too much was going on. Most of our squadron was down range or TDY,[34] so I had the pleasure of welcoming Mark to the team and getting to know him quickly. Within that first week, all Mark could talk about was becoming a JTAC and heading down range to carry out his quest to defeat as many terrorists as he could. And he did just that.

Mark's attitude was contagious. He volunteered for whatever he could and he'd help you out no matter what. A good example of this is when his teammates would go out on the town, he'd go along as the designated driver to make sure his buddies got home safely.

Mark showed his determination to becoming a JTAC and skilled operator on a daily basis. His green Tundra was often the last truck at the team room. His truck waited patiently as Mark would fine-tune his kit, study all things Close Air Support (CAS), or get in an evening workout. His commitment and determination are second to no one.

Even though some others complained, Mark's hard work and focus paid off when he was chosen to deploy to a location that is historically violent and has a reputation for requiring a great deal of CAS. Many of my peers questioned the decision to place Mark at FOB Cobra, but after we saw what he produced, we knew our leaders had made a good decision. Mark's performance during this deployment was truly spectacular, especially for a Senior Airman on his first combat rotation.

I spoke often with Mark, whether through email or Facebook. We talked a lot about the mission, but mostly about what we will do when we get home, training we wanted, and a lot of football. Anyone who knows Mark knows how he loves his Alabama Crimson Tide.

---

[34] TDY (Temporary Duty) refers to work assignments at a location other than the service member's regular duty station.

Matthew Sampson – Capt, Pipeline teammate

I attended three months of training with Mark near the end of his pipeline at Hurlburt Field, FL. I simply wanted to pass along how he impacted my life and what I thought of him. I know if anything ever happened to me, my mother and father would want to know what my peers thought of me.

Mark and I had a lot in common. We both were older students in the training with Bachelor's Degrees and a little bit of life experience under our belts prior to entering the service. We did this because we felt we were called to do so. I think this was the foundation of what started our friendship. Mark was the guy with the character to state his beliefs and not back down no matter how much peer pressure was put on him. Ultimately, I think it was a quality most of the younger guys aspired to attain. His maturity and work ethic naturally placed him in the leadership role among his peers—a role he filled admirably.

Mark always wanted to be in the action. We were on the same team during this training course so we performed a number of field maneuvers together. We got to the point where it was a running joke to give the other one a relentless hard time if we were put on a job for an operation that was a slower tempo—still important but lacking the action.

On one occasion, Mark and I were manning the command and control point for a surveillance/reconnaissance mission. This meant Mark and I hid out in the woods and manned the radios while the rest of the team clandestinely moved to observe enemy activity. I settled in nicely to my role but Mark couldn't stand it. His answer was to climb a tree in order to get a better look at the "action" (not advised in a real world operation).

Mark was half way up the tree when we heard someone walking through the woods in our direction. We didn't want to compromise our position, so I stayed concealed and Mark attempted to hide himself by freezing halfway up the trunk of a tree and behind a tiny branch. I remember laying there trying to contain the sound of my laughter while he tried to conceal his large frame behind a six inch diameter tree trunk. The instructor spotted him immediately and was speechless, except for the expletives; while I laughed hard as Mark just about fell out of the tree getting down!

There were other training exercises where I was in the action piece and poor Mark was confined to perimeter security or some other slightly more boring detail of the event. Every time, I harassed Mark as much as possible. It wouldn't have been so much fun—for me—if he hadn't been such a competitor wanting to be on the front line with his buds.

Mark took advantage of numerous opportunities to visit Patsy, Joseph and their kids in the different places they lived while Joseph went through medical school in the Air Force. She remembers:

I was personally so blessed to know and love Mark. He was around me from the age of 23-38. He watched me grow up also. He was around from me being a young married girl, to a mother of four (while he was alive). We now have 5 children. He and I had an amazing brother/sister (in-law) relationship. We would talk about everything, from girls to shopping.

He actually enjoyed shopping with me. (Much to Joseph's relief, I think.)My husband would take care of the kids when he was in town, and Mark and I would just go shopping and have the best time. He appreciated my advice on things. I recall a shopping spree we had when we lived in San Antonio. We went to the Lucky store at La Cantera and I had him buy jeans, shirts and a couple of shorts. We were having a great time, and then he picked me out a pair of shorts and a couple of purses. He was my buddy, and I loved spending time with him.

We moved to many different places due to my husband's medical and military career, and wherever we lived, Mark would come to visit us. Mark was my husband's best friend. They had so much in common, especially in Mark's

later years. They would bounce ideas and thoughts off each other and talk, text, and communicate in whatever way possible. Some of our fondest memories of Mark were during these visits. In San Antonio the boys recall going to *Schlitterbahn* water park. They would laugh about their experiences that would bring us all to tears laughing. In Colorado, we went skiing, snowmobiling, and sledding.

All of these experiences truly created a bond like no other. And if you could be a fly on the wall, you would have to have watched *Seinfeld* to really understand what was going on. These boys would refer EVERYTHING back to a *Seinfeld* episode. It truly was a sight to behold.

These times together often consisted of watching and quoting *Anchorman, Zoolander, Wedding Crashers*, and *Nacho Libre*. Mom even loved watching *Nacho Libre* with us. She still enjoys watching that movie. It reminds her of watching it with Mark and hearing him quote lines from it.

As mentioned before, Mark's training lasted about two years, a year of which was spent at Hurlburt Field in the Florida Panhandle. It is close enough that he could make regular trips to visit home, friends and me. With his good looks, quick wit and polite manners, Mark seldom lacked for interest from eligible women. Through college and training, he dated some and even had a couple girlfriends, but I can safely say only one woman ever really had his heart (after mom and Terri, of course). It was during one of his weekend visits to Tuscaloosa that he met Megan.

I remember the first time he told me about meeting this new girl. He went on at a length just trying to describe her "sweet little Southern accent." Looking back on it now, I realize how significant this was. We're Southerners and talk like Southerners, so the accent isn't really an accent to us. The fact that he took such notice of the way Megan speaks gives a good idea of the strong impression she made on him.

Now, Megan is also very pretty, but not in an over-done Barbie-doll way—she's genuine rather than showy. Although a little shy at first, she easily matched Mark's humor and powerful personality (which I'm sure is only one reason Mark liked her so much). She is just as committed to her values and vision in life as Mark was. Despite their strong feelings for each other, they felt compelled to fulfill callings that pulled them in opposite directions. This divergence is what ultimately kept them apart. Megan shares her memories:

It was October 2008. I was close to finishing my undergrad at the University of Alabama with a degree in Human Development and a concentration in Family Studies. John McDow (one of the "Three/Four Amigos mentioned in Chapter 9) was one of my upstairs neighbors in the apartments where I lived. He was friendly with me and many others in the complex, often stopping to visit as he came and went.

One day, he and a buddy were returning from shooting and he called out, "Hi Megan!" to see if I would respond. I came out and he laughed about seeing my car sealed in plastic wrap (some friends and I had been trading pranks on each other). I laughed too, saying that if they kept giving me trouble, I might have to borrow one of the rifles they were carrying. We chatted a little more, but I kind of avoided paying any attention to his friend. He was very handsome and friendly looking, but I felt shy, so I pretty much ignored him. (He told me later that he was impressed and intrigued by my big talk and apparent self-confidence.)

John and I finished our exchange, we said, "See ya later," and I went back to my homework without thinking too much about it. Later, though, John asked if I wanted to go with him and some of his friends to the big haunted house they hold in Tuscaloosa every year. It sounded like fun and I was hoping Mark would be there too.

The line in was huge, so the wait was nearly three hours. The time passed quickly, though, as we talked and visited. Given the size of our group, conversation shifted from the bunch of us to smaller, separate conversations between two or three people. It didn't take long before Mark and I found ourselves holding our own dialogue as the line crept forward.

One of our first common points was *Seinfeld*, and we kept each other laughing with references and inside jokes that only true fans understand. I remember Mark telling me about his brother in Tuscaloosa, and new sister-in-law. He liked her a lot and spoke very well of her.

The longer we stood in line, the cooler the evening became and we were feeling the chill. Mark looked down at my sandaled feet and said, "I'll bet they're cold...." It was a small thing, but that kind of consideration impressed me, and I have no doubt that if he'd been wearing more than a t-shirt, he would have offered it.

After the spook alley, we decided to try sneaking into the old abandoned Bryce Mental Hospital. It's supposed to be haunted, and it is very creepy looking, even in the daylight. We didn't get very close, though, because security is pretty tight, especially before Halloween! So we went back to John's place and hung out for a while. Mark showed me a clip from the *Anchorman* that practically left him and John rolling on the floor. The humor must be a guy thing because I just didn't think it was that funny. Mark seemed really puzzled by that.

The next day, I sent Mark a friend request on Facebook. He accepted and sent a message saying he was going to be in Tuscaloosa the next weekend. He said, "no one would be around" (meaning Thad or John) so he'd like to see me, if I were available. Well, I don't know why he felt the need for some kind of cover story, but I guess he wasn't ready to let me know he was willing to make a five hour drive just to see me.

Mark called Friday night as he got into town. I told him I was about to go meet some friends at Waffle House, and he kind of invited himself. He didn't order anything, but volunteered to say grace. Then when the check came, he grabbed it and paid for our food. I was impressed, as were my friends.

Mark had left his phone charger in Florida. He asked if I'd like to go with him to Wal-Mart to get a new one, and that he'd take me home afterward. I happily accepted. It was kind of late when we got to my apartment, but as Mark and I were having a nice time, I asked if he would like to continue our conversation inside for a little while.

I'd noticed on Facebook that he was LDS, but I didn't really understand what that meant. Some people I knew tried telling me things, most of it pretty crazy. I wanted to hear it from him, and the more we talked, the more I found that we really shared a lot in terms of our relationship with Christ and our commitment to living by His example.

We continued to play the "get to know you" game by starting each new item about ourselves with "Here's something interesting for you to know…" This went on for a little bit, when he made his move and we kissed. It was nice, but I pulled back and said, "Here's something interesting for you to know: even though you've driven over five hours up here, bought my friends and me dinner, and we've kissed, it won't go any further than that because I am saving myself for when I'm married." Mark rolled back a little, let out a deep laugh and with a big grin on his face said, "Well, here's something interesting for you to know: I am too!" We both had a good laugh at that.

We talked a bit longer, then, after we'd finally said, "good night," Mark got home just as Thad was leaving for work! We planned to meet for lunch after crashing for a couple hours. When he picked me up, I hadn't gotten myself "dolled up," but went for comfortable in jeans, t-shirt, a jacket and very little make up. It didn't make a difference to him, the first word out of his

Mark and Megan

mouth when I opened the door was, "perfect!" I loved hearing that. I could completely be myself and to him, it was perfect.

I was also impressed that Mark didn't plan the usual dinner-and-a-movie date. He had heard of an animal shelter that needed volunteers to walk the dogs so they could get some exercise and human interaction. That was a different date idea and I liked it. Unfortunately, when we got to the shelter, we learned that before we could handle the dogs, we had to have some training that wasn't being offered at the time.

Instead, we stopped by an art museum. (As Mark's brother, I know he was really wanting to impress her because we Foresters didn't grow up doing anything like that. I had a similar experience and took a girl to the same gallery. Mark remembered it and called me to find out where it was.) Mark started talking with the docent, asking things about the different works. He shadowed Mark and me as we moved through the gallery, and they talked to each other like they'd been acquainted for years. I was watching Mark closely, and I liked the way he was different from other guys I'd known. Being together was so natural for us that there was never a question of whether we'd see each other again. It was only a matter of when he'd be in town next.

When Mark was away, we talked a lot, preferring Skype to the phone so we could see each other at the same time. A couple weeks later, Mark and I went to an Alabama football game with my younger brother, Brian and his friend. Both had just begun their freshman year at UA.

Even though Mark and I had already talked for hours and hours, he hadn't said much about his job. I knew he was in the Air Force, but I hadn't thought about it much more than that. As we drove to the stadium and hunted for a parking place, Brian pressed Mark about his work. I didn't really notice at the time, but he was serious and kind of evasive.

We finally found a place to park—far away from the stadium-- and started the hike to our seats. Brian and his friend had gotten a little ahead of me and Mark when he stopped suddenly and turned me to face him with a seriousness and intensity I'd not seen before. He told me his job was very scary, and that he'd already seen how a lot of women couldn't handle being with a man whose work was so dangerous and took him away so much. I just said, "Whatever it is, if it's that important, we'll work it out."

I wish I could describe the relieved look on his face. We held hands and hustled to catch up with Brian. We found our seats and settled in. When it was time for the National Anthem, Mark was immediately to his feet, hand over his heart. After the music ended, I noticed Mark wipe a tear from under his sunglasses. His love of our country was true and deep.

During the Thanksgiving holiday, Mark and his buddy, Johnnie Yellock, stopped to see me while I was visiting with my family. We all had such a great time. They got along with my family who enjoyed their antics, including terrific silliness playing Guitar Hero.

At some point, the guys wanted to go out for a little target shooting. We hiked down to the creek on my parent's property. Mark and Johnnie could jump it, both being tall and in very good shape. For me, they actually moved a fallen tree to walk across!

By December and the Christmas Holiday, we had become very close. I loved all our time together, I loved him, and I know he loved me in return. To most couples feeling as we did, marriage is the natural next step, and we discussed it—a lot. However, there were serious issues holding us back. Our difference of faith was a big part of it, but it was less about different doctrinal beliefs than different callings we felt summoned by the Lord to fulfill. Looking back on it, I think the importance of these differences was probably exaggerated as a way to protect us, or to at least protect me....

We lurched between one of us wanting to move forward and the other holding back. It created major emotional conflict because while we couldn't see how we could ever be together, we just couldn't bring ourselves to be apart.

Mark would often say to Megan, "You are something else." By it, I think he was expressing his simultaneous awe and frustration with her and their relationship.

In May of 2009, I made a trip to Florida. I met up with his parents again and we enjoyed a very nice time, but as usual, it was overshadowed by the conflict of what to do with each other. Mark asked, "What are we doing??" We toned down part of the relationship, but what made it so hard was not just the love we felt for each other, but the deep friendship we'd formed. To think of ending our friendship caused a feeling of grief that was like thinking of a loved one dying. I don't say that to be dramatic, it's just how it was.

A little while later, Mark was in Tuscaloosa. Separately, we both had taken up kayaking with other friends. And we had independently planned to go that weekend with others, but those plans fell apart. Rather than giving up on it, and despite my conflicted feelings, I couldn't resist his invitation for a little adventure—or the chance to spend time with him. At some point that weekend, we were walking along, holding hands when we suddenly noticed the comically different messages our t-shirts proclaimed. My shirt was tie-dyed with the bible verse from John 3:16, and Mark's was camo-colored with "Infidel" written across the chest. It seemed a fitting metaphor for our lives and relationship. We wanted to be together, but we just couldn't figure out how to reconcile our divergent paths.

This is also the weekend that Mark broke the news that he had completed his training at Hurlburt and would soon be heading for Pope in North Carolina. It's too far for quick weekend trips.... but before he left, Mark bought a really good webcam for me. There was no way we couldn't stay close and we used it plenty.

In August, I'd finally completed my undergrad work, and was getting ready to leave Tuscaloosa. Mark came into town to visit Thad and Roz, and to see me off. Despite our conflicted emotions and the fact that we were not "an item," we couldn't help being as affectionate and loving to each other as we'd always been.

After graduation, I had plans to spend about four months in Spain doing an English teaching ministry there. Mark and I continued to Skype regularly. At one point, one of my roommates asked, "Who is *that* and *where's* he from??" She overheard us talking and thought Mark's accent was pretty funny.

When we visited, we talked about all the things going on in our lives. He'd tell me about his buddies, and some of the training. I'd tell him about my classes and the things I'd seen in Spain. We had been dating others, but it was always pretty disappointing. Mark would complain about the girls around him, and I'd tease him about it.

The people in Spain really do practice the Siesta life-style, resting during the day, and staying up very late in the evening. I came home late one October evening, logged into my computer and found Mark waiting for me on Skype. We "celebrated" our first meeting one year earlier.

After my time in Spain was up, Mark and I found ourselves in Tuscaloosa at the same time—entirely by accident, of course! Even though things had changed a lot, what was still the same was our deep connection. Mark went shopping with me and helped make sure I had the right clothes for my next area. Northern California early in the year is a lot colder than any of the other places I'd been so far.

Michael Madsen is a good friend of ours from our Tuscaloosa days:

Mark and I went kayaking for an afternoon on Lake Tuscaloosa while Mark was on leave in the summer of 2009. We spent a couple of hours on the lake paddling, swimming and talking. As I recall, Mark had just finished his Combat Control training. He told me stories about the training he had received and the nature of his job as a Combat Controller.

Mark knew that I had all but decided to join the military and that I had been exploring different options in different branches. When I went to the Air Force recruiting office in Tuscaloosa to inquire about opportunities as a Combat Controller, the recruiter told me one of his former recruits was going through the CCT pipeline. When I told him that Mark Forester was a good friend of mine he asked me, "Are you as tough as Mark Forester?"

I told Mark that the recruiter had informed me that I was too old and that the Air Force wasn't granting any age waivers for Combat Controllers. Mark paid me one of the greatest compliments I have ever received. He said, "That's too bad because we really need people like you." I know it's not true, but it sure made me feel good.

Throughout that afternoon on the lake I envied Mark. I envied his achievements and his experiences, but most of all, I envied the calm and the confidence that can only come from doing exactly what you want to be doing and what you know to be right.

I have been in the Army JAG Corps for about two and a half years now. I have two pictures of Mark in my office and always will. It can be very easy to forget the military part of being an Army lawyer and focus on the lawyer part. I am safely ensconced in my office in Maryland, thousands of miles away from any combat, dealing mostly with service members who represent the worst the military has to offer. The pictures of Mark remind me of what the standard should be. They remind me of the good people who sacrifice so much. They remind me of what service to country really means and of what it means to truly live a life of purpose and conviction.

In the five years I knew Mark Forester, I don't believe he ever did anything to prove something to someone else, only to himself. His decisions and actions were never motivated by hope of reward or to get a reaction, though he was destined to get a reaction from anyone who really knew him. Those who listened to Mark couldn't help but be shocked that someone had that much common sense and the courage to say things the way they were. He was not concerned with what other people thought of him, only that they knew where he stood. Mark would certainly not have been comfortable with all the attention that has been showered upon him, however, nobody is more deserving.

Mark didn't just endure the schoolhouse, he excelled. This fact was noted repeatedly. Sometimes the recognition was informal, other times it was formally established with positive reviews from his trainers and superiors and awards. Of these included the "Distinguished Graduate" award when he completed Combat Control School, class 08003. He received the award during the graduation ceremony on 19 June 2008.

Mark with Mom and Dad at CCS Graduation

Besides Combat Diver School, there was another time during his training that Mark was worried about his future, and in serious pain. Sometime during CCS, Mark and his team were scheduled to do a daytime static-line jump. Charles Ross, the medic that day at the 21st related:

> During the parachute opening, according to Mark, the groin straps pulled upward very forcefully. As he landed on the ground, he calmly hobbled over to me and said, "Sergeant Ross, I think I broke my nuts!" He explained to me that he wanted to stay in training but needed me to evaluate his situation. I know he was embarrassed, as we both were (knowing I was going to have to have him pull his pants down), I assisted him into the ambulance

that we had on site and I had to perform a scrotal examination on him; which is to actually "cop a feel". Sgt Noll, his instructor for the day, was trying to lighten the mood with some crude humor, which we all got a few good laughs at. But the fact that I was unable to palpate his left testicle, I had to rush him to the ER for an emergency Ultrasound. As we all know now, his exam was normal, which is to say he didn't actually "bust a nut!" The warrior that he was, he was taken straight from the clearance of the ER doc right back into training.

The reason Mark was worried about his future during this incident was because he wanted kids and didn't want this complicating things. When Mark told me this story, he conveyed pain in his face and speech. He said his harness straps weren't tight enough before he jumped, so when the parachute opened, the straps moved too easily. He said he was yelling before he hit the ground. We laughed about this several times after. For this very reason, I make doubly sure that my harness is tight and everything is in proper position before I skydive each September 29.

Little did I know that Easter weekend 2010 would be the last quality time I would spend with Mark. Mom made an incredible Combat Controller cake. She made a very impressive version of their logo on that thing. We hung around the house on Saturday, and then went to Bo and Sylvia Knight's home in Muscle Shoals. They had a going-away party for Mark. The Knights have been good family friends for many years. They have three sons who were our friends youngest, Brad, spent a lot of time with Mark in Tuscaloosa working out and preparing for the Air Force.

Their home lies in a beautiful setting on the Tennessee River. We had a great time sitting around on their screened-in porch and outside on the deck. They had a specially built dinner table that seats about 12 people, so most of us were able to all sit together and eat. (Eight months after his death, I was scrolling through the text messages on Mark's phone. I found one from Bo Knight sent just after that weekend reminding him to keep his head down while deployed. Another from Bret Knight reiterating how much he wanted

Mark to remove those bad guys from the earth. Mark replied to each of them with a ready, "will do, and thanks for having us over.")

After leaving the Knight's, Mark, Michael S., Rozlynn and I went to the mall, and then stopped by our friend Derek's house. Derek later told me how invincible and ripped Mark looked that visit. He also remembered talking to Mark shortly after he joined the military and Derek asked, "What if you get sent overseas to fight?" Mark replied, "That's what I'm hoping for." And later, "I would tell Pres Bush that I'd be glad and honored to serve my country." He continued, "God wants me to kill terrorists." He was focused on his mission.

Each time Mark visited during his training, I could easily notice how much bigger he was getting. His shoulders got broader and broader, and it seemed like he was even growing taller, even at age 28.

By this time Mark's beard was looking very good—not long, but very defined and trimmed. This is a picture of Mark and mom after church on April 4, 2010. (Mark wearing a tie mom got for both of us.)

One of the gifts Mark received for his last Christmas was a helmet camera. Mom and dad bought it for him and I really looked forward to hearing him narrate the clips when he returned from deployment. I guess there is a little irony that what was intended as a gift for him turned around and became a gift to us. It captured so much of his experiences, skill and humor during his life in Afghanistan, that I think we'd have paid anything to have those last, precious glimpses of him during those last few months. Joseph and I had begged Mark to keep a journal while deployed, but he didn't—this helmet cam became his journal.

While Mark was saying his good-byes to friends and family in Haleyville, he had another good-bye to Megan. She remembers:

> Growing up and going to school in Alabama, I've had lots of friends and acquaintances deploy for military service. I guess I expected Mark's deploying to feel the same as it had for all those others.

Before Mark left, he sent me a package he'd promised for some time. It included cookies he made himself and a CD with his mix of music he teasingly called, "Jesus Music"—some of the music he'd listened to during his mission. Mark said he'd found strength and comfort in it, and wanted me to have it too. In it, he included this note:

Megan,

I promised you a package a few months ago, so I figured I'd own up before it's too late. I also made you some cookies of all flavors. Remember me asking if you liked coconut? I tried experimenting with the ones with coconut in them. If only milkshakes could be sent in a package....

I also made a C.D. The first 8 I think, are normal songs and the last ones are Jesus Music! I figured since you're doing missionary work I'd throw on some songs that helped me on my mission. The song on there called "His Hands" is an awesome song. Unfortunately I couldn't find the version I like the most. I'll try to find it. I lost it when my hard drive crashed. Anyway, I hope you like them.

Enjoy your last couple of months. You better Skype with me! BTW, I can't remember the last time I wrote a letter. Consider yourself lucky! Send me some pics of San Fran.

   Mark

135

We spoke during his last night. He talked about what he wanted me to do if anything should happen to him. Looking back on our relationship, it almost seems like he must have had a feeling about how things would go. I didn't like this kind of talk at all, and after we hung up, I broke down and sobbed for quite a while.

I took off work that Monday so I could spend that day with Mark. We went to Cathedral Caverns near Huntsville. Our friend, Michael Shiffler, went with us. We had a great time. The cave was interesting and something we had never done. On our drive back, I kept thinking about Mark leaving for war, but not letting myself dwell too much on the dangers of it. It was hard to imagine him in extreme combat, because I thought that was few and far between, but I really didn't know how to envision it. One day later, I wrote in my journal, "It was good to spend more time with Mark since he's getting deployed to Afghanistan on the 20th. I will miss that booger. He's going into very hostile territory called 'Cobra'. He's highly trained though."

At some point, Mark told Mom that he had never been so sure about doing anything as joining the Air Force. Mom wanted him to be a dentist.

"You can't tippy-toe up in this humpy-bumpy!"
– Terry Tate, Office Linebacker (A Mark Forester Favorite)

CHAPTER 11

Making A Difference: Deployment

…[He] was a strong and a mighty man; he was a man of a perfect understanding; yea, a man that did not delight in bloodshed; a man whose soul did joy in the liberty and the freedom of his country, and his brethren from bondage and slavery;

Yea, a man whose heart did swell with thanksgiving to his God, for the many privileges and blessings which he bestowed upon his people; a man who did labor exceedingly for the welfare and safety of his people.

Yea, and he was a man who was firm in the faith of Christ, and he had sworn with an oath to defend his people, his rights, and his country, and his religion, even to the loss of his blood.

….And this was the faith of [Mark Forester], and his heart did glory in it; not in the shedding of blood but in doing good, in preserving his people, yea, in keeping the commandments of God, yea, and resisting iniquity.

—The Book of Mormon, Book of Alma 48: 11-14, 16
(Excerpted and applied to Mark.)

Citation to Accompany the Award of The Bronze Star Medal
(with Valor, Posthumous)

Senior Airman Mark A. Forester distinguished himself by heroism as a Combat Controller, 21st Expeditionary Special Tactics Squadron, Combined Joint Special Operations Air Component, while engaged in ground combat against an enemy of the United States on 6 August, 2010.

On that date, in support of Operation ENDURING FREEDOM, Airman Forester was serving as the primary Joint Terminal Attack Controller attached to an Army Special Forces Team conducting a combat patrol in Oruzgan Province, when the team engaged in an 8-hour battle with over 30 enemy insurgents. The team was initially pinned down by effective machine gun and rocket-propelled grenade fire.

With complete disregard for his own safety, he stepped out from behind his vehicle in the face of enemy fire, fired a smoke grenade to mark the insurgent positions, and directed two AH-64 strafing runs on the target. However, the sizable enemy force continued to fire and maneuver to within 250 meters of the team's location, wounding three Special Forces operators with machine gun fire.

Recognizing the team's dire situation, Airman Forester again exposed himself to enemy fire to mark an insurgent location and then eliminate it with A-10 strafing runs. Finally, he ran through a hail of enemy bullets to reach the front of the team's column to gain a better vantage point of the final enemy stronghold. Airman Forester launched smoke grenades to pinpoint the positions while simultaneously directing two 500 pound bombs onto the target from a flight of F-16's. His combined actions resulted in 37 insurgents killed and enabled the team to break contact, evacuate the wounded, and return to base without further incident.

By his heroic actions and unselfish dedication to duty in the service of his country, Airman Forester has reflected great credit upon himself and the United States Air Force.

In late 2009, a Dutch reporter, Hans De Vreij, visited Cobra. He offers some good insight to life there, *"Challenging is one way to describe the environment in the district of Charchino in this northwestern part of Uruzgan province. Firebase Cobra is completely surrounded by hostile forces."* He noted that in about two months' time, the Howitzers and heavy mortars had *"dispatched almost 5,000 rounds, from smoke and illuminating grenades to protect patrols, to lethal high explosive to hit the enemy when need be. This is Uruzgan's 'Wild West'."*[35]

Interesting the author used that term, because Mark used the same description in an email exchange with a buddy, Bryan Floyd, only two weeks before his death: *"Things are crazy where I'm at. It's the wild, wild west man, I'm dodging bullets left and right. Hopefully I can keep that up, but odds are one day they'll connect on one. I do feel that I have done my part to reduce the Muslim extremist population by a hefty amount. I can feel satisfied in that part."* I wish I'd had a better understanding of the dangers Mark would face when he deployed, but I suppose the only thing it would have changed was my worry for him.

About the time he earned the *Bronze Star with Valor*, I was Skyping with Mark at mom and dad's, along with Rozlynn and mom. He looked very worn and exhausted. We had a great time talking, though, and it was actually a sad moment because we could tell how tired he was, and he even told us he was tired, but he didn't want to end the conversation when I was trying to let him go. I thought I was doing him a favor because he clearly needed some rest before getting back to work. Mom even looked over at me and whispered "He doesn't want to hang up." It touched us. He never told me specifics what he was doing while deployed, but during that conversation he told me to remember to ask him about a battle that took place in early July. I made a note of it and couldn't wait for him to fill me in when he got home. That was the last time he and I Skyped. I wish I'd savored the moment a little more.

When I consider everything in Mark's life, it is safe to say that deployment was the ultimate expression of his values, personality, and passion (with the important exception of starting his own family). On deployment, everything came into sharp-edged focus: his intelligence, compassion, love of adventure, and good humor. Most important, though, was his readiness to be the sheepdog—putting himself between his loved ones and danger—and aggressively confronting that danger with deadly precision. Finally, he did this not for his own glory, but from his deep commitment to walk the path God had led him to. He did not delight in violence and killing, but did find deep satisfaction in protecting his teammates, serving his country, and fighting evil.

---

[35] http://www.rnw.nl/english/article/uruzgans-wild-west

Mark Forester
September 4, 2010

My anger at having to miss Alabama football for the next two months will be paid back 10 fold against these savages!

Like · Comment · Promote · Share   👍 17 💬 10

Peter Bradberry DO IT!!!
September 4, 2010 at 1:41pm · Like

Joseph Forester Let 'em have it brother!
September 4, 2010 at 2:20pm · Like

Victor Sierra Do it up Mark....
September 4, 2010 at 2:23pm · Like

Jonathan   thats what im talking about
September 4, 2010 at 2:52pm · Like

Douglas   Give'em some of my anger too!!!
September 4, 2010 at 3:23pm · Like

Terri Forester Woods Go brother!!!make them pay!!!!!!
September 4, 2010 at 6:55pm · Like

Thomas Simpson The single greatest status update I've ever read.
September 4, 2010 at 6:59pm · Like

Tara Beth Knight That just gave me chills! Be safe!
September 4, 2010 at 8:11pm · Like

Not long after that last Skype, he posted one of the best Facebook comments I've ever read. He displayed both his sarcasm and commitment to Alabama football and for those of us who knew him, we were laughing hard.

With the stories from many others while Mark was deployed, it's easy to get a feel for his personality on the battlefield and while talking to aircraft. He was comfortable in his role, and was in my opinion, after talking with so many who fought with him, a living legend then, and still today.

As soon as Mark knew he was headed to Cobra, he began communicating directly with **IshVillegas**[36], the CCT he would replace. For more than two months, they corresponded via secure email, phone, and even Facebook

---

[36] Ish was recently awarded his second Silver Star, joining an exclusive club as only the second airman to receive multiple high valor awards in the global war on terror.

(taking care to avoid OPSEC[37] violations, of course). By this time, Ish had been a CCT for thirteen years and was wrapping up his seventh deployment (sixth to Afghanistan). He is very experienced. Ish told me he was a little apprehensive about Mark coming to take his place, even with all the conversations and messages they traded while Mark was still at Pope. No one understood better how demanding this post would be for any operator, a rookie especially. That said, Ish was assured by everyone back at the 21 STS that Mark was "skilled, mature and that he would not disappoint."

When Mark's boots finally hit the dirt at Cobra, he caught Ish and the team a little by surprise. He wanted to get on with his job, so he caught a lift on a MEDEVAC flight two days ahead of his planned flight in. For the next two and a half weeks, Ish worked directly with Mark to make sure he was ready to be the lead JTAC for Cobra. Before that could start, though, Mark needed to settle in. Ish lead him to the concrete box that would be his home for the next six months. After a couple quick pointers, he left while Mark made himself at home.

After a while, Ish returned to check on Mark. Not surprisingly, he had his gear squared away, but that wasn't the first thing Ish noticed. Like many on the team, Ish had spent months decorating his walls with posters and images of attractive women (in his case, all were clothed). Stepping through the door, only bare concrete walls greeted Ish, rather than the girls. He blurted, "What'd ya do?!" Mark simply said, "Well, I'm here to work, and I don't want distractions."

"Fair enough," said Ish in his low-key way, "but what'd you do with them?" He knew some of the other guys wanted a few pictures for their collections. Mark had not ripped them down, but had taken great care to avoid damaging the pictures, which was not easy. They were in a tidy stack on the floor. It's another example of how well Mark balanced total commitment to his own principles without judgmentally imposing them on others.

I don't know how long Mark was on base at Cobra before his first mission, but I'm sure he showed no hesitation the first time he went

---

[37] Operations Security (OPSEC) is the process of protecting little pieces of data that could be grouped together to give the bigger picture. OPSEC is the protecting of critical information deemed mission essential from military commanders. Protecting this critical information is through the use of email encryption software, careful of who may be listening to you (like in a hotel bar), paying close attention to a picture you have taken (back ground) or not talking openly on social media sites about information on the unit's critical information list (military deployments, shortages of equipment or movement of VIPs).

outside the wire. "Mark was excited and had no fear of conflict, but he wasn't careless." Ish says he first saw Mark's desire to fight the enemy the first time they went out to the edge of their battle-space (the area under ISAF[38] control). Ish took him up on a ridgeline to point out landmarks and features. Ish kind of hunkered down behind a boulder a little, but Mark stood tall in the open, taking in the scene, as if surveying his new domain. Ish suggested he'd do well to stay down, but Mark told

him he wanted them to see him so he could figure out where they were and get them. He said, "God sent me here to kill terrorists." Ish drily replied, "Well, you are going to get that opportunity here, my friend."

Ish once told me he has a different kind of smoking habit—he only smokes when he's deployed. Sometime during the two weeks he and Mark were together at Cobra, Mark saw him smoking and without a hint of judgment said "you know that's not good for you." Ish told me, "I looked at him and I could see the disappointment in his face. It wasn't the type of disappointed look like he was let down, it was more a look that said 'Ish it's not good for your health and you can do better'. He wasn't speaking but I heard it loud and clear. I paused for a second and I remember thinking that it came from genuine concern. There was no hint of nagging or self-righteousness, and I knew I should listen to Mark."

I'm sure most smokers hearing this would feel defensive or angry. Instead, something in the way Mark said it, the look on his face, and the spirit he radiated made Ish feel a little guilty. Any time after that, if he was smoking and saw Mark, he'd try to hide the cigarette; feeling like he let Mark down somehow.

As the "turn-over" process progressed, Ish told Mark about his Nemesis. This Taliban Fighter acted as a spotter on the hillside just outside the base. He would provide early warning for the enemy and direct mortar fire against the team every time they left the base. Ish's Nemesis never managed to hurt any Americans on the team, but they had a lot of close calls because of this guy.

From time to time, Ish would see the enemy spotter, but could never quite get him. He says, "I spent many artillery shells and had helicopters fly around trying to lure him out so we could get rid of him. He was the one guy we needed to eliminate to move into those areas without worry of receiving accurate fire from the enemy. We train to direct fires, and so

---

[38] International Security Assistance Force

do they." Ish showed Mark where this guy hid and now it was Mark's mission to get rid of him for Ish and the team.

The two and a half weeks passed quickly, with Ish closely watching and coaching Mark through a number of missions. As good as he was from the start, there was plenty to learn from an old hand like Ish. On their final mission together, Ish pulled back completely, not giving Mark any feedback or instruction. As Mark worked the comms[39], coordinating with aircraft and other assets, he kept looking over his shoulder back at Ish. Finally, Ish pressed him, "Why do you keep looking back at me??" Mark shot back, "I keep waiting for you to tell me what I'm doing wrong, like you've been doing for two weeks!" He was doing fine, otherwise Ish would have kept up the critiques.

When that mission was complete, (the final one in the turn-over from Ish to Mark), it was time for the team to head back to base. Ish said that as they rumbled along, "Mark pops on the comm and requests a flyby of the convoy, in honor of my last mission." The pilots obliged and buzzed our line. Then, "Mark gets back on the comm to say thanks and then declared (full of irony), 'I've been consoling Ish for the last 24 hours because he's no longer the primary JTAC at Cobra.'" It's easy to see why people liked Mark. I think he was a breath of fresh air for everyone.

Even after Ish left, he and Mark stayed in regular contact. Mark told him a few times how close he'd come to finally getting Ish's Nemesis. One day Ish received an instant message from Mark letting him know they finally got the guy. They had gone into an area and Mark was able to get a good fix on the spotter's location. Ish admits he was a little disappointed that he didn't get this especially troublesome enemy fighter, but he was pleased that Mark had completed his assignment.

Amy Osborne worked at the 21 STS as an NCOIC (Non-Commissioned Officer In Charge) of Combat Arms[40], but the operators usually just call them "Armorers". She took good care of Mark, Bobby and the other CCTs as they got ready for their deployments. Later, as the 21 STS members

---

[39] This is military slang referring to their communications network.

[40] The job of NCOIC of Combat Arms entails running the armory and building/fixing/training on all weapon systems. The common term of Armorer is used by the operators, though in the Air Force, the term applies to a lower-level, menial job. The NCOIC of Combat Arms is far more skilled and knowledgeable about the equipment so they can effectively consult with the operators and get them the most effective tools possible for their trade.

embedded with Special Forces teams around Afghanistan, Amy worked from Bagram Air Base to support them with equipment and whatever comforts she could arrange.

I remember meeting Mark for the first time when he and Bobby Bonello entered the armory and began asking to be issued a weapon and all the accessories. I figured the guys on their team must have scared them to death, because every other word out of Mark's mouth was "Ma'am" in his calming southern drawl. I

would soon find out Mark wasn't scared, but that he truly meant all the respect when he would answer any of my questions followed by "ma'am" and/or "Sgt." I worked hard at getting him to call me Amy, which all the guys eventually came around to calling me. I did not like the "operator initials" (most often the first and last letters in their last name; Mark was "FR") assigned to everyone when they entered the unit; I preferred the personal feeling of knowing "the guys" on a first name basis.

It was not long before I found Mark darkening my office door more than any other operator. Mark would come in just to talk and tell me how things were going. I enjoyed listening to him talk, often teasing him about how much I loved his smooth Southern twang. Mark talked about many things, but mostly about his gear and his weapon. We became good friends, though, and he knew he could talk to me honestly and not be judged if he had personal issues bothering him too.

Over the next few months, I heard about his search for a church, about his problems with girls he would go out with, and finally, right before he deployed, I heard true happiness in his voice when he found a church he loved in Raleigh. Then shortly after, he talked to me about the most beautiful girl he ever met (I cannot remember her name) and she went to his new church.

A week later, he was telling me about how they had talked and he could not wait to get to know her better. Then, a few days later, he was crushed because the girl found out he was in the military and getting ready to deploy, and basically told him she did not want to talk to him until after he returned. I wish I remembered her name, because she deserves to know Mark did not give up on her, but was counting the days until he could see her again.

The day the controllers find out where they are deploying to is a strange day in the unit. Guys you hardly ever see in the building start hanging out, waiting for the announcements. Then it happens and when it is over, you can see the excitement and/ or disappointment in each man as he finally gets the news of his deployed area.

When Mark told me his location, I could see the excitement in his eyes, but honestly, I felt scared for him. As a new controller, Mark was amazing. However, during my time with the 21st, I had only heard of the most seasoned and experienced controllers going to FOB Cobra. Mark's maturity and exceptional skill are the only reasons for this assignment, but I worried a lot for Mark. I was not worried about him being up to the job—there was no doubt in my mind that he was up for this demanding assignment—I was worried because I knew what he would face and hoped it would not change him.

After the guys find out about their location, things in my part of the building begin to get busy. They all want to work on their weapons and gear to make sure everything is in the right place and everything works well together. Many days are spent on the range and in the office fidgeting to get just the right fit. Mark was no exception. He would be the first one I would see some mornings and often the last I would see at night. We would zero his weapon (set the sights) and then he would ask about some other piece of gear and we would add it and then go zero his weapon again.

Mark spent more time prepping his weapon to go than anyone. Maybe this was partly because he was among the first to deploy with the new, heavier weapon system[41] the unit just received. When he would show up with doubts or questions regarding his weapon or gear, we discussed it and then spent many after duty hours on the range (usually the only time I could find on short notice), so he would be confident in his equipment. I could not let him deploy harboring any doubts.

---

[41] SCAR-H - CCTs still had the option to use the M-4, but many appreciated the greater firepower of the new system, especially those embedding with smaller, 12-15 man units, as Mark did.

The unit said goodbye to them all in the normal fashion, with a shot of whiskey. We all watched to see what would be in Mark's glass—WATER!!![42] As if we should have been surprised! With

the final unit goodbye, most personnel would not see the guys again for six months; a few would stop by on the morning of their departure for the final farewell. Watching them all say goodbye with hugs and kisses to their families and friends is always sad. Knowing what they all feel makes it even sadder

when we have to finally close the doors on the vans and watch them drive away. Saying goodbye to Mark was hard. I knew I would miss our conversations and the kindness he showed me on a daily basis. Right before he left, I assured him I would send care packages and to call if he needed anything. It was the least I could do.

Shortly after "Blue" team's departure, I got a phone call from Mark. He loved his new weapon and offered a few minor suggestions that might benefit others who would later be issued the same equipment. During his calls, sometimes he'd ask for a few items to be forwarded to him, or he'd ramble about how he was doing, what he was doing, how things were, how some things were different than he expected, and how other things were exactly as he expected them to be. Sometimes, he just needed a sounding board, someone to just listen to him. Our conversations were limited because of the time differences and work schedules, but we still talked at least twice a week. He was starting to get excited about our unit deploying and taking over the operational control/supply ultimately responsible for him.

When I arrived in country, Mark called immediately. He was thrilled to have his unit "family" there to back him on his last three months of deployment. Quickly we settled into our work routines and as soon as Mark figured them out, I would get my daily phone call from him. He would tell me about his missions, about talking to his Mom and Dad, he talked about his plans for

---

[42] I asked Bobby Bonello about this incident. Here is his perspective: "Everyone would stand up in front of the unit and have a going away or farewell. All the deployers would take a shot together. People may have been surprised about Mark because even people who didn't like JD or didn't really like drinking would still take the ceremonial shot because they were in front of everyone. But Mark made it clear that he would not be doing this so he took a shot of water which was out of the norm."

when his deployment was over, he told me about the friends he'd made and about how he was ready to leave Afghanistan. They were typical Mark conversations, full of life with many plans in his head.

When Danny Sanchez was killed, Mark called and talked to me in a way we had never talked before. I was upset, and he was the perfect person to help me get through that time. Mark was definitely the best thing for me then. I only hope our conversations provided him the comfort he needed too.

When we arrived in Afghanistan, he arranged to get a Tempurpedic mattress he could use for the cold nights out on patrol. (It was a small, travel size one.) Mark would laugh and joke about it on the phone saying the guys were going to be so envious. Eventually we started calling it "Myrtle," because he figured the guys wouldn't steal a girl out of the mail, but a mattress they definitely would. It took at least two weeks to reach his location and the day it arrived, he called to let me know he had it and could not wait to use and make all the guys jealous. We had a good laugh and I could hear the guys giving him a hard time about how they were going to take it and make him sleep on the ground.

When Mark's belongings were sent back to be accounted for, one of the first things I noticed was the box we used to send the mattress—it was completely unopened. I know how much Mark looked forward to sleeping on that mattress, and how thankful he was to receive that item. Still, he did not use it because not everyone on his team could have one. It's just how he was.

We have heard from many aviators that working with Mark was different than working with most CCTs/JTACs. These stories are powerful to read and the contributors describe what it was like working with Mark in a very effectively way. Marine F/A-18 pilot **LtCol Frank Latt** has a great story that illustrates what made Mark stand out:

The first time I "met" Mark (on the radio, and I knew him only as Jag 28) I was supporting a Marine JTAC in southern Afghanistan when Mark's team got into a firefight. (He was in the same river valley as he fought on 29 September, only on this day he was about 15 km farther south.) I raced to Mark's location and switched up to his frequency.

147

As soon as I contacted him, I could tell things were serious because I could hear the gunfire in the background over the radio. He didn't waste any time telling me what he wanted as he bypassed the standard check in protocol. He told me he needed an immediate show of force up the river valley north to south at 500 feet and 500 knots. He told me he was under accurate fire and needed me to quiet the guns while he worked up a target for me.

Being the good Marine pilot that I am, I wanted to give him what he wanted immediately, no questions asked. The only issue was that just days prior, I had been on a mission with another JTAC who also asked for an immediate show of force and it almost ended tragically. The problem had been airspace deconfliction with other aircraft. During that show of force, I almost ran into two apache helicopters the JTAC had failed to tell me about. Then on the second pass, I almost ran into a contractor helicopter nobody told me about.

My lesson learned that day was to verify the airspace was clear below me before going down low for any high-speed passes.

Fast forwarding to Mark's request: I began maneuvering to the north for my show of force, but before I started descending, I innocently asked Mark, "Is there anybody below me? Do you need me to contact the airspace controller and clear the airspace or can you do that yourself?" Without any delay and with the firmness of Patton, yet with perfect Southern tact he retorted, "Vivid 22, I am the controlling JTAC in a troops in contact situation—I own the battle space from the surface to the moon, I cleared you for a show of force 500 feet, 500 knots and I need it NOW. Questions???!"

This squadron commander knows when he's been schooled and commenced an immediate split-S (pure vertical nose low dive) for the requested fly by. Mark had left no doubt that he was in charge and that he was a highly competent professional. From that moment on, I never questioned Jaguar 28 or hesitated with him again. I assure you I didn't give this same treatment to other JTACs who didn't earn my unquestioning respect.

In the end, that flight ended beautifully as he had me conduct three lethal strafe[43] attacks on the enemy before I ran out of gas

---

[43] An attack of machine-gun or cannon fire from a low-flying aircraft.

and then I handed over to a section of A-10's who he continued to control for more attacks.

As I started to check off station, I apologized to him for small delays during the flight. As the supporting element to Mark, I held myself to a high standard and wanted perfection. Showcasing his amazing personality, Mark replied, "No, I apologize to you for not getting targets for you faster and taking so long to get your ordnance off. I'll do better for you next time."

It is amazingly ironic that the guy getting shot at had any thought or concern for my desire to employ ordnance—your son was truly a remarkable man. He demonstrated his love for what he did in every transmission and from that day on I always looked forward to supporting Mark. I still smile whenever I think of this little incident.

Ben King – SSgt, US Army, teammate

It seemed the sun rose slower than usual that morning. I recall breathing in every second as I hung in the moments of darkness just before sun-up. We all prepared for the mission that would begin at sunrise, the silence of the motor-pool was broken by the roar of the gun truck engines. Air, fuel and fire breathed life into the hulking machines as ammunition came down from the shelves and began to fill every remaining empty space inside the trucks. We were armed to the teeth.

The smell of coffee, oil, breakfast and exhaust filled our nostrils as we quietly prepared for the mission. Beyond the walls, we were sure enemy messengers were passing the word that the infidels were preparing to leave their base. Our options to engage the enemy were abundant, we could choose any direction and find opposition. The enemy would prepare to meet us, but he had to guess where; only we knew which way we were heading.

Radio checks were good, everything was ready and we began piling into our trucks. After linking up with our partner forces, we pointed the trucks outside the wire into the dim, early morning light.

We moved as quickly as we could before the sun got overhead. The sky was cobalt with an inkling of light bursting over the ridgelines that surrounded us. You will never forget the Helmand if you have ever seen it, and you will never forget an Afghan sunrise.

It was just getting light, the early summer heat pulled a blanket of fog off of the Helmand River as we rolled up to the north bank, then, single-file, we crossed the river at a shallow point. Water gushed over my hood, filled the driver's side foot-well, and saturated my feet in cool water.

Some portions of the drive involved extremely unlevel terrain beside the river, and the trucks would lean alarmingly. During this portion, most occupants of the vehicles would hop out to mitigate a possible catastrophe. I remember one especially hairy spot, looking out the passenger window, strait down on the river below. Then, I glanced out my left window and there was Mark, standing in the grey dawn, arms crossed over his SCAR, grinning and smiling in approval as I drove my truck through that unnerving stretch. The image is burned in my memory and I'll never forget how Mark seemed to be enjoying himself, as if he were on some big safari.

We cleared through the village Doane as fast as we could; ahead of our convoy was the Garmab Pass. We followed a very narrow route up and over the mountain that took us around a river bend and into the wilder, more dangerous southern villages. Of course, this was our destination.

Our convoy was eleven gun trucks deep. The plan was for half the trucks and men to go to the more northern village, Garmab, while the other half, our half, would head one village south to Wrishem. The mission was expected to have us in and out by the afternoon but these areas were hostile and home to many insurgents. We planned to get into this area since the start of the rotation because all the intel pointed to it being a haven for the anti-Afghan Forces of the area.

We knew there was going to be a fight that day. The team leader had added extra time into the timeline for loading the trucks down with additional ammunition. We planned everything down to the final minute and smallest items, and ran through every rehearsal. This was so when things went wrong, our responses would be coordinated, just a branch or sequel to the current plan.

Our intention was to find two houses in the village and talk to the elders of the compounds. If everything went according to plan, it would be another boring, simple mission. But what if something else happened? Planning and preparing for the contingencies are what made this mission difficult before it even started. This was definitely the enemy's territory and though we hoped it would be routine, we were almost certain a fight was going to happen. It was just a question of when, where, and who would come out on top.

We made it to the top of the pass and stopped behind an outcropping at the southern exit of the pass. Our convoy was still screened from sight. We all had a lot on our minds as we looked down upon an ancient village. It was a chaotic smattering of tan boxes, surrounded by mud brick walls. Lines slicing through the bright green foliage connected the compounds. The village was tucked snuggly between the opposite bank of the Helmand River and the cliff face that rose hundreds of feet. At the top of the cliff was a cap of brown vegetation.

A few wisps of smoke rose from some of the compounds, but no life could be seen. Aerial imaging and maps cannot do this area justice. The trail down from the pass descended into miles of open space, which then gave way to the green zone. What you see on the map and what you see on the ground in the green zone often do not match. It's very easy to get turned around if you can't see the mountains.

Stepping into the green zone is like stepping out of a time machine. Very little has changed in these fields and villages for hundreds of years. Aqueducts cut through fields that are never fallow, just alternating from poppy to food to poppy to food, and so on through the generations. The sun was up now and the temperature rising.

Mark was in the first USSF (U.S. Special Forces) truck, which followed behind two Afghan HMMVs. My truck was the third USSF truck. Before we started rolling again, everyone did their final checks one more time. Weapons were hot. We smiled at each other, but in somber silence all minds were focused on what might come next. Time to earn our paychecks. I put on my helmet and shifted my vehicle into drive.

We raced down the hill. Our dust cloud was massive as we barreled through the wadi dividing the two villages. No American gun truck had driven these roads in at least a year. This is when the ambush started. As we banked past the first compound and headed towards the river and the main portion of the village to the southeast, we began to take sporadic gunfire from three sides. They were shooting at us from the opposite side of the river, across the wadi, and from the hill behind us. This caused the Afghan driver of the first truck to panic. He stopped rolling which caused a confusing delay at the front of our convoy.

The enemy position on the hill had the advantage of elevation over our entire convoy. As soon as the fire broke out from the hill to our rear, Mark responded by calling in 105mm artillery strikes from the firebase onto each of the enemy positions. We immediately gained fire superiority. This rapid response by the men within the convoy and the field artillery platoon allowed the ODAs (Operational Detachments-A, or A-Teams) enough time to get the Afghan trucks and their skittish drivers moving again.

My truck was able to lay down serious fire support with 50 cal., 7.62 and 40mm. We pushed through the narrow village entrance and made it to the western side of Wrishem. The village wall was the perfect height to cover our trucks, but still allow our turret gunners to shoot back at the enemy positions in the village.

All gun trucks were firing now. Dust was kicking up everywhere. In between our volleys, I could hear the whip of enemy fire all around us. I watched as the nylon cover on my 60mm mortar tube, strapped to the hood of my truck, was ripped open by a bullet or a ricochet.

I sat in the driver's seat, engine running, looking all around to keep my bearings and awareness. As I focused toward the front of the convoy, who did I see standing on top of a gun truck, staring down into the village? No surprise, I saw Mark Forester, on the comm, calling in the coordinates of enemy positions that he could pinpoint only from his exposed position.

Apache attack helicopters then tore over the mountain to our west and began honing in on the targets. The coordination was incredible to witness. I watched as the words left Mark's mouth, then became offensive action by the pilots, and resulted in devastation for the enemy.

For the next few hours, Apaches and A-10 Warthogs would bounce around between the two combat controllers. When Mark relinquished control, he grabbed an idle 240 Bravo medium machine gun and pumped rounds towards the enemy. I spoke with him several times that morning and I cannot explain how motivating it was to hear him joke and laugh in the middle of situations like that.

As the battle unfolded, I watched him hike up a hill to get a better view of the action when the Apaches came overhead. He confidently guided them towards targets while a couple Afghan soldiers shot off RPG's beside us. Mark asked to move to the top of the hill so he could better see the valley and control the aircraft. The team leader denied his request because he was vital to the mission and clearly could see well enough to get the job done. Besides, Mark would have been completely exposed and alone on the top of the hill. The team leader couldn't slice an element to go with Mark either because all available personnel were either returning fire or prepping to move to the compounds of interest.

Finally, we reached the compounds we were after and conducted a search. With that objective complete, the ODA left the village and occupied a position of advantage to the north to support the other ODA that was now engaging targets located across the river from them. While positioned here, they saw the other ODA's gun trucks being engaged from a cave opening to the south. Our team moved down to that location to see if we could support the lone gun truck that poured suppressing fire on the cave opening. Once our ODA arrived we took over firing upon the cave opening so the other ODA could link back up with their own elements.

Mark stood tall and led two Apaches in to make gun runs. These gun runs turned into Hellfire missile strikes. Together, Mark and the Apache pilots accurately fired missiles into the small cave opening.

A few of us drove up as close as we could to conduct a damage report following the missile strike. As the team moved in close to the cave opening, gunfire erupted. The BDA[44] team backed away from the cave opening in order to bring aircraft on the target.

The team leader was directing the Afghans back to their truck in order to move farther away from the cave opening on the advice of Mark. He said that we were too close to drop any ordinance from the A-10s overhead. As the team leader was yelling at the Afghans to get into their trucks, Mark mistakenly ran with them through the gunfire over to the Afghans truck. Half way to the trucks, Mark realized the team leader was talking to the Afghans, not to him. So, he then had to run back through the gun fire to catch a ride away from the cave. The enemy fighters were in the caves for the long haul and had somehow survived the barrage of fire we unleashed on their position, including multiple Hellfire missile strikes and lots of gunfire. We pulled out and then regrouped back in the desert.

A-10's were on station. They circled overhead and discussed the options. Finally, it was decided to collapse the cave entrance under the weight of the remaining ordinance from both A-10s. With that, the ODA called the mission complete and moved out back to our firebase.

Just another day at the office, right?

Nicholas Currie –CPT., US Army/AH-64D pilot who worked frequently with Mark.

The first time I worked with Mark Forester was around May/June of 2010. Mark operated out of FOB Cobra, a small base to the northwest of FOB Tarin Kowt where I was located. I was part of an Aviation Task Force that worked directly with the ground forces in the outlying areas of southern Afghanistan.

FOB Cobra was one of our most active bases. It seemed like every other day they were declaring a TIC (Troops in Contact)[45].

---

[44]   Battle Damage Assessment

[45]   A TIC, depending on intensity, can be simply responded to with a Ground QRF (Quick Reaction Force) or an Aerial QRF. We were an Aerial QRF and it is usually reserved for a more intense TIC. Sometimes they receive CAS (Close Air Support) as well, if these assets are near-by. CAS is specific to fixed-wing aircraft. CCAs, or Close Combat Attacks, are flown by rotary aircraft. The difference is that for CCA missions, pilots can work with anyone (e.g. an Army cook on the ground) while CAS must be done by a qualified observer.

Well, during one of our missions responding to a TIC, I came across a JTAC with the call sign "Jag 28." Not to offend, but the typical M.O. for an Air Force JTAC was to push the Army rotary wing off-station so they could bring in jets to do a "show of force" through the valley. A "show of force" essentially meant the jet came through the valley at 3,000 feet above the ground and dropped flares. Meanwhile, two Apaches would be left circling at 500 feet making a whole bunch of noise over nothing but dirt.

Mark was nothing like that. He would bring us in, right overhead and use us as his primary shooter/sensor as much as possible. He loved that we had no issue flying right above the ground and staying with his team, serving as an air-mobile maneuver force. Like ground forces, we are capable of denying the enemy freedom of movement, fixing his location, and destroy him. The fast-movers (jets) can't do this as well. His approach was so different—and refreshing—that after my first encounter with Jag 28, I contacted his platoon leader out at FOB Cobra and asked for his contact information.

After trading email and phone info, I really started to get to know Mark. Anytime Mark's team planned to push outside the wire, he would shoot me an email with the details. He knew we would respond anytime he called for us and we knew it was going to be a good flight. He and his team were going to hit the enemy hard, and he had the ability to make jokes and lighten the mood when most people would be cowering behind the largest rock they could find.

Another thing that stood out was his crazy Bama hat or Bama t-shirt that he wore every other day. One of my other pilots is a staunch Ohio State University fan and they would bicker a LOT over the radio. What it may have lacked in strict "professionalism," it more than made for in good humor and morale. No surprise that Mark usually won...

Mark's team was relentless. They conducted aggressive patrols into areas that were extremely hostile to coalition forces. They would drive right into known high-threat areas in vehicles that were no longer used by conventional forces[46]. One time, in

---

[46] They called these up-armored HMMWV's "gun trucks" because they carried a few small caliber machine guns on the back and a .50 cal on top, along with extra armor.

155

particular, I remember working with Mark to the south of FOB Cobra. When we came on-station, they were trying to find a couple of insurgents that had just conducted a drive by on his patrol.

Mark told us to start searching a local qalat (a compound with several small houses) about two kilometers away. We dropped to around 500 feet and started looking down into individual compounds for a specific male and a motorcycle. After about twenty minutes, we spotted a guy who matched the description and passed it to Mark. Mark acknowledged and said he was moving out with his scout force.

I expected to see the typical Mark vehicle (a HMMWV with two giant American flags flying on the rear). Instead, I saw an ATV with one sniper and Mark with a teammate driving the most sophisticated military vehicle available, of course: a golf cart, yes a *golf cart*! All the guys in the flight started laughing hard at the sight of an ATV and golf cart driving straight towards likely trouble!

We decided to maintain a continuous presence over the compound to reduce the threat against Mark and his buddies. Meanwhile, Mark drove straight up to the compound and hopped out to interrogate the male. When he was done, he called over the radio saying the guy denied any involvement. There wasn't much more they could do, and they were running out of daylight. It was time to return to the FOB before sundown, so we followed Mark and his teammates back to base and signed off for the night.

A little later, sometime in July, we were providing cover for a mission that was inserting multiple coalition Special Forces teams into the valley near Mark's base. They were there to conduct a good sweep of the villages for insurgents.

Initially, we were coordinating with a USAF JTAC who normally worked out of Kandahar. As usual, he pushed us off-station to the south to clear the airspace for a "show of force" and we just accepted our fate. But within about ten minutes, Jag 28 came on the radio, took over as JTAC, and directed us back overhead.

I asked for Mark's location and plotted it in our aircraft, [meaning we set the coordinates in our aircraft's computer]. When I slaved our sights over to his position, I could see he was kicked back on a hilltop, leaning against a large boulder, just watching the ground guys clear the villages below him.

One of his most notable characteristics was his ability to maintain a "quiet professional" demeanor even in the most extreme situations. One example stands out in my mind. We got word that FOB Cobra was declaring a TIC, so we headed straight to the west of the FOB and I called for Jag 28. He replied, saying calmly that they were being shot at by a sniper from the south of the river he was near.

We began searching all of the complexes and tree lines, but had a hard time trying to spot the sniper. After about five minutes, Mark called back and said, "Hey Thunder, he's still shooting, anytime you want to kill him would be great." I replied to his sarcastic comment saying, "We'll get to it when we feel like it!"

Eventually, we narrowed the insurgent's position down to a tree line that had an irrigation ditch running through it. Mark called back over the radio, this time a little more serious, saying, "Hey guys, he's getting a little closer, you're cleared hot on the tree line." We finally identified the position, and engaged the sniper before he could fire again.

Mark had been positioned on a rocky hillside just sitting on a rock. He was casual at first, but after about thirty minutes, he started to get a little anxious. However, not as anxious as most, considering that at one point the rounds were hitting within a couple meters of him!

We talked later on the phone about this engagement and he was laughing about the fact that the sniper rounds were slowly getting closer and closer to his position. He jokingly asked me what took so long. I just smiled and said, "At least we found him!"

We were sitting in our company command post one day when we received a call from our tactical operations center that said there were troops in contact at FOB Cobra again. One of the Soldiers had been shot so we were going to escort a MEDEVAC bird to the grid and provide cover. My co-pilot and I ran to our helicopter and quickly launched.

After about ten minutes, we started picking up the radio traffic. I could hear two different assets overhead talking to Mark on the ground. One was a French aircraft and the other was an American. Mark's voice sounded incredibly tense and we could tell he was in trouble. His ground force commander was trying to figure out where they could land the MEDEVAC aircraft and not get more people hurt in the process.

Every time he keyed his mic, we could hear gunshots in the background. Finally, he said, "We have to move the MEDEVAC LZ; right now situation is too hot on the ground." Then I heard Mark call, "Thunder, JAG 28." I responded back and he told us to standby. After about a (long) minute of silence, he came back and said, "Thunder, Thunder, Jag 28. I need you to come to me overhead. I need rounds north of my position on the west side of the river. We are getting lit up pretty good, buddy. If you will light up the tree line over there, I'll mark it with smoke." I told him to hold the smoke as we were still about two minutes away.

Within about thirty seconds, he called back saying, "Thunder, say your position." I told him we had friendly forces in sight and we were directly to his east. He said, "I need you to engage the corn fields directly to my west, that whole tree line... it needs to go bye-bye. I'll mark it with smoke."

I caught the smoke out of the corner of my eye and we rolled right to engage the tree line with rockets. Mark called back, "Good hits, shift farther north along the tree line." During our low pass, I identified several insurgents running through the tree line. We turned around and identified the area. I notified Mark we were in-bound and we shot another rocket as well as some 30mm into the tree line. Mark called back saying, "I need another re-attack," so we turned around and engaged the entire tree line with a continuous burst of 30mm.

In the meantime, the MEDEVAC aircraft was landing and picking up the casualty to the south, away from contact. We notified Mark we had about five more minutes left of station time and he said to put everything we had down on the tree line. We conducted multiple passes and shot several more bursts of 30mm and flechette rockets. By the time we left, Mark and his buddies were headed back to FOB Cobra in their small convoy.

That evening I got a call from Mark. I asked him how everyone was doing and he said a few of the guys got hit, but were recovering fine. He said all of the vehicles were pretty torn up by RPG and machine gun fire. Then he said thank you for everything we did that day. In the background, I could hear all of his buddies screaming thank you and cheering. He put me on speaker and I told them we were glad to help, we were just glad to take the heat off them and direct the fire towards us for a few minutes so they could catch a break.

A few days later, I got an email from Mark saying that they ended up killing dozens of insurgents that day. Additionally, our flechettes were very effective. The locals reported to Mark "The rivers are running red with Taliban blood," as those who survived the initial attack later died from their wounds along the riverbank.

Every time I read these words, they hit me powerfully. I think about all those who knew Mark could hear the sarcasm in his voice while asking when are they going to kill the bad guys shooting at him and his team. I'm glad they could appreciate his humor as much as I do just thinking of it.

Nick continues: I got to meet Mark only a handful of times throughout the time I knew him. I would fly out to FOB Cobra to cover a resupply mission and land when the mission was over to trade memory cards with him. He would take helmet camera videos and photos of his missions working with us while we would take pictures from our aircraft of his signature vehicle. Every time I landed, I knew where Mark was by the camouflaged baseball cap with a large "A" on it. When my co-pilot, who hated Roll Tide fans, saw the hat, he started going off on the radio. He told Mark how disappointed he was in him for loving such a team. Mark asked who his team was and my co-pilot told him, "Auburn." Mark dismissively said, "Well, that explains a lot."

On one of the resupply missions to Cobra, a Chinook was dropping several pallets of supplies when the crew chief for the aircraft got into an altercation with one of Mark's teammates. The crew chief began yelling at the teammate and even spit in his face! The situation was tense and the pilots called over the radio saying they were going to leave because of this supposed injustice.

I listened as Mark came on the radio and told them to stand-by. Next, Mark ran up to the aircraft and started working to calm everyone down. We threw our two cents in, calling over the radio telling the pilots to suck it up and drop the supplies for the guys. Mark and I talked later that evening on the phone. He said it was probably the most hostile (non-enemy) action he had seen the entire deployment. He also said it was the most awkward situation he had ever had to deal with.

Since Mark died, we've received videos from his helmet-cam[47] taken during some of his missions. It is not like watching a movie, because it's raw and unpolished. A movie or TV show leads the viewer through the story or action. With these, there is little context and no story, just action as observed from that one person's (Mark's) point of view.

Even with the limited context, certain things are very clear, and engaging. We hear Mark's voice, his accent, and his temperament in combat. The closest comparison I can think of is that it's like listening to football players and coaches talking on the sidelines in the middle of a game or practice.

To help me understand one of the videos, I reached out to one of Mark's team captains, **Wes Wilson**. Even if you're not seeing the video yourself, his words convey a lot about the realities of being in combat.

That video is what we call "Yakhdan #1". The video probably rolled somewhere between 0900-1100 in the morning on 06 AUG 10. Del R. & James S. were wounded in the afternoon that day.

Let me start with the terrain... the vehicles were facing west; Mark was gunning to the south. Matt D., Marc F., Del, Cal Harrison, and others were clearing the compounds on the south side of the river beyond the vegetated area you can see in the video.

The area we were driving in was believed to be heavily mined with improvised explosive devices (IEDs). In Afghanistan, dry river beds are used as roads because that's the smoothest, most level place you can find. Since the soil is also soft, it's also the

easiest place to dig, emplace, and camouflage IEDs, which is why we weren't driving around a whole lot and maneuvering on the enemy. The enemy likes to bait us into IED-infested areas.

---

[47] Personal helmet cam footage is now an officially prohibited practice.

When we went back to Yakhdan in January we found several [IED's]near where the trucks were in August. One was a 500lb USAF bomb, most likely from several years earlier, that hadn't exploded on impact. The insurgents moved it and attached a pressure plate to it. When the EOD (Explosive Ordnance Disposal) guys reduced it, shrapnel was thrown over 3km.

Matt & the other dismounts had spotted several insurgents at close range near the compounds, but the insurgents fled into the vegetated area between the mounted and dismounted area which made it difficult for the mounted element to support the dismounts because of the risk of fratricide[48].

Fortunately Mark planned properly and made Gridded Reference Guides (GRGs) for everyone. The paper you saw me hand Mark was a GRG. The GRGs are a tool we all use to quickly report to one another where we are on the ground. Mark numbered all of the buildings and had the Military Grid Reference System overlaid onto the paper as well so that we could relay our exact position to Mark so he could quickly report it to the pilots. In this instance where the enemy basically put us in a position where we ended up in a "Polish Ambush[49]" Mark used the helicopters to strafe down the middle, parallel to our positions, which was an effective way to engage the enemy without causing fratricide.

An hour or so after the video cut off, the mounted element moved back to the east where we dropped off the dismounts. The dismounts re-cleared the village, mounted up into the trucks, and we all moved to the extreme west where you saw the trucks

---

[48] The employment of friendly weapons, with the intent to kill the enemy or destroy his equipment and facilities, and which results in unforeseen and unintentional death, injury or damage to friendly personnel or equipment.
http://www.armystudyguide.com/content/powerpoint/Safety_Presentations/fratricide-2.shtml

[49] Also known as a "U" shaped ambush. "The U-shaped ambush is very similar to the V-shaped ambush, except that the U-shaped ambush is applied to the far ambush *only*... The coordination of troops and elements presents a challenge, but this formation has an optimal effect when implemented against large open areas, such as a narrow valley that affords good sectors of fire." "Difficult to coordinate? Inclined toward fratricide? You bet! But even more confusing for the patrol caught in the middle of such a defense." - Light Infantry Tactics: For Small Teams, Page 214 and 220, Christopher E. Larson, 2005

parked in the video. As soon as we reached that point again, we were heavily engaged from the west side of the river.

At that time the insurgents shot out all of our tires and we ran out of ammunition. We called Willie L.'s team, and the battalion headquarters for reinforcements and a resupply of tires and ammunition. We pulled forward again, this time with Willie's team, and faced heavy fire again. This time James and Del were wounded. An Afghan Army soldier was wounded as well. Mark was able to determine the enemy's location, based upon an exceptional map and imagery reconnaissance of the area. Mark had two A-10 jets drop their entire payload along several canals from where we thought we were receiving fire. We were monitoring enemy radio traffic indicating the air to ground munitions were effective. By the end of the day the enemy was reporting [dozens] KIA and 2 WIA. The next day it was [all] EKIA.

We were unable to cross the river and conduct battle damage assessment (BDA) for several reasons. The first time we tried to cross the river we were nearly wiped out by enemy fire. The mounted element was unable to maneuver into a position or across the river to where they could support the dismounts because each of the six trucks had one or more flat tires and the spares were flat as well due to enemy fire. We had run out of ammunition for the second time that day.

We also ran out of water for the second time too. It was Ramadan and the Afghans weren't able to eat or drink during daylight and they were all about to collapse after having been through the six hour firefight. The supporting aircraft no longer had any munitions to support the dismounts and we didn't want to risk waiting around for more aircraft to show up. It was not worth risking more casualties.

Wes also gave us other perspectives on working with Mark. He told me that when there were lulls between combat missions, he would go on civil affairs missions into the friendlier villages. Their objectives could include building rapport with the village elders, running medical clinics, passing out educational materials, etc. While he didn't let his guard down, Mark didn't think of Afghans as enemies (unless they were shooting at someone, of course).

Wes said Mark was always eager to join these missions, even though there was no real obligation for him to go. Mark especially enjoyed contact with the kids. Wes said they couldn't just hand out candy or other goodies because they'd be swarmed and overwhelmed by the young villagers.

Mark, Wes and others would discretely get on the roof of a building and then start tossing out the treats. Aside from the delight it clearly gave the kids, they enjoyed messing with the kids a little too. Wes and his guys would start tossing over to one side. Naturally, the bigger kids would dominate the "treat-landing zone," and when they were concentrated in one place, with the smaller kids on the fringes getting nothing, the team would start tossing the best goodies on the opposite side. This evened things up so everyone got something nice.

Another thing was that Mark made extra effort to learn other teammates' specialties. And he trained other guys on the JTAC role. He'd help teach his teammates how to guide supply aircraft for airdrops to the landing zone that would eventually bear his name.[50] Other times, he'd set up practice sessions with the helicopter pilots. The pilots enjoyed this cross training and eagerly supported it. The value of Mark's initiative really paid off after Mark's last fight. As the battle ground on without him, his teammates had enough skill to support George, and coordinate with the pilots to keep the pressure on the enemy fighters.

Wes told me that a particular passage of New Testament scripture always reminds him of Mark. It's from the First Epistle to the Corinthians, chapter nine:

> 24 Do you not know that in a race all the runners run, but only one gets the prize? Run in such a way as to get the prize.
>
> 25 Everyone who competes in the games goes into strict training. They do it to get a crown that will not last, but we do it to get a crown that will last forever.
>
> 26 Therefore I do not run like someone running aimlessly; I do not fight like a boxer beating the air.

---

[50] "The Mark Forester Tactical Drop Zone"

27 No, I strike a blow to my body and make it my slave so that after I have preached to others, I myself will not be disqualified for the prize.[51]

Chad Hall—CCT who worked with Mark until he was replaced by George Earhart.

In 2010, Firebase Cobra was the most dangerous—and desirable—place for any Combat Controller in Afghanistan. The CCTs coveted that spot because doing the close air support portion of the job is virtually guaranteed. Everyone knew, you *will* practice your trade. You *will* protect friendly forces. You *will* take the fight to the enemy. And Mark was ready: he was intelligent, motivated and consistently surpassed his peers through the training pipeline. Even though it was his "first rodeo," he had a knack for delivering serious pain to those who were looking for trouble.

He shares a good experience that shows the power and reputation of the CCTs:

Three rivers connect in a T-shaped intersection a half-mile south of Firebase Cobra. The western branch of the river intersection was probably the most volatile in the Firebase Cobra area of operations—at least until Mark and his team decided to go that way and the fighters in the village of Yakhdan tried to stop them.

In that battle, Mark had Apache attack helicopters and fixed-winged fighter CAS (Close Air Support) allocated to him. He orchestrated these assets into a deadly symphony, turning pandemonium into a targeted, controlled use of force. The extended firefight left an estimated 75 Taliban fighters dead, 90% of them resulted from Mark's close air support coordination.

Most Special Forces team members have one radio and one radio antenna. The CCT, though, always carry two radios: one for the team, and another for the aircraft. The extra antenna makes him stand out from his teammates a bit. The Afghan populace

---

[51] This is from the New International Version (NIV) of the Bible, and these are the exact words Wes thinks of.

knows that the American with all the antennas is the guy who talks to the aircraft and brings the bombs. Combat Controllers try keeping these antennas subtle to avoid unwanted attention on the battlefield. Up close, though, they are obvious.

This came into play a couple days after the battle of Yakhdan. Mark's team was sent to the village of Sekzi. Before approaching the village, the team stopped and was doing a quick spot-check of their gear (you don't want surprises with your gear if there is a surprise from the villagers) before entering Sekzi. While the team was doing this, they watched a group of old men approach the team.

The men were the village elders. They demanded that the Special Forces team not enter the village, "We don't want what happened at Yakhdan to happen here." Going away was not in our plan; at least some of our team had to check things out in the village. The village elder doing the talking pointed to Mark and spoke something more in a forceful tone in Pashtu (one of the native languages in Afghanistan).

Mark asked the terp (interpreter) what the old man said. He laughed deeply, then explained the uproar. The old man said, "You cannot come in...and HE (pointing to Mark), the man with all the antennas, *definitely* cannot come in." The elders were almost more afraid of Mark and his antennas (because 75 dead bad guys is a lot of dead bad guys) than they were of the whole team going into the village.

One of the direct benefits of that battle at the village of Yakhdan, and Mark's role in it, is that an American VSO (village stability operations) site was established. The constant American presence lead to consistent security for the native villagers, improved infrastructure, and increased economic activity. This battle was just one of Mark's many engagements while in Afghanistan that produced similar results.

Much later, I learned that when Mark showed up at Cobra, Chad was surprised. He asked Mark what he was doing there and who he knew. Mark was so new to his team at the 21 STS that Chad suspected some kind of favoritism had been in play to get Mark to Cobra for his first deployment. Mark quickly earned Chad's respect on the battlefield and in the weight room. Chad was strong and when Mark asked him if he wanted to work out, he accepted. They did "wall balls," a CrossFit workout. Chad went first and felt good about his count. Then Mark blasted him. Chad was surprised and soon realized Mark was a force to be reckoned with on the battlefield and off.

David G., US Army

We both liked Keen hiking shoes a lot and wore them in Afghanistan. However, he'd also brought sandals. One of my favorite mental images of him is once, during a firefight, I looked over to see him up on the back of a truck shooting grenades at the enemy and I noticed he'd worn sandals on the mission. I don't know if I can explain to a civilian why that was funny, but the image of him lobbing grenades (if you've seen *Inception*, that scene where one guy tells the other one that he isn't thinking big enough, and then pulls out the grenade 6 shooter; it was that gun) in those casual shoes was pretty hilarious.

Those kinds of things aren't stories though.

Mark truly made you all proud. When we found out that he was on his first combat tour, we were astonished. He was the best CCT I've worked with. I know people always say that kind of thing after a guy is KIA, but the thing is, we were saying that about him *before* it happened. Mark was the real thing: tactically proficient, great at juggling multiple air platforms at the same time, kept his cool or lost it in a funny way.

One time we were getting shot at from…...well, that was the real issue. We didn't have any idea where it was coming from. So he starts shooting up the side of the mountain, and he starts yelling at me to shoot, and I'm like, "At what? Do you have a target?" "No! But shoot something!" That was terrible tactical advice, but it was pretty funny and we had a good laugh about it later. He didn't lose track of his faith down there, but he didn't judge either. It's common to see people who do a bad job of living their faith and still judge other people. Mark did the opposite. Probably the best witness that I've ever seen.

David K., – teammate:

CCTs and SOT-As[52] interact constantly on and off the battlefield. Mark was always professional in all of my interactions with him. Everyone agreed that even though he was relatively new to the job, he was one of the best, if not *the* best, JTAC that we had the honor of serving with.

We spent many nights on and off missions discussing life, faith, what we were doing there and such. He seemed very resolved that he was doing exactly what he was supposed to be doing. I'm not sure if you've heard the story from my friend David G. or not, but the short version was that while I was in a sniper position with one of the team's weapons experts, we began to take fire.

Mark and David G. were in the next highest position and began to return fire to draw the attention away from us. The enemy shifted their fire and pinned Mark and David behind their truck. After a few minutes, the team began to pull everyone back, including Mark and David from their position on the hill. David had a few pieces of gear in the open. As David turned to leave the protection of the truck, Mark pushed him back and grabbed the gear for him instead. This is the kind of man that Mark was and inspired all of those around him to be.

David G.'s Perspective:

I've been working with Mark at FOB Cobra for the last three months, and he was hands down the best CCT that I've ever seen, despite the fact that this was his first combat rotation. To come straight out of the schoolhouse with the level of professionalism and competence that he displayed speaks volumes about his work ethic and the pride that he took in what he did.

Because of the nature of my job, I often got to work in close proximity with Mark, and one mission (shortly before his last)

---

[52] SOT-A special operations team A—A team with specialized equipment designed to provide threat warning and/or situational awareness information to a supported commander through SIGINT/EW operations. These teams can operate independently or as augmentation to another SOF element. - http://www.fas.org/irp/doddir/army/fm3-05-102.pdf

we found ourselves sitting together, just the two of us, on the top of a mountain while the rest of the team gave medical aid to local villagers. During our time on that mountaintop, we talked about our families, our love for our country, and—more than anything—our faith.

We spent several hours like this, working and sharing stories of our lives, and then just as we were preparing to leave the village, we began to receive fire from across the valley. Because the enemy fire was dangerously accurate, we ran behind a military vehicle that we had taken to the top of the mountain and took cover. Then, upon receiving the command to leave the hilltop, I told Mark that I was going to run to the front of the truck to gather up the gear we had left there when we were attacked.

As I started to step out from behind the truck, Mark put his hand on my chest and pushed me back, running forward to gather our equipment while bullets struck the ground all around him. When he came back, I was angry. I yelled at him and asked what he thought that was all about. He simply told me that it was the right thing to do under that situation. He said that God would approve. That was the kind of man that Mark was, a brave man in the face of danger, one willing to put himself in harm's way when he saw a chance to protect others, a hero.

Mark was a great man, and during our time working together, where many people compromise their beliefs in one way or another, I never, ever saw him act in any way that was not completely consistent with his beliefs, and he was someone that was I honored to call friend—someone I'll never forget.

Don Richardson – Maj USAF, Navigator on an AC-130H Spectre with the 16th Spec Ops Squadron

Our job on the AC-130H Gunship is to provide Close Air Support to Special Operators on the ground when they come under enemy fire. Combat Controllers like Mark direct us where to look with our cameras, point out enemy positions, control all the aircraft in their area, and give us clearance to engage targets. They do all this while taking fire from the enemy, and returning it from their own weapons.

On a September night, just hours before Mark's death, we checked in with Jaguar 28 sometime after sunset, and Mark started to direct us to all the positions where they had taken fire during the day (most of the fighting had stopped once it got dark). Mark also knew the enemy was only 150 meters away, watching him from a building. He pointed out the high ground the enemy used for fighting positions, and he told us about a ferry on the Helmand River the enemy was using to supply positions on the east and west sides of the river; the ferry was about 2,000 meters north of his position.

All the while Mark and his team were discussing who the greatest rock band was. Our crew thought it was pretty funny and threw in our suggestions. It often amazed me how men like Mark could make light of their situation even though they were face to face with the enemy and possible sudden injury and death.

We located the ferry on the west side of the river and reported back to Mark what we found. I told him we could help eliminate the ferry and the enemy's ability to supply the fighters on the east side of the river. He responded with, "I like the way you think," in his smooth southern accent and started to work the clearance for us to engage the ferry. He also worked up some other targets in the same area for us to engage.

Ten minutes later, Mark informed us we were cleared to engage the ferry and all other targets. After a few minutes of firing our guns, the ferry broke in two and sank. We were also able to snap the guide wire they used to get it across the river. During the engagement, Mark's team picked up radio transmissions from the enemy saying they heard "bombs near the port" and one individual was asking, "How is my boat?" Bad news for that guy!

Once the targets were engaged, we reported back to Jaguar 28, "All targets destroyed." Mark then informed us the next morning they were going to move to the north and clear the Taliban so the locals could return. As our crew searched the valley, it was obvious that Mark and his team had cleared the Taliban between their current position and FOB Cobra to the south. Directly to Mark's north, only 150 meters away, the area showed no activity and no visible life. All the local Afghans had fled the area as the Taliban moved in.

Mark and his team brought safety to the locals; they trusted Mark and his team to protect them from the enemy.

> *"Nobody developed the battlefield like Mark."*
> – Brian A., US Army teammate

George Earhart is a USAF NCO, seasoned veteran and TACP[53]. He joined the military in 2000 and saw action during multiple tours in Iraq and Afghanistan. "I was not formally responsible for Mark, but I still regarded him as my troop. Part of my job was to show him the ropes, and see to it he was prepared in every way to live and fight at Cobra."

Even though Mark never had the chance to tell me many specifics about the guys he worked with at Cobra, I have learned a lot about them since his death and I have a clear idea of Mark's feelings about them. Bobby Bonello told me, "I know George very well and I know that the two of them had a great friendship. George is a very easy going guy who is well liked."

He continued, "George is a very experienced JTAC and Mark learned a lot from him. JTAC's tend to gravitate towards each other when deployed because most of the time there is just one of us attached to all Army dudes. I know Mark and George spent a lot of time hanging out with each other in their free time. Mark mentioned they liked to play video games and watch movies together sitting on Mark's bunk. There is no doubt in my mind that Mark learned a lot from George. They both fed off each other because they're two of the most outgoing guys I know."

George recognized the same admirable qualities others have commented upon, but he also said, "Mark saved my life—and not just on the battlefield." The casualties of war reach far beyond the dead and wounded. The regular, extended separation of deployments causes tremendous strain on marriages. Well before his deployment in 2010, George's marriage had succumbed to the stress. (He actually signed the papers finalizing his divorce while stationed at Cobra with Mark.)

---

[53] TACP (Tactical Air Control Party) - AFSOC TACPs are composed of Joint Terminal Attack Controllers (JTACs) who provide terminal attack control and fire support expertise for all three Ranger Battalions, the 75th Ranger Regiment's Reconnaissance Company, U.S. Army Special Forces Operational Detachment A teams (ODAs), U.S. Navy SEAL Team platoons, and other Special Mission Units.

The break up left George hurt, bitter and angry. Before deploying, he found himself looking forward to it. Though he had never been a big drinker, in the weeks before leaving, he sensed a habit beginning to form of relying on alcohol to ease his stress and pain. As harsh and dangerous as the war zone can be, there would be relief in the challenging, focused work. And, the bases are dry. "How messed up is that?" he thought to himself.

Once deployed, he did find some relief in the constant, demanding work. And he drove himself hard: planning missions, working out, maintaining his gear, patrolling, training, etc., from the moment he woke until he finally hit the rack. He seldom let himself unwind, even when there was time and opportunity.

George says, "Some of the guys would be around a campfire, hanging out and getting some much needed relaxation. I couldn't do it, though. I would usually find something else that needed to be done; and that was not just bad for me, but bad for my guys too. To maintain a strong team, we need those times as much as we need the rest of it." He continued, "But you know, special ops guys don't open up. We don't want to be seen as weak, so we bottle up pain, contain it, and focus on the mission."

George and Mark spent plenty of time together, and got along very well. But the inner struggle seeped out at times. The only thing Mark wanted more than putting the hurt on the enemy was to marry the right girl and start a family. Whenever he talked about it, George admits he could be kind of rough on him, trashing marriage, women, etc.

George and Mark playing air guitar to Guns-n-Roses for an air drop.

George shares, "Finally, one day Mark asked me, 'Hey man, are you O.K.?' I told him I was. He wouldn't take it. 'Are you really sure you're O.K.?' He wasn't confrontational, but he was persistent and sincerely concerned. I felt it.

Well, I wasn't O.K., and I don't know exactly why—maybe it's because his experience as lay clergy made him better at reading people and making them feel safe—but I just spilled my guts out to him. That was when I finally started to heal. I don't think I could have ever forgiven my ex-wife and moved on if Mark hadn't refused to take, 'Ya, I'm O.K.' for an answer. And when I think of the path I was on before deployment—I hate to think of what it would have been like after that deployment.

When George remembers Mark, the thing that stands out most is "his selflessness and empathy. He always put others before himself." Others have shared many of the more obvious examples. George adds, "When some guys in the unit would bad-mouth the ANA soldiers, Mark would stick up for them, pointing out some who were good guys." He continued, "We talked a lot about staying in and getting out. Most guys, when they talk about getting out of the service, they are usually disgruntled in some way. When Mark talked about it (and it was never his plan to make it a full career), it was for the unselfish desire to be fully dedicated and available to his family—one he didn't have yet. He didn't even have a girlfriend!"

Josh C. – US Navy EOD, teammate

On July 4th, 2010 one of our camp dogs at Firebase Cobra, in the boonies of the Uruzgan Province of Afghanistan, had a small litter of puppies. In typical Afghan fashion, the males were quickly taken away, their ears and tails chopped off to begin the harsh life of dog fighting for local entertainment.

Left behind were two female puppies, Satchel and Dixie. I immediately took to Satchel and she became my little piece of sunshine in a place where we were getting shot at every time we left our firebase. Mark claimed Dixie and they brought entertainment and something to look forward to for all of us at Firebase Cobra.

From the very beginning, Mark and I planned to do everything in our power to bring these dogs back to the states and ensure they lived a good life. Mark, however, was killed during combat operations a few months ago, yet the team stepped up and continued to take care of Dixie and are working on getting her back to the States. Satchel has been with me throughout the entire deployment, on combat operations, in firefights, and by my side through thick and thin.

Josh was still deployed when he wrote this. Since then, both dogs have come back to the states. He has Satchel, and teammate Danny F., adopted Dixie. It's hard to believe, but the process to bring them back to the states cost about $5,000, *each*. Josh and Danny were ready to step up because they are so attached to the dogs, but fund raisers were set up that fully covered the costs.

Nicholas Currie -- CPT., US Army (sent to us about a week after Mark's death):

> I thought I would send you this little update. I know you won't see it in any news story, but I wanted you to hear how things are going. The area where Mark was working has had a HUGE turn around in the past few weeks. Things have changed big time. The enemy is running away, the continual strikes have resulted in the insurgents cowering. Most have left the area and given up on the fight!
>
> We have been going up there quite often and even made a delivery of ice cream with Mark's name on it. I read the update on your website, about the battle that Mark was a part of. Mark worked hard with one of our teams that day (the two Apaches mentioned) and they did a great job. I came up about three hours later with a MEDEVAC aircraft to pick-up the wounded soldiers. We were a single ship AH and Mark was a little stressed. In the next 15 minutes, Mark told us to make the tree line go bye-bye. I was glad to see he got an award for that day.[54]
>
> We joked around a lot about that day because his buddies were thanking us for wasting the tree line, and we kept thanking them for being our heroes. Someday, I have some pictures I will have to show you..... yeah we were both vain and liked to see pictures/videos of ourselves! It's funny to see it from Mark's point of view, looks like Call of Duty!

During his speech at the memorial at Pope AFB, Bobby said, "Mark was a natural born leader; nobody ever had any doubts when it came to following him. This translated to when he was deployed, his Special Forces team leader would consult Mark prior to making any final decisions to whether

---

[54] This is the battle where his actions won him the Bronze Star with Valor.

they would go on a mission or not. Mark knew the area like it was his backyard and if he thought something wasn't right then they respected his opinion enough not to execute the mission. This is the kind of leadership Mark displayed and he quickly gained respect from each team member for having this quality." This is completely consistent with everything we've heard from all of Mark's teammates, friends and leaders. Further, he was positive and almost never complained. The only report I've heard otherwise is that apparently, he sometimes complained about the French combat pilots[55]...

---

[55] In fairness, it probably had more to do with the Rules of Engagement (ROE) NATO partners worked under than animosity toward French aviators in particular. On one mission, they were getting a lot of action and Mark called for aerial support. All US assets were occupied elsewhere, so they got a single French Mirage. Between the Alabama and French accents, Mark and the pilot struggled to communicate. Then, as Mark tried to talk the pilot onto the target, he wouldn't (or couldn't, flying NATO rules) descend low enough to get a fix on the target. Reportedly, Mark let fly plenty of his G-Rated curses, to the amusement of his teammates.

"If you start something, you're gonna finish it."
– Ray Forester

CHAPTER 12

He Was Ready

NARRATIVE TO ACCOMPANY THE AWARD OF

THE SILVER STAR (POSTHUMOUS)

TO

SENIOR AIRMAN MARK A. FORESTER

Senior Airman Mark A. Forester distinguished himself by gallantry in connection with military operations against an armed enemy of the United States in the Uruzgan Province, Afghanistan on 29 September 2010.

On that day, while performing duty as a Combat Controller for Special Operations Task Force- South East, Firebase Tinsley, Combined Joint Special Operations Task Force-Afghanistan, Airman Forester demonstrated extreme valor while engaged in combat with a well-equipped and tenacious enemy.

Airman Forester participated in a deliberate assault against an insurgent safe haven in Jangalak Village,[56] supporting a team of

---

[56] There is some ambiguity about the name of the place where Mark died; sometimes it's called Shah Mashad, and other times it's Jangalak. To clarify, I asked Wes Wilson, team captain of the ODA Mark was attached to. He explained, *"When looking on a military map, a person would say that [the battle] took place in Jangalak. However, the locals call the entire area Shah Mashad, as did the ODA for the duration of the deployment following that battle. Due to outdated maps and no distinct borders, it's easy to confuse the two areas.*

four United States Army Special Forces Soldiers and eight Afghan National Army Soldiers on a patrol to secure possible enemy ambush positions to provide security for a mounted patrol.

As the patrol moved into the village, it came under intense enemy machine gun and sniper fire. Airman Forester, without hesitation, exposed himself to enemy fire in order to identify enemy positions and coordinate close air support. As the enemy fire became more accurate, the patrol was forced to bound through an open field in order to secure a defensive position in a compound.

As they approached the compound, one of the Afghan Soldiers suffered a fatal gunshot wound from an enemy sniper. Airman Forester was able to quickly maneuver a pair of AH-64s over the enemy positions, which enabled the patrol to reach the safety of the compound. Once inside the compound, Airman Forester assisted in its clearing and moved into a position to flank the insurgents.

As the team flanked the insurgent position, they again came under effective enemy machine gun and sniper fire. When a United States Army Soldier was fatally injured by the sniper, Airman Forester again exposed himself to the enemy and immediately killed the sniper. Airman Forester then organized a team to retrieve the injured Soldier. Airman Forester led the team back into the enemy's line of fire in a valiant effort to rescue a fallen comrade when he was fatally wounded by insurgent fire.

Airman Forester's steadfast courage in the face the enemy led to the elimination of twelve insurgents and the capture of multiple weapons and hundreds of rounds of ammunition. By his gallantry and devotion to duty in the dedication of his service to his country, Airman Forester has reflected great credit upon himself and the United States Air Force.

The official account of Mark's last action (above) covers the core details, but offers a limited perspective of that day's events. I've spent numerous hours talking with the people who were there that day, trying to understand—as fully as possible—exactly what happened. I suppose I am motivated by a number of things. It offers closure to know what, how and why the battle played out as it did. Also, the better I understand what happened, and how Mark reacted, the better I can share and inspire others

with his example of selfless sacrifice. Lastly, it helps me appreciate the sacrifice of everyone who rises to the call of being a sheepdog, placing himself or herself between danger and the people they love. I will continue to ask questions as to what happened that day, but for now, the Silver Star citation and the details below will suffice.

The following is what I understand to be the events of that day. These words are heavily drawn from the sworn testimony of other servicemen who witnessed Mark's actions. Much of this derives from a particular individual who had a bird's-eye-view, and is largely responsible for Mark's sacrifice being honored with the Silver Star Medal. He does not want to be named here because he wants no attention drawn to himself. As another said, (paraphrasing) "We did nothing brave that day, but *Mark* did and I want no distractions from that."

The enemy in Cobra's AOR was not like the disorganized and ineffective Taliban discussed in other places. These fighters were determined, well-armed, trained and disciplined. We've been fighting each other a long time. We know their habits/strengths/weaknesses—and they know ours. All this contributes to why the area around Cobra was just about the most active combat zone in all of Afghanistan. They owned a big chunk of that territory, and they had the means and determination to fight for it bitterly.

On 28 September, the operators at FOB Cobra launched a mission to sweep an area, located about three miles southwest of FOB Cobra, of insurgent fighters. It is a green zone, and like most of these areas in Afghanistan, it is characterized by dense vegetation, hedgerows, irrigation ditches, and scattered, high-walled compounds. All of this is set into a narrow, heavily canalized strip along the Upper Uruzgan Helmand River with steep hills and mountains on both sides to the east and west. It is ideal terrain for defending fighters to put the hurt on an offensive force.

The 28th was a very active day with multiple engagements. Mark was in a mounted element, coordinating the JTAC role with George Earhart who worked with the dismounted element. On these missions, they took turns on who walked and who rode. On day one, Mark was mounted, working closely with Wes Wilson, their team captain. George was dismounted and out pounding the dirt with their Special Forces teammates, clearing compounds and fighting the insurgents. The next day, it was George's turn in the truck.

The overall plan called for the men to stay overnight in the field, ready to continue the mission the next morning. Bivouac sites were selected in the walled compounds belonging to the local farmers. George recalls, "The night of the 28th was peaceful and I remember looking up at the stars. Mark and I stayed on the radios with each other and coalition aircraft until about 2100 hrs. I found a good spot for us in the corner of a compound with shelter in case of rain, and I made sure Mark had a good MRE. He was settled into a good spot, and felt it was best to stay put for the night. I had been on foot that day and was super tired. I slept like a rock for about 6 hours. I didn't know it, but that was the last good night's rest I'd get for six months."

It may seem counter-intuitive, but the more dangerous position was manning the gun trucks. They are big, easily spotted, and a focus for attack with everything from small arms and RPGs to massive IEDs. George operates a lot like Mark; he wants to be the one in the more hazardous spot, where he can protect his buddies. George felt good knowing Mark was doing the "safer" job the next day.

They braced for another day like the last, with action right away. Instead, the quiet of the night continued from the time they pushed off at around 0600 hrs through the morning. The day ticked away and it was so quiet, George said, "We were *almost* a little bored." He can't remember the exact time now, but sometime around noon, the quiet time ended with an attack on the mounted element that included an IED strike on George's truck. The blast gave him a concussion and the team leader offered to send him back to base. George stuck it out, though, not wanting to leave his buddies right when things were getting busy.

As the situation started heating up, a TIC call was sent to the Task Force at FOB Tarin Kowt at approximately 1300 hrs. A pair of AH–64D Longbow Apache helicopter crews responded and set out on a direct, 20-minute flight to Mark's team, roughly 7 km southwest of FOB Cobra. Upon arrival, they checked in with Jag 28.

Mark told the fliers that his team of US Special Forces troops and Afghan National Army Commandos had taken small arms fire from a large qalat structure approximately 150 meters to his southeast. The pilot of the lead bird reported[57]:

As the low bird aircraft in the flight of two Apaches, I descended to approximately 200 feet above ground level (AGL) to fix the forward line of troops. Through ground signals, I fixed Jag 28's position and then stepped to Able 12E (another dismounted element) and Bravo 05 (the mounted element where George was located) operating on the left and right flanks of Jag 28 respectively.

---

[57] These details were cleared for release by this pilot's assigned unit.

After fixing all positions, Jag 28 informed my flight that his team was going to move south and clear the qalat where he had previously taken fire. My team requested that he mark the structure to ensure my aircraft had eyes on the correct qalat. Jag 28 fired in a 40 mm red smoke grenade round which landed slightly in front of the structure, confirming that my team did indeed have our sensors on the correct objective.

Mark's team, consisting of 10 to 15 Afghan National Commandos, moved south at the same time the other dismounted element, Able 12E with 20 to 30 Afghan National Army soldiers, followed a parallel and southerly course. This enabled them to support Mark's team and cover their left flank. George and his group maintained an elevated, supporting position to Mark's right flank.

As the low bird, I moved my aircraft in an east to west fashion at roughly 200 feet AGL, back and forth from Able 12 E's position to Jag 28's position. This enabled me to maintain situational awareness on their progress, while my wingman, the high bird, held a higher orbit around the entire objective area. As Jag 28 moved upon the qalat structure which he was about to clear, he contacted us and stated he was preparing to enter.

At this moment, my aircraft observed Afghan National Police (ANP) moving 10 to 15 military age males toward the rear of the qalat structure, which we surmised to be an action to move back the local populace that had been moved out of the area during the clearing operation.

The qalat structure was a large rectangular dwelling oriented west to east with a courtyard at its most westerly side and another at its most easterly side partially obscured by large hardwood double canopy trees with living areas centrally located within the structure. It was at this easterly side that ANP trafficked their populace back into the community, traveling in an obscured canal system adjacent to the easterly wall of the subject building.

As these personnel traveled under the vegetation outside of the easterly wall of the qalat system, Jag 28's team entered the westerly side. As I observed this action, I had completed my orbit and was moving toward Able 12E's position as he entered the heavily populated qalat system, also obscured by double canopy vegetation. It was as I flew over Able 12E's position that Jag 28 called out "shots-fired" inside the qalat and he had a man down. I immediately moved to Jag 28's position with a 3 to 4 second time of flight and descended to 130 feet AGL, holding a tight left orbit around the structure so as to be prepared to observe and engage the enemy as directed by Jag 28.

Upon my first turn around the structure, roughly 10 seconds after the call of "shots fired," ANA commandos exited back out of the westerly doorway where they had originally entered, dragging a dead ANA soldier by his feet, then lying him in front of the doorway.

At this time, the ANA soldiers began firing into the qalat structure adjacent to the objective building with small arms and rocket propelled grenades (RPGs). As I continued the left orbit around the qalat, numerous military age males, upon hearing the weapons fire, fled from under the vegetation on the easterly side of the structure where the ANP had lead them.

Communications between my front seater and our sister ship were taking place throughout this sequence of events, ensuring both aircraft were situational aware. After making numerous left orbits, Jag 28 made a curt radio call stating that he had a second man down, was taking fire and rounds were impacting all around him. Alarmed, I descended farther to ascertain his location, holding a very tight circle around the structure. It was at this time that I was surprised to see Jag 28 emerge from the easternmost portion of the living quarters into the open courtyard, slightly in front of the large double canopy vegetation that overhung the wall and part of the courtyard.

My front seater and I assumed that Jag 28 and his team were still in the westerly entrance with the ANA commandos. It became obvious that Jag 28 and others had continued farther through the structure in pursuit of the insurgents who had killed the ANA commando; however no call had been placed to our aircraft from Jag 28 stating this fact.

As I came around and achieved eyes on Jag 28, he made his call of taking fire and rounds impacting all around him. I observed him advancing from the cover of the living quarters out of a doorway and towards the double canopy area of the courtyard, crouching with his weapon up, firing and advancing. As he continued to move forward, I could see the recoil of his rifle bucking his shoulder back and the muzzle flashes from the barrel.

My front seater and I instantly looked forward to the direction of his fire and attempted to see where his rounds were impacting under the tree line, which was a distance of 20 to 25 meters. Unable to observe the enemy, I looked back at Jag 28 and began to observe rounds impacting to the left and right at his feet and the wall around him. As the insurgent rounds impacted, Jag 28 continued to advance, firing his weapon at the enemy. I continued my left turn around the easterly side of the qalat where his location was briefly obscured by the vegetation. As I cleared back around, I again obtained eyes on the courtyard and saw Jag 28 lying prostrate on his back with his weapon beside him. Shocked at what had happened, I continued around once again and was able to see another US soldier on his back beneath an archway directly under the double canopy vegetation in front of where Jag 28 had fallen.

My front seater and I determined that the insurgent fire had come from the roof of the qalat where the enemy was fully obscured by the hardwood branches overhanging the courtyard. As I came around again, I called out four insurgents fleeing the eastern side of the qalat from underneath the double canopy trees, armed with AK-47s. I immediately called this out to my front seater and made a transmission to my wingman stating that I had armed military age males fleeing the site.

I was so low at this time that as I passed the enemy in orbit from roughly 80 feet away they turned and looked from the qalat structure they had just left to determine the noise behind them. As they turned and looked at me, their mouths literally dropped open, realizing that we had observed them and they began to run easterly along a narrow canal system. I was so close that we could not bring our 30 mm cannon to bear. I then handed over the enemy and their position to my wingman while my front seater requested from Jag 28 clearance to fire. We did this only because of the high human traffic behind the qalat system at the time of the shots fired and we knew that Jag 28 would be able to positively identify the personnel who had engaged him.

We received no response from Jag 28 and I continued to relay the insurgents' movements to my wingman. Just before the insurgents were able to move into a nearby qalat structure, I gave my front seater permission to engage the enemy, concurrently my wingman picked up the impact of our rounds and engaged the enemy as well. Communication intercepts from the enemy determined that we killed three insurgents during the engagement.

My flight was unable to reestablish communications with Jag 28 or anyone else within the compound. My front seater walked Able 12E onto Jag 28's position and Bravo 05 departed his over-watch position and linked up at the compound. I then confirmed to Able 12E our ability to facilitate MEDEVAC 9 Line[58], he replied that Jag 28 was KIA.

The insurgent sniper and his comrades did not leave Shah Mashad alive.

As a senior AH–64D Longbow Apache aviator rated as Pilot In Command and qualified as Air Mission Commander, I have never witnessed such an act of heroism in my three years of fighting in combat. I have over 2,700 hours total time with 1,500 hours of combat time in both Iraq and Afghanistan. My only regret is that I was unable to prevent Jag 28's death. I will carry that burden indefinitely. Jag 28 continued to advance on the enemy while taking intense enemy fire, and continuously fired his weapon in an attempt to get to his fallen teammate and destroy the enemy. I can only hope to live up to such an example.

George, in his position with the mounted element heard all the communications, and instantly knew what had happened. He told me the hardest thing he has ever done was suppressing the rage that exploded

---

[58] This refers to the military's procedure for initiating a MEDEVAC flight that covers 9 points of information deemed vital to the evacuation. One place to see the points is: http://www.armystudyguide.com/content/army_board_study_guide_topics/First_Aid/9-line-medevac-request.shtml

in his heart in that moment. Viscerally[59], he wanted to sprint across the battlefield, straight to Mark's side. The nearly overwhelming compulsion was to help Mark and hurt the enemy he'd confronted. He wanted to do anything other than what he did, which was to stay disciplined and on-task. I don't know what else can demonstrate such a high degree of commitment and professionalism. He still had a job to do, and now that Mark was down, it was even more critical that he keep doing it. (It's also good that he didn't evacuate after getting blown up and suffering a concussion by the IED about an hour earlier, earning him a Purple Heart.)

Frank Latt – USMC F/A 18 Pilot, was one of the "high birds" that day. As noted in earlier chapters, he knew Jag 28 well from previous missions. Shortly after we lost Mark, he wrote to me explaining as best he could what happened. This is his perspective:

> I am restricted somewhat in what I can say regarding some of the specific details (dates, locations, call signs, etc.) based on classification rules but I am happy to describe the events from my perspective in generalities. Also, realize that as an aviator my perspective of the battlefield is a God's eye view, but very much limited. Our only situational awareness comes from the communications from guys like Mark. We are not plugged-in to the ground force command net, etc. There is a lot that goes on behind the scenes that we never see or hear, and sometimes what we think is going on is slightly askew.
>
> Mark and his element were not alone on the battlefield that day. They were conducting a fairly large clearing operation (large for SOF and larger than what I had usually witnessed in that Area of Operations). They were clearing a river valley of insurgents in several small elements all working with the Afghan National Army and Police. This north-south river valley has a very distinct and narrow "green zone" along a river. This green zone is littered with fields and small structures and groupings of structures that ultimately form the semblance of small rural villages. Many of

---

[59] Definition of VISCERAL
    1: felt in or as if in the internal organs of the body: deep
    2: not intellectual: instinctive, unreasoning
    3: dealing with crude or elemental emotions: earthy

the fields are bordered by lush tree lines, and within these tree lines there are often ditches and trenches. The green zone is bordered to the east and west by mountainous rocky ridgelines and high ground barren of foliage. The transition from desert mountain to lush green zone is amazingly distinct from the air. The battlefield is very canalized and focused on that green zone, only about 1300-1400 meters wide in the area where he fought that day. With so many Special Forces operatives combing over the green zone and so little space to maneuver, the enemy had little choice but to put up a fight. They really didn't have anywhere to go.

On previous missions, the enemy would often use the high ground to fire on Mark and his team, or report on the coalition force movements to enemy fighters below in the green zone. The fighters in the green zone often used the tree lines and trenches for cover as well as civilian compounds. This made targeting from the air challenging but Mark always made it happen. On his last day, things were no different.

When my wingman and I arrived on station (mid-day), we relieved a section of A-10 pilots who had been working with Mark that morning. I believe the A-10s had delivered some ordnance during their time on station but I do not have those details. If they did employ against the enemy, I have little doubt that Mark had a part in that handiwork, as he was very good at finding, fixing, and killing the enemy with air fires.

We conducted a battlefield turnover with the A-10s and they left for home base. It was fairly quiet for about 45 minutes. Originally, I was working with another of Mark's Air Force controller buddies a few km to his south, and my wingman was supporting Mark. Nothing significant occurred so my wingman went to a tanker to refuel and I stayed on station to cover both controllers.

Shortly after my wingman left, my controller urgently told me to flow north a couple km and switch to Mark's frequency—he was in a firefight. I quickly switched up his freq and he expertly began building my situational awareness of what was going on and what he needed. This is not easy to do, and doing it as well as Mark did is a gift.

185

I recalled my wingman from up above on the tanker and within minutes we were employing our 20mm cannons on insurgents in a tree line to Mark's east and southeast. It took me a minute to realize it, but I don't think he was the one originally in the firefight. I believe it was a sister element that was getting pummeled from a tree line and their controller couldn't see where the fires were coming from. Mark, from over 4km to the north, took charge of the situation and expertly guided our eyes and weapons to the target in order to relieve the unit under fire. He controlled several gun attacks, adjusting our aim-points along the tree line until the enemy fire stopped. This kind of battlefield situational awareness and ability to step in and take charge of a situation is noteworthy.

Shortly after these attacks, Mark started taking fire from the same tree line but farther north of his position (about 1,200m east). He controlled more strafe runs from us and partially quieted the enemy. About this time, he started taking accurate mortar fire from an unknown location to the southeast.

As you may or may not know, mortars are difficult to deal with because they shoot from far away and are indirect, not line-of-sight, weapons. They are lobbed high in the air, and then drop on their target. All the enemy needs is a spotter and some sort of communication method to adjust where they land.

It is difficult to determine their point of origin and without knowing that, you can't knock them out of action. Mark knew these were a threat to him and he asked me to try and find the point of origin while they handled the direct fire threat.

I searched for the mortars but it is literally like looking for a needle in a haystack from up high. I could not find them. Mark's fire support team eventually started firing their own counter battery mortars. He then redirected me to search the original tree line to his southeast for insurgents. I found some in the tree line and he was trying to get approval for me to drop a laser guided bomb on them (more lethal than strafe).

Someone on the net mentioned the target's close proximity to a compound just north of it as an issue. (We try not to damage civilian compounds if possible). Mark didn't miss a beat as he said, "There are so many trees around that compound to absorb the blast, it won't be damaged—and even if it does I'll personally walk over there and slap some mud on it!" I laughed out loud in my cockpit with my wingman and we both said what an awesome guy that is down there.

We were in lock-step with him as we too wanted to kill those insurgents. Unfortunately, while Mark was working the approval, the other team I mentioned earlier started moving farther south, and were exposed with no fire support. About this time, two Apaches showed up overhead and Mark decided to have the Apaches cover him while I went to cover the element on the move.

In many ways, I wish he could have followed through on his bomb mission as just maybe we would have killed or greatly demoralized the very insurgents who ambushed him just 15 minutes later. Giving up his air assets and that bomb to another controller was a selfless act. We all knew there were still enemy in those trees.

I must pause to recount a funny moment that I'm sure you will appreciate knowing Mark, especially in the midst of what was an incredibly stressful battle. Sometime in the middle of the above series of attacks, I was trying to pinpoint his position on the ground so I could ensure I didn't accidentally release ordnance too close to him. He talked my eyes on to the vicinity of his location and I saw a large tree line, parallel and to the west of the enemy tree line. Being a Marine and having spent my fair share of time as an air controller on the ground, I naturally assumed he was hunkered down in this tree line away from the enemy's observation and fires.

I asked, "I see the north-south tree line—are you in that?" His response made me chuckle, "No, I'm 30 meters to the east of that tree line standing in the wide open brown field all by myself like a big dummy." I surely wish I could type that wry sense of humor and Alabama twang in an email but I'm sure you can imagine it perfectly. He was standing out in the open so he could see and control the airplanes while everyone else was in the trees. Wow. I think "unflappable," "selfless," and "brave" say it best.

Per his request, I moved my sensor and orbit to the vehicle convoy on the move just to his south, and that convoy was almost immediately engaged from their south by effective fire. Just another feather in Mark's cap highlighting his awareness on the battlefield, as he knew they would need over-watch on their route.

By this time, my wingman was on the tanker again, so it was just the two Apaches and I left on station. I was monitoring three frequencies, talking with two controllers, my wingman, and working with the command and control network to ensure we had a relief in-bound, as I was again getting dangerously low on fuel. Because of the multiple frequencies and chaotic events to come, my recollections are incomplete. While I might not know everything that went on in the following 15-20 minutes, I remember vividly Mark's role in it as if it were happening right now.

I must pause and tell you that up to this point, Mark was amazingly calm and in his element. Quite frankly, I think I was more nervous for him and his crew than he was and I was in a relative sanctuary of safety up above the fight. Fighter pilots often joke about dying doing what we love "in a ball of flames" because much of what we do is dangerous and it helps relieve our stress. I have great confidence that Mark died doing what he loved—he was loving his job and purpose in life to the end, and died in his own ground combat version of "a ball of flames."

While I was talking with his fellow controller trying to locate the source of the enemy fire to the south, I heard Mark talking to the Apaches about more mortars. He said the enemy mortars had them "dialed-in, dead to rights" was the line he used, I believe. Mark then said he and his element were on the move because they were really getting pounded by the mortars. He also described their plan to move forward (north then southeast) in order to clear out of the mortar impact area.

Shortly after this, I heard him calmly announce to everyone that the compound we had previously been strafing around (the one we were going to bomb next but hadn't) was now occupied by his element. They had successfully crossed the field and entered the compound. The compound was actually a cluster of about five adjoining compounds amongst the enemy tree line. Up to this point, I was still working the troops in contact situation to his south with the other controller and could see the Apaches circling over his position in over watch. While I knew there would surely be more fighting, I was ill-prepared for what came next.

All of a sudden the radio came alive with a new sense of urgency I had not heard from Mark before. It was not panic, because in my observation he was no doubt incapable of losing his bearing. Rather, it was a dire, passionate and professional plea to come to his team's aid—*immediately*. I knew I heard the closest thing this man could display to panic and thus it was apparent he was in a bad spot. I could hear the gunfire and impacts on the radio in the background as Mark transmitted that he had a man down, that he needed air support NOW; they were taking heavy and effective fire from the east, and reiterated he needed air NOW.

In events like this, you get a sort of slow motion time compression so I am not positive of the exact timing but it was merely seconds and minutes from this point forward; it all happened very fast. Mark only made about three transmissions after the first indication of trouble in the final minute or so. He said there were rounds landing all around him and he couldn't tell where they were coming from but kept saying it was from the east.

After the first transmission, I immediately told my controller I had to switch back to helping Mark and I told Mark I was overhead, on his frequency and had a visual on his compound. I told him I would give him anything he needed right now, but we both knew I needed a little more information. I was too high to see people (about 6,000' AGL) so I needed either a rough "no closer than range" (I had no way of knowing if any friendlies had pushed east of the compound or not) or a rapid target description (i.e. "hit the tree line east of the compound"). With either of these instructions, I could have strafed in seconds; but without them, I could not be certain I would not harm friendly forces.

The Apaches had a similar issue, but slightly different—they could see people relatively well, but I'm sure they couldn't discern the good from the bad without Mark's help. As I've said before, Mark was the best controller I've seen, so I have no doubt the enemy fire was so withering that no controller could have gotten this done. Mark's transmissions ceased as quickly as they had begun and sadly, I knew in my heart that he had just given all.

I do not have the exact details from the ground but I have no doubt they were ambushed from the tree lines just to the east of the compound ranging from just 50-150m from his position. That is extremely close on today's battlefield with modern weaponry. The fact that his team fought their way out of this attack is a tribute to their warrior ethos, training, and brotherhood.

As soon as Mark's trouble calls went out, other SOF ground elements nearby started making their way to his position. With the help of the Apaches and my Hornets, we vectored them to his location. The Apaches were able to find some of the bad guys and lit them up pretty good. By this time, I was mainly focused on getting the southern convoy turned around, passing the info I had to the Navy F-18s who had just checked in to relieve me, and I was organizing the stack of jets that were rallying to the sound of the alarm.

Once my handover was complete, I could delay no longer. I hated to leave and I so wanted to hear Mark's voice back on the net. It was not to be.

I am based on an aircraft carrier and it took almost 2 hours to refuel and get back to the ship. While I had no confirmation Mark had been killed, I was sick to my stomach because I knew it in my gut.

I'll have you know I am a religious man. That being said, I don't make a habit of praying much when I fly—but I did several times on this day. I did not know Mark's family or friends, but I prayed for Mark and you at 24,000 feet over Pakistan on my way back to the ship. I prayed that Mark was still alive, I prayed for God to comfort you if he was not, and I prayed that he did not have a wife and kids who would have to mourn and endure his loss. Perhaps God gave me two of the three.

-Frank Latt USMC F/A 18 Pilot

Mark had said for several years that he wanted a job that would provide him with the greatest opportunity to serve and inflict maximum damage on our nation's enemies. He wanted to find a job that allowed him to kill terrorists. He found that job. Many other members of his squadron believed they deserved to be at Cobra because they had several deployments under their belts—they'd earned it. I think this is one of the reasons he told me not to tell anyone when he got his assignment. He knew others he worked with wouldn't understand. Now we know that decision his leadership made to send him to the most coveted area for CCTs was completely justified. And I'm pretty sure his teammates agree.

"It is foolish and wrong to mourn the men who died.
Rather we should thank God that such men lived."
- General George S. Patton, Jr.

CHAPTER 13

Aftermath

I lay down my weapon
And put on my Beret
To mourn in the loss
Of a great man today
So surreal
Can't believe it
Never seems real
But Can't ignore it
It's something I feel
And will always store it
No "maybe next time"
No "see you later on"
It's different this time
I know that you're gone
There'll be no more jokes told
No dumb movie quotes
No more screaming "Living on A Prayer"
And missing all the notes
No more smoke-filled clubs
(You hated that scene)
But you always went out
Keeping watch o'er the team

No more Chick-fil-A Oreo shakes
No more Texas Roadhouse steaks
No more coconut cake
Your Mom loved to make
A short list of things that we'll never share
But I know you'll have plenty of the best that's up there
Finally, now you're on eternal relaxed grooming
So let that hair grow till its full and booming
And at The Gates as you embrace all your Buddies
They'll all pause to say, "Wow, nice Duggy!"[60]
I can't speak for all, but my life's been truly blessed
Of all that I've known, you're the greatest I've met
I remember you now as you join all the rest
I say a final HooYah, and WILL NEVER FORGET
I'll pick up my weapon and as today turns into night
I'll honor my friend and return to the fight.

I Love Ya Brother,

YK (Johnnie Yellock II)

Mark's death deeply affected more people than we will ever know. What follows is a sample of the messages we received. Not only do these words hint at the emotions felt, but they testify to the difference each of us can make when we strive to be the best person we can, and do good for those around us.

In the Notification chapter, I gave my account of what happened when we were given the news of Mark's death. I had many questions, later on, for the men who notified me. Questions like, when did they find out? How long had they been waiting near my home and my parent's home? How did they prepare? Etc. Below are their accounts of that most dreadful day of my life.

---

60 The reference comes from a song about the singer's great hair do. Johnnie and
   Mark had many laughs about it.

Sean Gleffe – CMSgt, USAF/Mark's Commandant of the Combat Control School

The day of the news...

I was attending the Chiefs Leadership Course at Gunter Annex in Montgomery, Alabama. I was there with Chief Markham (CM) and we were in the last days of completing the course. I remember I was in my room that neighbored CM's and I heard him on the balcony talking on his mobile. I heard him utter a loud "F***" as he kicked his door and, of course, I went to see what was up.

Standing there, I waited for him to hang up, then he told me that Mark was confirmed KIA. He was a ball of emotion ranging from anger to sorrow. I offered my assistance and he willingly took it as he went to coordinate with the school's administration to excuse him and me from the remaining curriculum so that we could execute next-of-kin notification, according to Mark's written desires. The school's leadership was more than accommodating and committed to assisting as much as possible.

In Mark's next-of-kin notification request, he specified simultaneous visits be made to you (Thad) and his parents. That led to CM and me getting in a rental car and navigating to your parent's home using the GPS in our phones. We were in continuous contact with CM's home unit Acting Commander, Major Loughran who in-turn was in communication with our higher headquarters Commander. A plane with the Major was en route to rendezvous with CM and me at Haleyville's local airport. Aboard were more members to assist in making the simultaneous notification as Mark had requested [the team included a medic]. CM and I finally got to Haleyville and we had to make a quick, inconspicuous run by your parent's house to make sure people were home and that we were at the right place to make the notification. Once we confirmed the house, we headed to the airport to wait for team two.

When Team Two arrived, Capt Bair, another teammate of Mark's, was identified as team leader for the second team. He and I re-boarded the plane in order to fly to Tuscaloosa to make your notification. Once we arrived in Tuscaloosa, the Captain and I had to do the same thing that I did with CM in Haleyville: find and confirm your house. While all these moving parts were ongoing, we were coordinating and planning by phone with team one (CM and the Major) to be sure that we were knocking at each door at exactly the same time. The fear was that one of the families wouldn't be present and that we wouldn't meet Mark's desires. We were able to synchronize the dual notifications to within seconds.

In the time leading up to your notification, Capt Bair and I discussed how we would break the news that you had lost Mark in combat. We trouble-shot our approach and thought we had a good plan. Neither of us had made next-of-kin notifications before, but thought we knew what to expect, we really didn't, though.

The next series of events that I recall may not be completely accurate, but I think they are pretty close. We knocked on your door and as you may or may not recall, you were greeted by the two of us in dress blues. What I remember is feeling shocked by your close resemblance to Mark. It took me back at first.

It seemed you were totally unaware of why we were there. You had a shocked look on your face and probably started to put two and two together that we were teammates of Mark when you focused on the berets.

"What's up guys?" were your first words. We responded appropriately to the current awkwardness at your doorstep so as not to give away any signs of the news we were carrying. Capt Bair asked if we could come in and you invited us to do so without hesitation. You guided us to the living room in the back where we met your wife. To be honest, I think she knew why we were there before you did, based on her body language and the distraught look on her face. Capt Bair made the notification as quickly as possible so as not to keep the suspense. Clearly, you were both stunned and immediately hugged each other as you struggled to process the news we had just delivered.

You had many questions about how and why Mark had died which we tried to answer in a way that was truthful, yet sensitive to the situation. Your wife began crying before you, but I don't recollect you doing that. We also made mention that your mom and dad had just been notified as well and either right then you received a phone call, or you made a call to mom and dad. I don't remember how that transpired.

Sometime during all of that, we also let you know that the squadron and career field were going to be with you every step of the way through this challenging time.

You know the rest, you and your wife planned to hit the road to spend time with the rest of the family in Haleyville. The Capt and I said our good-byes so that you could do that as quickly as possible and we made sure that you didn't need anything more from us at that time.

You asked how I prepared for it all. Really, you can't prepare for this sort of thing. The one thing the Capt and I wanted to do was to be as sympathetic to your needs and situation as possible and convey the sentiment for all those who couldn't be there at that moment in time.

Andrew Bair – Capt, USAF, former Team Leader

The following is what I remember from that morning. Parts of it I won't ever forget, but other events are already a little hazy. Overall, though, I think it is pretty accurate. I'm glad you are writing a book, it's important for people to remember and recognize Mark and others' sacrifice.

That morning, a little while before I left for work, I got a call from the squadron saying I needed to come in and see the Commander (Maj Loughran was the acting commander while Col Hughes was deployed with the squadron). With the loss of Danny still fresh, I instantly assumed it wasn't good news. The drive in was not easy and seemed a lot longer than normal.

Maj Loughran was in a meeting so I waited outside his door. When they were through, the door opened up and one of the senior Controllers walked out with tears in his eyes. I sat down and he told me that Mark had been killed and he needed me to help track down and notify his family.

AFSOC/Gen. Wurster made one of their jets available to take us down to Haleyville so that we could notify you and your parents as soon as possible. While we waited for the plane, I grabbed my blues and the details of where you and your wife lived.

Our plan was to meet Sean Gleffe at the airport in Haleyville. (He was attending a school in Montgomery, but was driving up.) Then, he and I would go to notify you and your wife at the same time that Maj Loughran, Chief Markham and their team notified your parents.

Once everyone in the notification party was ready to go, we proceeded out to the flight line to wait on the plane. It landed and I think we took off late morning or early afternoon. The plane ride was extremely quiet, as we were all spending the time thinking of what to say to you and your family.

We landed in Haleyville and re-discussed the plan for notifying you and your folks. Basically, Maj Loughran and Chief Markham would drive out and find your folks' place while we found your house. Once we had the locations and knew that all parties were at home, one of us would call the other to "initiate" the notification.

We left the airport and drove to our locations. Maj Loughran and Chief found your parent's house but your mother and father were not at home. They either parked someplace close by or drove by the house every couple minutes to keep an eye on the place to see when your parents got back. We found your house without trouble, saw the car in the driveway, figured you were at home, and let Maj Loughran know. After that, we drove down the road a little while and slowly meandered through one of the neighborhoods waiting for your folks to get home.

I'm not sure how long we waited, but I don't think it was more than 30-45 minutes. It was late afternoon/early evening. Maj Loughran called and let us know that your folks had gotten home and he set a time for notifying you and your parents (3-5 minutes after the phone call). We drove over to your house, parked in the driveway, got out and rang the doorbell. During all the training and missions down range, I don't think I have ever been more nervous.

You answered the door. I'll never forget the next couple of seconds. When you first answered, you had a smile on your face and the friendliest look in your eyes. After a second or two, I think you recognized the fact that two strangers in Air Force Service Dress don't usually show up unannounced at one's door, and something was wrong.

Your face got kind of pale and your demeanor changed. I introduced Sean Gleffe and myself and asked if we could come in to speak with you. You invited us in and I sat down while Gleffe remained standing in your living room. I can't tell you exactly how the conversation went, but this is how I remember it:

I'm not sure how I started, but I told you and your wife that Mark had been killed by enemy fire a short time ago. Both of you began to cry and started asking questions: "Had it been friendly fire?" "Did he die quickly or did he suffer?" "Did he have medical help on hand?"

Looking back it seems like we talked for about an hour, but I don't think that could have been the case because (unfortunately) we didn't have a lot of information at the time concerning Mark's death, plus your father called shortly thereafter so I don't think it could have been more than 10 or 15 minutes. We left shortly after. You and your wife thanked me for traveling down to tell you. I'll never forget that, either: how you could get such horrible news and still be so friendly and accommodating.

We left your house and returned to the airport. The pilots were waiting for us so we took off shortly thereafter.

Reading their accounts of the notification still stirs a lot of emotion in me. That scene is one I'd watched in movies or TV and now it actually was playing out in front of me and to my parents. As I was talking to Joseph on the drive up to Haleyville that night, he said, "Oh brother, I'm sorry you had to experience the notification. I should have been the receiver instead of you."

Below are more messages sent to us from Mark's teammates and leaders, both in the U.S. and down range.

Dave – SSgt, 21 STS Blue Team

It hit me hard when I learned of Mark's passing. Not only was FR my troop, but he was my friend, my brother in arms. It has been a rough summer for our tight-knit family in Special Tactics.

But the more I've thought about Mark, and the way he lived his life, a feeling has set in that has calmed my emotions. Then, I began feeling proud. I am proud to have known Mark, to have trained with him, and to have mentored him. I'm proud to know that I am cut from the same cloth.

We can never replace one of our fallen; we simply place another hard-charging operator in his position. The world is a lesser place without Mark. I don't know how long it will take me to get over losing FR, but I can tell you what I will do. Everything I do from here on, I will at some point think of Mark. And when I think of Mark, I will be reminded that I have to attack every day and everything like he did, just so I don't let him down.

After this deployment, I will become an instructor, and I almost feel bad for the students I will train, because they will have an incredibly high standard to live up to. That standard was set by Mark Forester, and although it will not be easy, I know it will make them better operators—and better men.

Matthew Sampson – Capt, Pipeline teammate

I still miss the well-timed "Gosh dang-it!"[61] Mark would throw out instead of the "colorful" language his comrades used. His sharp wit and desire to be the best at whatever he attempted can never be replaced. I looked forward to crossing paths with Mark through the years as we served our nation together.

Bryan Floyd – Pipeline teammate, friend

It's been one year since we lost Mark. I know, we all lose people. Death is just a part of life. Most people in our lives leave impressions on us, and we cherish these feelings and memories. No matter how hard we try to hold on, these impressions fade as time moves forward.

But every now and again, someone special comes along. Someone different from all the rest; someone who leaves more than just an impression. Mark was that person for a lot of people.

---

[61] I asked Matthew to confirm he didn't mean "dad-gummit", because this was a common phrase Mark used. He said he knows that phrase well too, but was certain Mark said "gosh dang-it".

He was that way for me. He was that friend that showed you how to be a better you. Every day I wear a blue bracelet that reads "Be Like Mark". I think that if I follow that advice, I can't go wrong.

Ben King – SSG, US Army

Not a day passes that I do not remember Mark. He showed up on our camp with his Alabama t-shirt and his richly cultivated hair-do one afternoon in early Spring. In the gym, we watched him performing strange exercises he called "CrossFit." We set down our weights to gawk at a grown man in the hand-stand position against a wall performing some sort of push up. Today I check the CrossFit[62] workout of the day and throw my feet above my head and perform those same pushups. Mark was clearly different, in the way a breath of fresh air is different.

However, CrossFit tricks are at the bottom of the list of valuable things I learned from Mark. He set a simultaneously humbling and inspiring example in everything he did from his G-rated swear words in our intense basketball games to witnessing him practice his craft with precision, skill and discretion during hectic firefights that significantly lead to one success after another for coalition forces.

John B. – CCT Instructor at STTS, Hurlburt Field

Dear Forester Family, I'm so terribly sorry for your loss. I had the pleasure of meeting and training Mark at the STTS, Hurlburt Field. Mark's class was my first when I arrived as a new instructor to STTS in Mar 2009. I had many talks with Mark through-out the three months of teaching him in the ORT (Operational Readiness Training) phase of STS. Most of the talks were about his faith and why he joined the military. I've been teaching over 18 months and around 150 students and not one of them could stand above your son. You should be so proud of the fine man you raised; he is truly missed by so many people, and will never be forgotten. My heart, soul and prayers go out to your family and the many people that had the pleasure of knowing your son, Mark.

---

[62] In May 2012, CrossFit introduced the "JAG 28" Hero Workout of the Day (WOD) in honor of Mark.

AJ – Sergeant, US Army

> I worked with Mark almost every day during my time at FB Cobra; I have not met a better example of a "Quiet Professional." He was wise beyond his years as everyone who worked with him knew. I usually sat beside him in the back of our gun truck while we were out swapping stories about home and what we would do when we got back. It pains me to know I can never see his shining example of how to be a good soldier, professional, and friend again.
>
> To his family and friends back home, you should know he was one of the greatest warriors and professionals I've ever worked with. His passion for his beliefs and his job here were unmatched. He may be gone, but he is never forgotten. He was the guy who would go out of his way to help anyone, right up to the end. I hope you find comfort in the fact that he will live on forever in our hearts. RIP Mark, I love you bro.

Nicholas Currie – CPT., US Army/AH-64D pilot

I just wanted to tell you he was the bravest, most amazing soldier and controller I have ever, ever worked with. I joined several of my fellow aviators on the ramp when Mark left us late that night. It was a quiet and simple farewell to a wonderful man. I just wanted to let you know you have an amazing brother.

This is by far the hardest loss we have suffered here. Even though Mark was not a member of our Task Force, we all were extremely sad to see him leave. I have particularly had a hard time with his passing. Your brother was a true warrior and died a brave, brave man. I will miss him a lot.

I learned that your family is LDS. I never knew this as Mark and I never discussed religion much! I know Heavenly Father is proud of Mark. He was a superb example of an outstanding soldier and man. A true Stripling Warrior.

Please know that my thoughts and prayers are with you and your family. God bless you all. Thank you for letting me know Mark. He has definitely left an impression on my life.

God bless you and your family. Families are forever.

Brandon Hodge – CW2, US Army/AH-64D pilot

I'm so sorry and shocked to hear about all of us losing Mark. He was a great guy to work with and he will be deeply missed by all of us who had the pleasure and honor to work with him. Flying and working up in the vicinity of FB Cobra will not be the same without having him on the other end of the radio. He was truly outstanding at his job. In fact, I can honestly say that he was the best JTAC that I have worked with in two tours flying attack helicopters in Afghanistan.

Working with and seeing him grow as a new JTAC on his first tour, anyone could see the level at which he had advanced to being absolutely great at his job. He and I had a technique on how to do our jobs together to best affect the battlefield and to find and fix the bad guys every time. Mark and I were in constant communication throughout his tour and we would plan things out so that we would be overhead in the *right spots* where we knew that he could walk me in on the bad guys and get the job done.

I cannot say it enough at all, but Mark is going to be deeply missed by all of us Apache pilots. I'm sorry that I will not be able to make the funeral services for him. However, I will visit him when we return home and pay my final respects to the man who gave it his all 110% of the time and paid the ultimate sacrifice for the love of God and Country.

I'm going to miss hearing him tell me, "red smoke's out" on the bad guys' positions.

Benjamin Hubbert – Former SSgt, USAF

I know we have never met, but I was one of Mark's instructors at Lackland AFB, TX when he went through the first phase of CCT training. Over my 4 years at Lackland, I met thousands of students.

We had such a high wash out rate that I only kept in touch with the best of the best. Mark was no doubt my favorite student from the first day that he opened up to me and started talking football. Mark carried himself in a way that I will never forget. It was like he was an angel on earth! He made everyone around him better—including his instructors. :)

Some of the most important things people have done for me are just the little things. I deployed four times, so I know how difficult it can be to stay in touch. On 21 September 2010, Mark sent me a message wishing me a happy belated birthday. That meant so much to me because he took the time to write when it is hardest to make time for things like that.

When I got the news it truly broke my heart. Your son meant so much to me because he gave me hope. Knowing guys like Mark were willing to go through some of the hardest training known to mankind and fight such an evil enemy made me realize that our country will get through this war.

You and your husband raised one of the most outstanding Americans I have ever met! Please know that your family is in my prayers and please let me know if there is ever anything I can do for your family.

Huey – CCT Pipeline teammate

Misses Forester, I just got back from visiting Johnnie Yellock[63]. I am very relieved to see how good of shape he is in, all things considered. He asked me to let you know he's thinking of you and looks forward to speaking with you soon. He was adamant that I make contact with you. I can tell he sees the Foresters as family and cares about you all deeply.

I am not a very emotional person, but I have to admit being touched by Johnnie's behavior. He was more worried about how his family and the Foresters were doing than he was about his own condition! I am sure you know, but Johnnie truly has a bond with your family that words can't express. It is still very early and I am no doctor, but he looks like he will be able to make a full recovery.

Seeing Johnnie made me think of Mark. I think we sometimes glorify people when they pass, but with Mark there's no need. Mark was truly the most remarkable person I have ever met. Mark and I were very different in how we lived are lives, but

---

63 About nine months after Mark was killed, Johnnie was seriously wounded in an IED attack. His recovery has been long and painful with numerous surgeries, physical therapy, etc., but is making great progress.

Mark never judged me once. Mark is truly the most righteous man I have ever met. In my experience, people like that are few and far between. I just want to let you know you raised a remarkable man. I am sure I will never meet anyone like Mark again and your family deserves a lot of credit. Please pass this message to the rest of the Forester family.

Wes Wilson – CPT., ODA Detachment Commander

SSG Tommy Peterson has returned to our detachment. He escorted SFC Calvin Harrison's remains back to the US on the same flight that took Mark home. Tommy said that he met you and your family briefly at the airport [Dover] when Mark & Cal landed in the US.

I've been very hesitant to write since Mark was killed. I didn't know what to say at the time, and I've come to the realization that I will never know what to say. I do want you to know that I think about him all the time. We have a radio frequency that only the aircraft use. Each time a helicopter or jet checks in, I catch myself listening for Mark to respond. I'm still just used to hearing his voice.

Tomorrow will be Thanksgiving. I remember Mark telling me on several occasions how much he was looking forward to being home for Thanksgiving. I know this Thanksgiving and Christmas will be hard for your family.

On the topic of Thanksgiving, the village elder of Shah Mashad, where Mark and Calvin were killed, is still very thankful for their sacrifice. The elder's name is Mohammad Ismael. I ate dinner with him a few nights ago and he asked what perception Americans have of the Afghan people. He wanted to make sure that Americans know that not all Afghans are Talib. I told him that educated people understand that, but a few people do think that all Afghans are bad.

I told Mohammad Ismael that if he is worried about the perception and feelings of Americans, then he should write a letter to your family and to the two daughters that Cal left behind. He intends to do so. He asked me to repeat Mark & Cal's names several times throughout the evening so he would be sure to remember.

Naturally, your family will never forget Mark's actions, nor will those of us who served with him ever forget. However, it will never be forgotten by the people of Shah Mashad. That village was under Taliban control since before the US invaded Afghanistan. They are enjoying freedoms now that they had been denied for over a decade. The people of Shah Mashad continue to show their gratitude for the sacrifices made for them. The motto of Special Forces is "De Oppresso Liber" which translates to "Free the Oppressed." Mark's work definitely helped make this possible wherever he went.

This Thanksgiving, I am thankful for having known and served with SrA Mark Forester.

God bless you and your family.

Jeremy Glenn – Franklin County Operations Manager, Northstar EMS

I have been to funerals of EMTs, Firefighters and Police officers killed in the line of duty, retired military funerals, funerals of the very old, and the very young, and funerals of family and friends. However, Mark's funeral was completely different. In the days leading up to the funeral, it was very chaotic for the city. There was so much going on, from the talk of Westboro Baptist Church protesters to being unable to find American Flags for sale in three counties.

On the day of the funeral, I was very busy working the truck and I stopped to get fuel. Two motorcycle riders pulled up with flags flying. On the front of those bikes were yellow ribbons saying MILITARY FUNERAL. These guys were part of a group of veterans and other riders called the Patriot Guard Riders. Their primary job at military funerals is, at the family's request, to lead the procession and stand guard in front of any protesters that may disrupt the services.

As the day drew longer, I began to research everything about Mark, the Patriot Guard Riders, and other things related to military funerals. As time drew near for the funeral, out of respect, I chose not to attend because I felt that was for people who knew Mark. However, a few of my dearest friends and I decided to attend the procession and pay our respects.

After choosing our spot among hundreds lining the procession, I was able to witness one of the most respectful and powerful things I have ever witnessed. Hundreds of people standing quietly with flags waving and hands over their hearts, totally speechless. Mark's whole unit from Pope Air Force Base was in attendance, probably 200 men and women standing strong and proud while fighting back tears. The Patriot Guard Riders surrounded the burial and everyone in attendance stood shoulder to shoulder with flags in each hand.

I want to thank all of our military who serve this great country and a special thank you to those who work (on our team). I like to put feelings with songs. I encourage each and every one who is reading this to go online and look up the song "Angel Flight" the tower remix and listen to it. It is by Radney Foster and it is a very powerful and touching song that I think is fitting to this situation. What made me think of it was when I saw pictures of Mark's flag draped casket [at Dover] being unloaded off that plane at night in the rain with soldiers lined up with nothing on their mind but honoring their fallen comrade. I thought to myself how powerful that was. Godspeed Mark Forester!

Don Richardson – Maj USAF, Navigator on an AC-130H Spectre

I was sorry to hear about Mark, I cannot imagine how you feel or what must be going through your mind since his passing. I was stationed at Hurlburt Field, Florida for 15 years prior to moving to New Mexico with the 16th Special Operations Squadron. I have many friends who are Combat Controllers and part of STS; Mark was among an elite group of soldiers.

As a constant reminder to us all when one of our brothers falls in combat, the flag in our compound flies at half-staff for three days. One day in September, I remember walking into work and seeing the flag flying low on the pole. It always made me sad to think someone had been taken from us in battle; most Special Operators take it personally; I know I do. Most of us never think, "It will be me," even though we know it can be. Even though news like this travels quickly, I only knew we had lost a Combat Controller the day prior. I did not know who it was or his call sign.

Then, I got a message from my wife asking if I knew Mark. After I got the email, I went back and checked my logs and saw that in late September my crew had been launched to support a team from FOB Cobra. They passed us a radio frequency, the team location and a call sign. The call sign was Jaguar 28, Mark's call sign. I cannot describe how it felt, realizing the awful news, but I know you can imagine it.

The Combat Controllers are a rough group of men, but among that group Mark was special, he stood out for his expertise and for sticking to his principles. The men Mark worked with recognized that unbending characteristic is what set him apart from his peers. I imagine Mark's perspective on service was a lot like mine. I read where someone said Mark had told them "He was here on this earth to defend America," I have those same feelings myself.

One thing that keeps me focused on what I am doing while deployed is reading the Book of Mormon. My favorite part is Alma Chapters 40-63. If only we had leaders like Moroni and Helaman. I have read those chapters more than I can count and I realize, like Mark did, there are certain things worth fighting for. If all men could be like Moroni, *"...he was a man who was firm in the faith of Christ, and he had sworn an oath to defend his people, his rights, and his country, and his religion, even to the loss of blood"*. (Alma 48:13).

Although I never met Mark in person, I have heard and read what so many have said about him that I have to think this description applies to Mark also. I find comfort in these chapters of Alma, reading them has helped me through some difficult times as I have returned home and adjusted to "normal life." I'm sure Mark knew the dangers of what he was doing. Mark died doing what he loved and fighting for what he knew was important. Most people never figure that out.

May God bless your family and comfort you in this time of loss. Have faith that you taught Mark the right things and that our Heavenly Father has a plan for Mark and your family in the years to come.

Mark's Brother in Arms and Brother in the Gospel.

Below is an excerpt **LtCol Frank Latt** wrote to his squadron's families two days after Mark's last mission. At the time he wrote it, he did not know Mark's name, but has since become a good family friend.

Checkerboard Families,

Things on the ground have heated up a bit since the Afghanistan elections and our presence in the skies is more important than ever. Just yesterday, I flew a life-changing mission in support of some great American heroes who I will never forget. These "kids" were bravely patrolling through a village deeply entrenched with enemy fighters. Their mission was to clear the enemy out of the village and provide a secure place for the locals to live and prosper. Shortly after our arrival on station, the patrol started taking heavy and effective fire and my wingman and I were there to protect them with fires from the air. The situation lasted for hours as we continued to cover their movements and engage the enemy on and off. Apache helicopter gunships were brought in below us and things seemed to settle down for a while. It was quite a gratifying feeling to help those guys the way we did- they could not have succeeded without us.

The combat air controller on the ground directing our contribution to the fight was one I had worked with on several missions in the past and I had built a rapport with him- a rapport forged under the stress of combat and the feeling of ultimate teamwork, sacrifice and trust. It is funny that I consider him a brother to me, a brother in arms, a friend, yet I don't even know his name or rank- just his call sign, and he only knows mine. This bond is one of the most special things about military service.

Unfortunately, there is more to the story. All of a sudden, all hell broke loose on the ground as the patrol was ambushed by enemy forces at very close range. The patrol was immediately pinned down. They took immediate casualties, and I heard my "friend" yelling in the radio to "his friends" in the air for help. All he could say was, *"I need you now! I need you now!"* It all happened so fast and then the radio fell silent. I knew what had happened. My *"friend"* had given all.

We eventually were able to engage the enemy from the air and vector ground reinforcements to their aide, but it was not in time to prevent the loss of two American heroes. As I replay the events over and over in my mind, I struggle with the thoughts of what I could have done better. In the end, perhaps we did our best and it just wasn't ever going to be enough- war is an ugly thing and people really die. This is my cross to bear.

I do find solace in the fact that surely more would have died had we not been there to support. What is not lost on me is in his final moments alive on this earth, in a situation he knew was dire, he was crying out for help from above ...he knew his only hope for his team was from the superiority of aviation fires. *"I need you now! I need you now!"* This fact emboldens me to work harder than ever before to ensure our machines and people are ready to support these heroes at all costs. It also solidifies my resolve to endure this time away from my family. Your sacrifice as families IS making a huge difference to a lot of people, far beyond VMFA-312. And remember, no matter how hard this separation may seem at times, we have it easy. Our hardships pale in comparison to the sacrifice my *"friend's"* family just made.

Thank you for listening to my difficult but important story. As always, thank you also for your amazing support. I've never witnessed a unit with a group of families of your caliber. God bless you all and Semper Fidelis.

When Michael Shiffler set up Mark's website within one day of his death, he had the chance to communicate directly with many people we would get to know ourselves later. Here is one of those communications:

My name is CW3 **Matthew Longanacre** and I am an AH-64D Apache Pilot stationed at FOB Tarin Kowt, Afghanistan. I was the Pilot-In-Command of one of the two Apaches that were overhead when Mark and Calvin were killed.

I met Mark in person only once, for a few moments on the LZ at FOB Cobra. During that time and the many missions that I flew overhead cover for his team, while working on the radio with him, he managed to make what will surely be a life-long impact on me.

As a previous ground guy, I could not be more committed to the mission of protecting Mark and his team here in Afghanistan.

We pride ourselves on doing whatever it takes to protect these gifted warriors on the battlefield. This is why the loss of Mark has hit me harder than any in the past. I was overhead that day and unable to prevent this tragedy. I just hope that his family and friends can find some small measure of comfort in knowing that he took the fight to the enemy right until the end. Very few in this world can say the same. Rest in peace brother. I'll see you on the flip-side, BC 20

Megan Pike

During the five months of Mark's deployment, each of our lives got very busy, he was fighting the bad guys and I was still working with youth in the ministry in Northern California. We would still communicate regularly, though the longer he was there, the less often we could connect, again on Skype and I.M. Often, we couldn't speak because of others being around, so we'd turn on the cameras to see each other, and write messages back and forth.

One time late in his deployment, he tried calling me directly. Unfortunately, I was on a mountaintop in California with no coverage. Later, my phone buzzed when I had service again and his message got to my phone. All I remember was that the sound of his voice was unlike any other time I'd heard it. More than tired, he sounded weary and completely exhausted.

A couple weeks later, I was home again. My dad was in the hospital on September 10, 2010 for a minor procedure. I had my netbook to help pass the time as my family and I waited. Mark happened to be online and we chatted via Facebook. Mark told me he was really looking forward to going home, but that he was thinking of volunteering for another tour. He figured that if he redeployed, then some other CCT could stay closer to home. Many had families, and Mark felt it was better for him, being single, to spend the extra time than for some other guy to have to leave his family.

I told him he should "just come home." As far as I was concerned, he'd done more than his duty already. Before we could say much more, a doctor came and said there was a serious complication with my dad. I told Mark I had to go. Before logging off, he assured me everything would be fine, and it was—after dad spent two weeks in the ICU.

The following days passed in a blur. Somewhere in there I got another message from Mark, checking in. He said he knew everything would be fine and to give my mom a hug from him. My dad eventually went home, but he was still very ill and needed a lot of care. While I was preoccupied helping my folks, I was surprised when my phone rang on a Thursday evening and I could see it was my old friend John. I said aloud, "Why is John calling me?"

I answered and he asked, "Have you heard about Mark?" It couldn't be true. I collapsed to the floor of my room for I don't know how long. When I finally got up, I felt completely numb. I attended the services in Haleyville, and rode with Tony and Bobby [Bonello]. It only became real to me when I saw Mark in his casket. Before that, my mind refused to accept it.

On the way from Mobile to Haleyville, Megan stopped in Tuscaloosa to have her hair done by the dresser she'd used the whole time she lived there. They had talked all through Megan and Mark's relationship. She truly sympathized with Megan and talked about how horrible it was to lose Mark. "But at least he didn't leave a wife and children…" Then, she froze and whispered in disbelief, "Megan, you could have been that wife."

For weeks I went through the motions of my life in a surreal haze, often feeling disconnected from my life and those around me. He appeared in many of my dreams. Often, he'd have his eyes fixed upon something ahead, not upon me. Other times, though, he would be himself, funny, attentive and warm.

I had to keep myself from thinking about the "what ifs". It was too painful, and I just couldn't let myself get lost in there.

I know Megan took it very hard when Mark died. Even though their relationship was hard to define, there is no doubt they shared a unique and deep bond; losing him hurt her very much. When she said she feels their differences over religion were maybe exaggerated to protect her, I couldn't help asking whether it would really have been worse to have been a widow. She paused a long moment, then replied that in the eyes of many who knew her, she was. In closing, she said, "I was the girl he loved and I loved him back just as much."

Johnnie Yellock II, Pipeline teammate, friend[64]

Words cannot express how I felt when I was so casually passed the news that I had lost a true brother today. That's how all of these letters start out isn't it?... "Words cannot express." Unfortunately, in my current position, I need to try to make the most of my words since it's all I have. My team leader asked the lot of us if we knew anybody by the name of Mark Forester. Although I felt the truth in the forefront of my mind, I held out in disbelief and prayed that the question was only to boast about yet another of Brother Forester's many accomplishments as of late. The next quick, concise (almost flippant) phrase, "He was KIA today," brought about an all too familiar realization that yet another great man is actually gone.

I walked outside and hit my knees to pray for the Forester family who meant the world to him. Mark almost didn't have a choice but to be a great man, coming from parents such as his. Mark's mother is kind, giving, and compassionate. Traits that I had to apply to two weeks of working out after a Thanksgiving I was blessed to have spent with the Foresters as she was constantly preparing amazing snacks! (Brochette, protein balls, and the best coconut cake ever.) His father is caring, stern, headstrong, and a great leader of his vast family. Mark embodied all of the best of his family and religious upbringing and was able to apply these traits to better the lives of all who had the pleasure of knowing him. He made me always want to be a better person.

He was a natural leader, and a great follower, traits of every good soldier. Long before Mark began taking orders from his Uncle Sam, I imagine Mark as a child taking orders from his father, having their fair share of disagreements, I'm sure. And as he grew in his spiritual walk, I know his orders and unwavering direction was coming from The Father. A fact he would make known upon arrival to each new school throughout our training. We would all have a go-around-the-room session where the new instructors would get a chance to know us better. "Where are you from? Why did you enlist? Why CCT?" It was always a

---

[64] Johnnie was deployed to a different part of Afghanistan the same time Mark was at Cobra.

213

slightly different story that each of us would tell and heard each other tell time and time again; but we always looked forward to Mark's turn. Mark had the same response every time. "I joined the military and Combat Control for one reason, God told me to KILL TERRORISTS." We would laugh, instructors would be flabbergasted, and Marks face was stern; he was serious and, I can't speak for everyone, but I always believed him.

The last thing I said to Mark was a short message I sent that, as it turns out, arrived several hours before he passed. We hadn't had the ability to communicate much lately but his name kept coming up with the awesome job he had been doing over here and I felt compelled to ask him something. "What's up bro? You still finding time to read your Bible every day? I know you're out there doing God's work."

He was a strong, charismatic, funny, opinionated bright beacon of what we should all aspire to be. Mark was in top shape in every aspect of life, he was physically fit, an outstanding controller, loving friend to all, and as close to God spiritually as he could have been. He was taken from this world, by our standards, all too soon, but Mark was also an overachiever and had completed the task bestowed upon his life with quickness and valor. He was ready.

WE WILL NEVER FORGET!

Lt Col Parks Hughes, Commander, 21 ESTS (Comments read at the memorial for Mark, 8 Oct 2010, Pope AFB, NC):

On behalf of the men and women of the 21st Expeditionary Special Tactics Squadron in Afghanistan and Iraq, I am honored to share some words in remembrance of Mark Forester: son, brother, friend, teammate, selfless servant, skilled professional and courageous warrior.

As many of you know, I served as Mark's commander both at the 21 STS at Pope, and also here in theater. As such, I have been uniquely positioned to observe Mark's accomplishments and witness the vast circle of people that he so positively influenced.

When Mark showed up at the 21 STS, he was clearly more mature than most Senior Airmen, and as I got to know him better, I quickly realized how truly exceptional he was. Mark graduated from the University of Alabama with a degree in Business Finance. As a devout Mormon, he completed a mission, followed by college, and afterward, Mark made a very deliberate decision to join the Air Force, specifically to pursue a career in Combat Control so that he could fight our nation's enemies. Mark excelled throughout the training pipeline and rapidly achieved combat mission ready status at the 21 STS. And when it came time for Mark's team to deploy, I had to determine who would go to Firebase Cobra.

For most of you, Firebase Cobra probably has little significance, but for the operators at the Mighty Two One, that location is valued by many as the premier spot in Afghanistan. And it is not because of the great food and plush accommodations; in fact, Firebase Cobra is exceedingly austere. No, Cobra is popular for one reason only—it is a place where you are all but guaranteed to confront the enemy every time you step outside the wire. For most people, that would be a reason to avoid it, but for the operators at the 21 STS, and this is why I love 'em, they fight for the opportunity to go there.

To be sure, Fire Base Cobra is not where you would send your average Senior Airman on his first deployment, but then, Mark Forester was anything but average. The decision to send Mark to Cobra wasn't one that I took lightly, and it was one that displeased a fair number of guys in the unit who thought that seniority should be the determining factor. But I talked to the guys who trained Mark, I talked to Mark's team leader, and I talked to Mark himself, and in the end, I was confident that Mark would excel at Cobra just as he had excelled at everything else in life. Of course, as we all know now, Mark stepped up to the plate and knocked it out of the park.

I talked with Mark's Special Forces teammates, and they all spoke of his sense of humor, his positive attitude, his professional skill, his courage, and most of all, his selflessness. To a man, they said that Mark was a guy who ran toward the sound of enemy fire. They remarked how he always made his way to the front of the formation, even when his combat controller duties did not require him to be there. His Special Forces TL [team leader] sent me a note a month ago recommending Mark for a Bronze Star Medal with Valor. In it he wrote: "Let me just reiterate how well Mark is doing here. He carries himself as someone who has far more experience and rank than a Senior Airman on his first deployment. I couldn't ask for a better controller. He has been an invaluable asset to ODA 9876." (The Green Beret team Mark supported.)

The team also recalled with laughter Mark's antics to fight the hardships of life at the firebase. One of Mark's efforts was to get ice cream airdropped to the team. As his teammate, George E. said, "If you ever went a couple of weeks eating nothing but 'hot dog soup,' you would appreciate the significance of this quest." For months, airdrops would come and go with supplies, ammunition, food and water, but never ice cream. Mark, you will be pleased to know that a few days ago, as the men at Cobra recovered the most recent airdrop bundles, they were pleased to discover that ice cream was on board—mission success my friend."

Mark was also highly regarded by pilots across Afghanistan. He was known to them by his call sign, which is now retired in his honor. Many have told me that he was one of the most talented controllers they ever worked with. One of these pilots was the Wing Commander at Kandahar Air Base. To honor Mark, he scheduled himself to fly on the day of Mark's memorial in Afghanistan, and during the ceremony, he made a pass in his A-10, low and fast, over the gathering. It was quite the gesture.

At the 21 STS we have a tradition that involves a toast each time a unit member departs for deployment, because we know, as much as we don't want to think about it, that any one of those individuals may not return. Our toast is modeled after the tradition of the Spartans, at least as depicted in Steven Pressfield's book, *Gates of Fire*.

The Spartan toast involved wine, our toast involves Jack Daniels; however, true to his faith, Mark Forester's toast was with water. When we toasted Mark and those who departed with him, I read the following words from Gates of Fire, which King Leonidas spoke to the Three Hundred prior to their departure for the battle at Thermopylae. I think they are a fitting tribute:

"Nothing good in life comes but at a price, and sweetest of all is liberty. This we have chosen, and this we pay for. We have embraced the laws of military service, and they are stern laws. They have schooled us to scorn the life of leisure, which this rich land of ours would bestow upon us if we wished, and instead to enroll ourselves in the academy of discipline and sacrifice. Guided by these laws, our fathers for twenty generations have breathed the blessed air of freedom and have paid the bill in full when it was presented. We, their sons, can do no less."

At the time of his death, Mark was engaged in a strategically significant operation in Oruzgan Province, Afghanistan. During this operation, he distinguished himself, as he did throughout the deployment, as a skilled combat controller, a courageous warrior, and a selfless teammate.

On 29 September 2010, while assaulting an enemy ambush site, Mark performed his professional duties superbly. He covered the team with close air support, provided suppressive fire with his personal weapon, killed several insurgent fighters, and maneuvered his element into position to flank the enemy. When his teammate and friend, Sergeant First Class Calvin H., was shot by a sniper in the open, Mark organized a team to go get him.

Mark led the recovery element out of the compound in which they had taken cover. As they advanced in the face of enemy machine gun fire, Mark was struck by a bullet in the upper chest and went down. When the team sergeant returned to check on Mark a few seconds later, he was unresponsive. He and Calvin were subsequently evacuated by helicopter to the nearest surgical facility, where they were both pronounced killed in action.

Mark Forester could have pursued countless professions that did not involve risking his life in a faraway land. But Mark Forester would have none of it. He sought out the path that he was on. He enrolled himself in the academy of discipline and sacrifice. He braved great dangers knowing full well the risks involved. He did so willingly and did not ask for anything in return. Mark Forester gave his life for his teammate Calvin and in defense of the people of the United States, many of whom will never know the price that he paid on their behalf. But his sacrifice will not go unrecognized, and our nation will continue to exist as the greatest on earth because of the service of extraordinary men like Mark Forester.

To Pat and Ray; to Terri, Thad, Joseph, and David; to the rest of Mark's family; on behalf of everyone here, words cannot express how sorry I am for your loss. The nation is eternally indebted to Mark and to you, and the 21 STS stands ready to assist in any way possible.

To everyone else, Mark Forester set an example of professionalism, courage, and selflessness that most of us can only hope to match. But by striving to achieve the standard that he set, may we continue to honor the sacrifice that he made. Like many of you, I will never live up to that standard, but I will try, and I will consider myself forever blessed to have had the opportunity to serve alongside Mark Forester.

Our thoughts and prayers are with you all as you celebrate the life and mourn the loss of a true American hero.

Another person who was profoundly hurt by Mark's death was our Uncle William. Through the years, it was never his habit to hang around our house, we were together mostly for holidays. However, Mark saw a lot of him when they were hunting. After Mark died, Uncle Will was at our home every day from getting the news until the funeral. He didn't say much, he was just there in sad silence, providing support. One thing that did get some words from him is the rumor that protestors might show up at the funeral. He was so mad he had tears in his eyes and said he would not let it happen! He was very passionate about it, as were some other family members.

Uncle William unexpectedly died himself almost a year after Mark. I have no doubt the two of them had a tremendous reunion on the other side.

Through our years growing up, and later living together as roommates, Mark and I frequently went outside and tossed the football back and forth in the yard or street. It was about the ball, about relaxing, talking, just enjoying life. Recently, on a nice fall day, I actually grabbed the football and headed out the door, as I'd done hundreds of times over the years. Then it hit me, I didn't have anyone to throw with, or rather; I didn't have Mark to throw with.

"Floyd, I thrive on positivity."
– Mark Forester

CHAPTER 14

Legacy

Every May 15th since Mark's death, I go to Chick-fil-A and order a milkshake in his honor. While I enjoy other things at Chick-fil-A throughout the year, there is something special about the milkshake that I have to save it for Mark's birthday and enjoy in his honor.

In the weeks following Mark's death, only the superficial things in life settled back to their familiar routines. I went back to the office and started to catch up on the work I'd missed. I took up my responsibilities as Branch President (lay minister of our congregation). However, grief and thoughts of Mark crowded my mind and emotions. It was almost impossible to focus on anything other than my lost brother and the next event or ceremony. Even quality sleep was rare. My wife, Rozlynn was amazingly strong because I wasn't really around much, even when I was home. For weeks I got up early and stayed up late working on this book, the web site, the foundation and planning memorial events.

My family's determination to do more than just keep Mark's memory alive began to fill a little of the space Mark's death left. We had a new normal take hold as we found opportunities to share Mark's inspiring example. Fortunately, Mark's influence was such that my family and I were far from alone, and we would soon learn that people we'd never heard of were already hard at work building upon Mark's legacy.

In January of 2011, a TV crew from the Lifetime Network was aboard the aircraft carrier U.S.S. Harry S. Truman. They joined the crew in Spain as the ship sailed back to her home port of Norfolk, VA following a seven-month deployment to the Arabian Sea in support of Operation Enduring Freedom. During the voyage across the Atlantic, they interviewed sailors and filmed the happy reunions with their families who were interviewed by another crew back home.

Alex Walton was the producer leading the carrier-based TV crew. His team was there at the invitation of the U.S. Navy, and was authorized to talk to Navy personnel. However, there were plenty of Marines aboard too. As they did their work, filming operations aboard the carrier, talking with the crew, and soaking up carrier life, a Marine aviator called out to Alex on a few occasions, "Hey TV dudes, I've got a story you really need to hear about."

Frank Latt was that pilot and had already decided that he had to personally deliver the flag he flew in his cockpit the day Mark died to my parents. It was only after Mark's death that Frank figured out his name. Until then he'd only known him as Jag 28. Frank told Alex about Mark's exceptional skill and bravery, especially the day he died. He conveyed the powerful impression Mark made upon all he dealt with, and his plan to carry the flag all the way to Haleyville.

Frank's story moved Alex, and he knew it would make a compelling program. However, it was outside the normal scope of the program: happy reunions of men and women in the service with their families, not fallen heroes. Well before landfall, Alex took the idea to his bosses. One was Tim Rogan who told him to go ahead and start working with Frank, they would sort out the details later—like whether Mark's family would even be willing to participate.

Frank first contacted me shortly after he was back stateside. He told me about his working with Jag 28, and that losing Mark as he flew top cover had deeply affected him. He told me about the TV guys he'd spoken with on the ship and their interest in doing a show on Mark. Frank was earnest and clearly doing his best to be respectful. It was a huge risk for him, not knowing much more about us than that I was Jag 28's brother. It must have felt like walking into a mine field.

The first words out of my mouth were, "I can't believe you asked that...." He about died, certain he'd stepped on one of the mines. I was so stunned because I had just been thinking about what I could do to honor my brother. I didn't want to just move on with my life. I was (and continue to be) driven by a deep desire to expand and increase Mark's legacy and calling.

I was thinking about how I could interest different groups and media in picking up the story when Frank called me.

I quickly put him at ease, assuring him the news was an answer to my prayers. Frank gave me Alex's number and I called him to get the details of what he wanted. He also had a number of questions. I took his info and got to work lining up my family's support.

Frank wanted the flag to be a surprise for my parents, so it was a secret between him, the producers and me. No one else knew about it. Mom and dad were given a flag and flagpole by Mark's squadron, but it wasn't up yet. Lifetime paid a contractor to get it in place before it was time to film the show.

The thing came off well and we were happy with how the crew treated our family, friends, town and Mark. It also offered a valuable springboard to create mutual support for other events and activities that have helped us further Mark's mission in this world. The show was called "Coming Home" and Mark's episode was the only one in its two seasons to feature a fallen hero. All others were happy reunions.

Recently, I visited with Alex and Tim to get their perspective on doing the show. They said it was profound to see the tremendous grief and pain mixed with outpouring of love, goodness and hope from everyone connected to Mark. They said the city and community were great. Specifically, they noted how generous, welcoming and down-to-earth everyone was. It was a great experience for them too. One funny example Tim mentioned was the food served during the filming. In the world of TV and Los Angeles, events and gatherings are normally catered. And when the food is good, guests and hosts will discuss which caterers they have used and what they have done. Most of the food served for our out of town guests, hosted by my mom and sister at Terri's house, was homemade and *delicious*.

I asked what makes Mark's story so compelling. Tim suggested—from a story-teller's perspective—that Mark was the hero who wasn't *supposed* to die. It offends our sense of justice when the hero dies. He and Alex both noted that Mark was the real-deal, but still accessible. He wasn't super-human, but another regular man who used his gifts to accomplish more than most. As so many others have said, Alex and Tim agree that Mark's example and direction is encouraging and infectious.

Mark was featured on National Geographic's "Eyewitness War" on August 5, 2013. They showed clips of his helmet camera footage from a battle in

May 2010 where he displayed true leadership. A few of Mark's teammates, Chad, Ben, and Jarrod, were interviewed to describe the footage and entire situation. They also interviewed me to get the side of Mark the viewer didn't see. This was another great opportunity to share Mark's example with the world.

Looking back over the two and a half years, I am amazed by the number of memorials, events, and ceremonies we have attended in honor of Mark and other veterans. For the first several months after his death, there was an event almost every week somewhere.

One ceremony that we didn't attend took place shortly after we were notified of Mark's death—it was at Kandahar. **Lt Col Jeremy Kokenes**, Combined/ Joint Special Operations Element Commander in Kandahar, shared many details of finding out about Mark's death, notifying the LDS church leaders, preparing for him to arrive, reviewing his Form-93,[65]and participating in the ramp ceremony as he was carried by his STS brothers onto the C-17 that would return him to American soil. Here are his somber words:

It was dark when we walked down to the ramp where the C-17 was waiting. There were thousands in attendance to bid them (Mark, Calvin, and a Marine) farewell. We lined a pathway leading to the ramp. It was windy, but I could hear the bagpipes playing. The crowd was huge, and they brought Mark in on an MRAP surrounded by his brothers. As the sun started to rise, he, along with others, were carefully, slowly, and honorably taken to the back of the C-17 followed by Lt Col Hughes and others to escort them and pay final tribute and salute. The sun was up enough by this time to feel its warmth, and simultaneously I felt the Spirit confirm to me that Mark was ok, and that his mission on the earth was complete [all was according to His plan]. Once Mark and the others were secured, the ceremony was completed. I turned from the C-17 and saw three CV-22's (Osprey) coming home, flying in formation with the sun behind them. It was magical, sad, encouraging, emotional, and

---

[65] "DD Form 93 (Record of Emergency Data) is the official and legal document that designates the beneficiaries of certain benefits in the event of a Soldier's death or if they are determined missing. This extremely important document is used to identify the primary next of kin (PNOK), the secondary next of kin (SNOK), beneficiaries of death gratuity and unpaid allowances, and designates the person authorized to direct disposition of remains (PADD)." https://g1arng.army. pentagon.mil/processes/ddform93process/pages/default.aspx

everything in between. We savored the moment. I think of Mark often, and this experience.

How I first met Jeremy is pretty incredible. He was in a small women's boutique with his wife when he noticed a man "looking like a Forester." He felt prompted to ask, "Are you Thad Forester?" He doesn't know how he knew it was me, he just knew. This is crazy because this was in Birmingham, AL and he is from Niceville, FL (five hours away). I was in this store with my wife as we waited for a seat at a nearby restaurant. I have been blessed to meet many people connected to Mark as I've researched for this book. How else could I have "bumped" into a stranger in a rather large city? I remember being taken back and not extremely responsive while talking to him, but the encounter left me distracted the rest of the night. (Turns out he had already met Joseph and Patsy through their church in Florida.)

The University of Alabama Center for Veteran and Military Affairs renamed their annual *Student Veteran of the Year* award to *"The Mark Forester Memorial Award for Excellence."* I spoke at their banquet in November 2010 when this change was announced. When asked to speak, I wanted to make sure everyone understood the standard Mark set as a man and a warrior. As of this writing, I have been privileged to attend two of these banquets. Calling it an honor to represent our family, and Mark, is an understatement. It is also a comfort to meet young people who are inspired by Mark's story as they strive to achieve and make a difference in the world.

Rocky Mountain Mattress began offering a $1,000 scholarship per semester in honor of Mark via a patriotic essay contest. So far, two scholarships have been awarded. This is their way of supporting one purpose of *The Mark Forester Foundation*, which is to "Honor the Heroes".

On Memorial Day weekend in May 2012, *The Place of Refuge Church* and *The Welcome Home Heroes Foundation* honored Mark by dedicating the 11th panel of their traveling tribute to Mark. It was a spectacular tribute. My wife, parents and I spent a few days in Manteca, CA and were blown-away by the patriotism and the special honor shown to Mark by the city and sponsoring organizations. I was able to speak a few times to different crowds for this event too. Frank Latt and his family were there and he spoke as well.

This entire weekend came about because the organizer, **Pastor Mike Dillman**, saw the episode of Lifetime's "Coming Home." He was moved and inspired seeing how Mark had wrapped his body armor in the flag.

Pastor Dillman is a Vietnam veteran. He saw hundreds of bodies and body bags of servicemen and women, but said he'd never seen anything like that.

Through some research, he discovered Mark was a member of The Church of Jesus Christ of Latter-day Saints. This increased his desire to honor Mark because the local LDS church helps with this event every year, and Pastor Dillman's good friend, David Crockett is a local church leader (President of the Manteca, CA Stake[66]). He thought it would be best to have a fellow church member call us, so he put David up to the task of tracking us down. He didn't have the heart to call my parents, so he reached out to me. Once I got a feel for the event and their intentions, I knew it would be a good thing and mom and dad would be supportive.

Then, when the folks in Manteca, CA found out Mark served his two-year mission in Oakland, CA, they just knew this was right to have his story play a central role in that year's events. Of course, we were ready and willing to participate in anything they wanted us to do. We also could not ignore the feeling that this was all more than a coincidence.

During one of my speeches that weekend, I mentioned that Mark once told mom she shouldn't be worried about him going to Afghanistan, because he'd lived in Oakland for two years and survived. They seemed to appreciate his humor (fully understanding Oakland's reputation).

Besides the pastor, we have heard of others who were deeply inspired by the presentation of Mark's story in the Lifetime special. After graduating high school in June of 2010, **James Hill** (pseudonym) considered college, but he was restless to do something more meaningful and important— something to really challenge himself. He wasn't sure what that would be, so he kept working different jobs, from a supermarket to a furniture moving company with his two brothers, while he contemplated his options.

When we connected with him in February 2013, James had completed Combat Control School (CCS). He was at Hurlburt Field working through Advanced Skills Training (AST), and recently met Joseph and Patsy. He has a very interesting story about what took him from his hometown to AST in Florida.

---

[66] The basic congregations of the LDS church are called "Wards" or "Branches," depending upon the number of members in a geographic area. Usually, 300 to 500 members form a Ward, while smaller units are Branches. Typically, about 10 Wards/Branches comprise a "Stake." The term derives from the Biblical references in Isaiah 33:20; 54:2.

James told me:

> It was honestly just a huge coincidence, really; and crazy how everything ended up. So the first weekend I came into town, my buddy and I decided to go to the mall. We were there for a while and right before leaving, my buddy said, "Hey, let's go back and check out American Eagle."
>
> So we ended up back inside, and I noticed an attractive girl who was also shopping with a friend. I was helping my pal choose some clothes while she tried on jeans and I couldn't help but compliment her on how nice they looked on her.
>
> We didn't say much more before my friend was ready to pay for his stuff and I had a pair of sandals to buy. The two girls continued shopping as we left, but as my buddy and I were heading toward my car, I kept thinking about going back to try and speak with her some more.
>
> Finally, I made up my mind and said, "What the heck, why not" and went to look for her. I found her in line paying for her things, so I waited until she was done. Then I asked her name— Sara—and told her I'd like to get to know her better. We quickly became good friends.
>
> For the next couple of weeks we hung out as often as we could, including going to church with her. One day I pulled up YouTube and showed her a couple of videos of CCTs to try and show her a little about my job. Then I pulled up Mark Forester's website because I remembered that he graduated from Alabama and she is a huge Alabama fan herself. It just seemed right to show her Mark's page.

About a year and a half earlier, still trying to figure out his next move, James Hill was channel surfing at home one afternoon when something made him pause on the *Lifetime Network*. The episode of *Coming Home* that featured Mark and Frank Latt's story first aired in March of 2011, and they ran it frequently. James stopped in his tracks. He was struck by the comments people made about Mark. He listened as they spoke of his humility (clearly evident in his photos, James says), his courage and integrity. He was impressed and inspired by the descriptions of how Mark led his life and felt a deep desire to live so that he might earn the same kind of respect and admiration. He watched that episode many times, each time confirming he had found the direction he'd sought since graduation, almost a year earlier.

> As we looked through Mark's site, Sara kept saying that the name seemed so familiar. Then she saw that Mark was a Mormon and it clicked. She remembered that she knew Patsy and the Forester family. She gave Patsy a call, told her about me, and wanted me to meet them.

> From there, I met Joseph and last night I got to meet Mark's Mom and Dad! It just feels like it was all meant to happen. I always told myself I would do my best to try and meet them one day from the time I first saw the *Coming Home* show and it's just amazing how things happen.

When I first heard James' story, I was eager to visit with him and make sure I understood everything correctly. When we spoke, he mentioned that when he's "feeling the suck" going through the tough training, and his instructors say, "Remember why you're here," he thinks of Mark. It stiffens his resolve and he pushes harder. He says, "Even though I didn't know him, I still feel that I do know him, in my way. He's certainly played a role in my life."

I asked how he'd like to be mentioned in this book. He said he'd rather not be named (hence the pseudonym). Basically, even though Mark is his role model, and he often pauses at the mural of Mark in the training room, he doesn't talk to others about it. It's too personal. I respect him for it, and I am glad he was willing to share his story because it is a great example of how Mark's life continues to inspire others, even though he's not here in person.

The mural James refers to was painted by Airman

Josh Chambers in the STTS gym at Hurlburt Field. Before Pope, Mark was stationed at Hurlburt during the CCT pipeline. Some of his instructors considered him a "gym rat," therefore they felt it would be appropriate to use Airman Chambers' talents to honor Mark by hanging this 4' x 7' painting to watch over everyone who uses that gym to build their strength and skills. The plaque at the bottom of the painting reads: "Faith Driven – Never Ending".

On at least one occasion, Mark was found in the gym by instructor(s) on weekends or during off time, and was told he could and should take a break. Mark responded, "I can rest when I die."

Among the many honors the Air Force has paid to Mark, another is naming the drop zone at Cobra for him. This article covers the name change, but more importantly, it gives another window into the challenging work Mark and other CCTs do. Cobra is so remote, that without consistent deliveries of everything—ammunition, food, fuel, spare parts, etc.—the base would have to be abandoned.

2AS Delivers the Goods: Pope Aircrews Fly Airdrop over Newly Named Forester DZ

By Staff Sgt. Jacob Maywald, 43 Airlift Group Public Affairs

Not often are we given a chance to fittingly honor a fellow Airman's sacrifice. While we all mourn our fallen brothers and sisters in arms, the opportunity to conduct a tribute worthy of their service rarely arises. Recently, two aircrews from Pope Field were given the privilege to do just that.

Crews from Pope Field's 2nd-Airlift Squadron recently performed a historic mission over the newly named Forester Drop Zone in Afghanistan. They were the first all-Pope aircrews to perform an airdrop since the DZ was renamed in honor of the 21st Special Tactics Squadron combat controller.

Senior Airman Mark Forester, a combat controller assigned to the 21 STS at Pope Field, was killed in action (KIA) during a large scale clearing operation of an Afghan village on September 29, 2010, while attempting to render aid to a fallen comrade. He was submitted for a Silver Star for his actions that day. His actions resulted in the opening of a vital transit route and increasing stability in the volatile region. He was posthumously awarded the bronze star with valor for his heroic actions on a previous mission the month before he was KIA.

"I heard about the formation drop to Forester DZ approximately two days before its execution, and at that time heard the story behind it," said Capt. Jake Thirsk, an instructor navigator assigned to the 4551 Expeditionary Operations Support Squadron at Bagram Air Field, who flew on

U.S. Army Soldiers prepare to gather fuel supplies being dropped from a C-130 Hercules aircraft onto a landing zone at a Forward Operating Base in Afghanistan. A two aircraft formation of Pope Airman airdropped similar Container Delivery System bundles into Forester Drop Zone 7 April 2011. (U.S. Army Photo/Spc. Tia P. Sokimson)

the mission as an observer. "We thought it would be a nice tribute to him and meaningful to the 21 STS at Pope and his family to have an all Pope Formation Drop."

Captain Thirsk coordinated with the scheduler from the 7741 Expeditionary Airlift Squadron in Bagram to have crews made up of entirely Pope Airmen assigned to the mission. The operation consisted of a formation of two C-130 Hercules aircraft tasked with resupplying a Special Operations team with food, water, fuel and building supplies. The daytime drop consisted of 32 separate bundles weighing over 51,000 lbs.

"We were all very proud and privileged to be a part of the rededication of Forester DZ and to honor SrA Forester's great service and sacrifice," said Capt. Adam King, the aircraft commander of the #2 aircraft. "Since we fly as a hard crew and mostly single ship, it was an exciting change of pace to fly alongside a fellow Pope crew on such a prestigious mission."

Mountainous terrain makes the OEF Theater particularly difficult to airdrop supplies into. Because of a lack of direct line-

of-sight, radio coordination with the team on the ground was impossible. The crew instead relied on visual cues, smoke in this instance, to positively identify the Special Operations team.

"The terrain made flying low to the ground hazardous and limited aircraft maneuverability during the mission," according to Capt. Robert Bittner, who flew as the lead aircraft commander. "The terrain also created difficulty acquiring the ground party on the radio. Due to the lack of radio reception, the ground party provided a visual signal for the airdrop by popping a smoke canister. This canister marked the DZ and enabled the aircrew to judge the winds."

The lead aircraft dropped their load on the first pass, guided by the visual signals by the ground crew. Due to wind conditions the second C-130 aborted on the first attempt and had to circle around and reattempt the airdrop. Shadowed by the lead aircraft, their second effort was successful and all 32 bundles of the dropped cargo were recovered by the DZ party.

"The crews executed the airdrop with precision and great professionalism and were thrilled to dedicate the drop to Airman Forester," said Captain Thirsk.

"While at Pope prior to my deployment, I had heard about Airman Forester's death in combat and I prayed for his family and the 21 STS team," said Captain Bittner. "It was an honor to lead this mission as a tribute to Senior Airman Mark Forester, an American hero."

In June 2012, we attended Mark's Silver Star ceremony at Hurlburt Field for his heroic actions on that fateful day of 29 September 2010. It was another tender and touching occasion. All of our immediate family attended. We learned that Mark was killed on his 78th combat mission. Considering he was only in country about 153 days, I consider that a pretty significant number. He loved what he did, but I also know he was ready to come home when his time was up. I imagine it was much like his church mission to California—he worked his tail off while there and only when it was time to go home did he stop. In this case, he only stopped when that bullet pierced his heart. Up until then, he was moving forward, looking in the face of the enemy. We are honored that Mark's memory is being kept alive, so we are always eager to share; at the same time, though, these ceremonies and memorials are physically and emotionally demanding, especially for mom.

While we were in Ft. Walton Beach, FL in October 2010 for the Combat Controller Reunion, Chief Calvin Markham, who made it his mission to escort us that entire weekend, told me of a memorial walk he did for one of his friends who was killed a few years prior. As I listened to Chief, I felt impressed to hold a Memorial Walk each year on Mark's birthday, walking one mile representing each year of his age. This also meant increasing the distance by one mile each year. I remain as committed to this walk as I am to any other important part of my life.

Many people have said "What are you gonna do when you get to 50 or 60 miles?" My answer is simple: walk it. Even if it takes two days, I'll still walk it. When Mark was killed, there was a commitment burned in me to keep his memory alive. Starting this book was the first, and then came the memorial walk. Of course, all the speaking opportunities are much appreciated.

In December of 2010, my 30-mile Memorial Birthday Walk training began. I walked with weighted backpacks and without weight. I walked all over Tuscaloosa. The actual walk would take place as close to Mark's birthday as possible. Soon, some friends wanted to host a race in Haleyville in Mark's honor, which would raise money for *The Mark Forester Foundation*. We decided to hold both events on the same day. Of course, it was clear that the walk was my baby. Our dear family friend, Lauren Tinker does a fine job as the race director.

The first annual 30-mile Memorial Birthday Walk, held 14 May 2011, had 35 participants. Mostly, they were Mark's teammates from the Air Force, some family, friends and even a few strangers who heard about it. It was a special day and event.

The following year, 2012, we had 70 participants, double the previous year. Many were repeats from the first year; and in 2013, we had 40 walkers. This event is special to me. One important stop during the walk each year is at Mark's grave where we have a few words and share in memorial push-ups. In 2011, they were led by Mark's element leader/ CAS instructor, Matt Mueller. In 2012, they were led by Lt Col Parks Hughes. In 2013, they were led by one of Mark's team sergeants, Dennis Bernier (Mark and others called him "Big Sarge").

There is part of me that wants to keep it small, but another that wants it to be huge so that people will travel from near and far to participate and will make Haleyville, AL a household name, as well as the name of Mark Forester. I have been in awe at the support so many have shown by being willing to walk 30+ miles to honor my brother. The terrain is hilly and we walk relatively fast. I feel like I'm on a high the entire walk. I love talking to the different walkers and asking those I don't know how they found out about the walk and how they knew Mark. It's a special 12+ hours for me. There are many volunteers who help with food, drinks, trailing cars, and of course, the Haleyville Police Dept. that has at least two cars and officers to escort the walkers

Each year as we prepare the week of Mark's walk and race, it's a strange feeling to me as I drive around Haleyville and see banners and signs all through town with Mark's name as advertising for the events. How could I have envisioned seeing a road I drove on every day while living in Haleyville now named after Mark, and seeing signs up in town and his name engraved on the war memorial wall at City Hall? I'm honored that he's my brother, but it doesn't really bring any peace.

Everyone I've ever talked to who's done the walk has told me it was an amazing experience, and not just because of the blisters and very sore muscles. Of course, many of those who have walked were those who knew Mark, but there are others who never met him. Consistently, they have described profound experiences participating in this event. One is Dan Dyer. We were missionaries together in 1996, and this year he came over from Bentonville, AR to take the walk:

> I'm sad to say it, but before the experience of the walk and being
> around all the guys that Mark served with, my attitude towards

the military was sort of apathetic. I appreciated their service, but since I had never really been around any servicemen before, it was just a basic appreciation that I'm supposed to have at the least as an American.

Last summer my family stayed with Thad for a night as we were on a family trip. He told me the whole story of Mark. It was honestly one of the best nights of my life. It left a deep impression on me and I knew I had to make the walk after that. No way out.

And then to be at the walk, see their "swagger" and hear their individual stories, that appreciation is no longer apathetic or basic. The two events of staying with Thad and the walk have definitely given me a more humble attitude for Mark and those like him.

The night before the walk in 2013, Terri hosted a dinner for many of the walkers at her house. As we all sat around talking, a couple of guys who'd walked the 31 miles the year before started laying the horror-stories on Dan: pain, MANY blisters, toenails falling off, etc. He finally started to show some worry and they switched their line, telling him how fulfilling the experience was, and that he would not regret it for one second.

Dan held up well for the hike, taking every step of the 32 miles. At the end, one of those guys caught Dan just as he completed his final steps. He asked if it was as bad as he'd been told the night before. Dan nodded an exhausted "Yes!" Then, when asked if it was as great as they'd told him, Dan mustered some extra strength and said it was at least as good as they said.

Another person profoundly impacted by Mark is Julie Edgin. I think it's a great testament how Mark continues to inspire others to dig a little deeper to accomplish their goals. Here is what she had to say:

Mark Forester and I were "virtually" introduced through mutual friends while he was serving in Afghanistan. Over the last couple months of his deployment, we frequently exchanged emails, instant messages and even Skyped face to face on one occasion[67]. I knew enough about him to really look forward to meeting Mark in person after his deployment, but later realized how very little I understood about the kind of person he was.

---

[67] This conversation happened only one day after the battle in which Mark's actions earned him the Bronze Star Medal with Valor. Julie says he never gave the slightest hint that he'd just been through something that intense.

Not long before our introduction, I had finally been accepted to MBA school, only two weeks before the program started. The road to that point had been hard. I'd previously applied and been rejected, and took four tries to pass the GMAT. I only pursued it because of a strong impression--maybe even a calling--I felt that it was something I needed to do. As good as I felt about achieving my goal of getting into the program, I didn't realize that the truly arduous part of the journey had just begun.

Despite the surety that I was where I needed to be—and that the way had almost miraculously been opened for me—I felt very much out of place. Compared to my classmates, I had no real business experience, and I did not fit the business woman mold. Only a month into the program, I was feeling completely overwhelmed, discouraged, and inadequate. Then, in the swirl of mid-terms, interviews, and loads of homework, I received the news of Mark's death. My world stopped.

Despite everything going on, or the fact that I didn't know Mark well, there was no way I could miss his memorial and funeral. I quickly made arrangements and set off for Haleyville. While there, I soaked up every story I could and worked to piece together who he *really* was. Mark's ultimate sacrifice of giving his life for a fellow brother and our country is absolutely remarkable; however, it was clear to me that was simply the tip of the iceberg. He wasn't great because he acted heroically. He acted heroically because he was great. Understanding him and the example he set impacted me deeply, then and now.

It was said a number of times throughout the memorial that Mark *knew* what his life's mission was. He was supposed to fight terrorists. He knew it and he became one of the very best at it. As I sat listening and admiring his dedication and discipline, I had an inspiration or a realization come to mind reminding me that, like Mark, I had felt strongly that I was to do something. I *knew* I was supposed to be in MBA school; however, at that time, I had permitted my vision and knowledge to become foggy as the pressures mounted.

As I sat wrestling with these thoughts, I found myself awed by Mark's dedication to pay the price to do the job he knew he was meant to do. A picture comes to my mind of Mark in his BDUs carrying some sort of log on his shoulder. The sun is out and he is drenched in sweat. The look on his face was one of utter depletion—and pure determination. What Mark accomplished was extremely difficult, even for him. He worked hard and in the end accomplished what he set out to do. A feeling told me, "Julie, you are made of the same stuff. You have it within you to do whatever you want to, but it's up to you to succeed." Mark's example was on full display and it awakened in me a realization of who I am and what I am capable of. It renewed my commitment to live up to it.

On the drive out of Haleyville and the flights back across the country, I tried to process all I had seen and heard. I had been reminded of what I was supposed to be doing with my life and reassured that I could do it, even the hard things. I decided that I only had one shot at MBA school, and that I would give it my all. I had a renewed understanding that I could succeed at it.

Back in the grind again, there were many times when I wanted to quit, but that picture of Mark carrying that log came into my mind and I would literally tell myself, "If Mark could do hard things, so can I." Right before my final semester, I was one of ten students who were awarded the school's most prestigious scholarship. This recognition comes through top grades and nominations from classmates and faculty. I couldn't help but cry as I received the award from the very school that rejected me just two years earlier. Remembering Mark's example not only helped me to survive MBA school, but actually excel at it and make a distinct contribution.

That was more than a year ago now and there's always another challenge around the corner. I continue to feel impressions that tell me what I am to do with my life—and they aren't always easy to follow. In fact, they rarely are easy. There are still times when the picture of Mark carrying that log comes into focus and I am reminded that I have a mission to accomplish and I can do hard things. Mark would often end his instant messages to me with "Be Good". I think I finally know what he really meant.

The *American Fallen Soldiers Project* presented our family with a portrait of Mark, painted by artist Phil Taylor. It was presented on November 16,

2012 at The University of Alabama "Veteran and Military Affairs" Grand Opening of their new facility on campus.

Phil said he painted about four different portraits of Mark before he got it right. He said the one he presented us was the right one. He captured Mark's eyes, compassion, determination, patriotism, and even his little smirk.

Phil and his wife Lisa are selfless Americans who present about three portraits per month to families of the fallen. It would do you good to read more about him and his organization. And since he's a big Alabama fan, we were able to attend the game together the following day.

A full size print will be displayed inside the *Veteran and Military Affairs* office at The University of Alabama. We thank the University for allowing this presentation to be part of their grand opening ceremony.

The box carrying the portrait easily catches people's attention. Phil likes it that way. Since the portrait doesn't leave his side while in airports, he oftentimes has opportunities to talk to others about the purpose of the portrait and about the hero himself.

Please visit their website (www.americanfallensoldiers.com) to learn more.

This year, we were honored to have "**The Welcome Home Heroes Traveling Tribute**" come to Haleyville for the weekend of Mark's race and walk. The display was set up at the high school near the football field on May 16-18, 2013. I am amazed they came all the way from Manteca, CA directly to Haleyville, then returned right around to make it back home in time for their regular Memorial Day weekend celebration the following weekend.

"The Welcome Home Heroes Traveling Tribute" is a memorial that was built six years ago bearing the names of those who have fallen since 9/11. Pastor Michael Dillman, a Vietnam veteran and passionate supporter of our troops and Gold Star families, created the memorial as a center piece to the "Not Forgotten" event that takes place every Memorial Day Weekend in Manteca, CA which has an annual attendance of more than 20,000 people and is the largest Memorial Day Weekend commemoration on the west coast. Currently, eleven panels make up the memorial with each panel bearing the image of a fallen hero and the names of more than 6,400 who have given their lives in sacrifice for our country. This is the same tribute we saw the previous year when they dedicated Mark's panel.

Several years ago, Allied Supreme Commander General Craddock personally viewed the Tribute and said it was one of the most beautiful memorials to be found anywhere in the nation. Each panel lights up to create a beautiful memorial of light after nightfall. The Traveling Tribute has been displayed up and down California from football invitational games to professional hockey games to patriotic events in an effort to honor all who have served, remember our fallen, and remind our citizens that freedom is not free.

With the establishment of *The Mark Forester Foundation* in December 2010, one annual donation we commit to is awarding The Mark Forester Price of Freedom Scholarship to at least one deserving Haleyville High School student for help with college tuition. 2013 was the third year we've awarded a scholarship winner, and the 4th recipient. When enough funds exist, we will present as many scholarships as we can to as many deserving students possible. We appreciate the Tennessee Smokies' commitment to fundraising for Mark's foundation in 2011, with an auction of baseball memorabilia. Because of their efforts, we were able to award two scholarships in 2012. This is another way we can continue Mark's name and example and also give back to the community and encourage education, integrity and excellence.

In Chapter 12, **George Earhart** said the night of 28 September 2010 was the last good night's rest he would enjoy for many months. After Mark's death, the war and those fighting it pressed on as Mark's teammates continued their drive to push the insurgents out and those fighters resisted with everything they could. Only seven days later, George was on a mission not far from Cobra. He was riding in the back of one of the gun trucks as it rumbled across the face of inclined terrain. The trucks are extremely heavy with armor, weapons, ammunition and gear. The ground under the low side gave way; the truck listed and then rolled over. George couldn't jump free. Although it easily could have killed him, the accident broke his back, shoulder and crushed his hip. He now had no choice about taking the MEDEVAC Wes Wilson offered after his concussion a week earlier.

I ended up spending about six months at Walter Reed. The docs told me I'd never walk normally again. I was in serious pain, so they kept me pretty doped up. I'd been through a lot: the divorce, the deployment, the concussion, losing my friend and teammate, *the guilt I felt that it was him and not me*, the pain, my helplessness.... I'm not too proud to say I was severely depressed. The opiate-based painkillers made it even worse.

My sister came and started to look after me and—more important—to advocate for me with the medical staff. But I was not a nice person to be around and a very difficult patient. At one point, she was trying to help me with something and I lashed out at her. She broke down. All I really remember is her telling me, "You're not you!" It kind of shook me, I guess, and I finally started fighting to get better. Also, she pushed the docs to get me off the meds.

As I healed, I got more mobile. I needed less painkillers, and my head started to clear. The docs told me I'd heal and walk, but not normally. I'd likely have a bad limp, and that would force me to accept a medical discharge. I was determined that I would not let that happen. When things were really hard for me, I would think of Mark, and I'd push harder. I'd think of him watching over me and encouraging me. I didn't want to let him down.

Even before I got out of the hospital, I felt a duty to go see Mark's family, especially his parents. I was very nervous about it, though. I wasn't sure how they would receive me, or even how I would be able to talk to them. What would they think about my motives, and how would they react to seeing me? It was all swimming around in my head, even though I'd talked to them on the phone a couple times, and Rozlynn had even visited me in the hospital.

Finally, I was well enough to make the trip and the arrangements were set. At first, it felt like a pretty normal road trip. But the closer I got, the more anxious I felt. Just crossing the state line into Alabama was spooky! I kept going, but had to stop several times along the way to calm myself down, especially when I started seeing signs for Haleyville.

Once I pulled into town, it got very surreal. I saw signs[68] for Mark and thought about all the stories he'd told me of growing up there. I made my way to the Forester's home slowly and deliberately, sort of like I was watching someone else go through all this in one of my dreams.

I found their street, went down one hill and up another. I got to the house and pulled into their driveway. I parked the car, got out, and expected—braced myself for—a long, awkward moment on the door. I stood there a long second, then knocked.

A couple footsteps from inside, the door swings open and before I can say anything or react in anyway, Pat throws her arms around my neck in a huge hug. Every fear and anxiety instantly vanishes, and it is immediately like being with family.

I stayed with them four days. Sleeping, eating and visiting in the same house where Mark grew up. I really wanted to do something for them, but I didn't know what. I told them everything about Mark that I could, from the first time we met to the aftermath of our last battle together. I told them about my challenges, and how his influence continued to help me. They told me about the boy and young man Mark had been. I told them about the friend and warrior I had known. We laughed and we mourned together. Finally, I realized that just being there—sharing memories and stories about the different sides of Mark that each of us knew—was the best thing I could do for them, and it was the best thing for me.

Every day since Mark died, I have thought of him. For a long time it gave me a sad feeling, but not anymore. Now, I think of the good times we shared, even the dangerous ones. He was not just there with me on deployment, I have felt him there beside me many times since, and someday I want to hear him tell me, "You did it right."

---

[68] He's referring to Dime Road being named "Senior Airman Mark A. Forester Memorial Drive".

I am certain George will hear those words from Mark someday. I remember being excited to meet George on this visit. I was very impressed with his maturity. I guess when you go through what he has, you're forced to grow up. He and I went to Wal-Mart and I remember thinking, "If only these people knew what kind of hero is walking beside me." We met someone I went to high school with while there and he expressed his condolences about Mark and asked me what happened. I was honored to say "Meet George. He was with Mark on that final battle." I am in awe at all of Mark's teammates who I meet and spend time with. I always wonder how many people know how hard they work so that they can risk their lives for us.

A few things that George shared with us during this visit stood out for me. He told me that of all the combat he's experienced during his six deployments—from Fallujah with the Marines, to 10 months in Afghanistan in 2007 to his deployment with Mark—he's never seen anything as intense or as close as the last mission with Mark in Uruzgan. "We definitely had a fight on our hands. It's a miracle that we didn't lose even more guys."

Since his first visit to my parent's home, we've all kept in close contact. We talk and he visits when he can. He's recovered well. Physically, he was good enough to join us in May 2012 for every step of the 31-mile Memorial Birthday Walk. Then, he got himself fit and qualified to deploy again in early 2013. However, he was injured in a parachute training exercise that broke his back, so he's back to rehabbing his body. The good news is that his spirit has healed well and while I'm sure she was not happy to see George get hurt, I know his fiancé, Annie, is happy to keep him close to home for a while yet.

Shortly after Mark's death, my brother-in-law, Steve Bartholomew, shared these thoughts:

> The first and only time I met Mark Forester was at my brother and sister-in-laws' wedding, in Millville, Utah. When I remember Mark, I see him wearing a tuxedo, a huge smile, and storming down a country lane in a '65 Ford step side pick-up with the other groomsmen, as they made a memorable, rowdy entrance at the wedding reception.
>
> It would only be in later conversations with my brother-in-law, Thad, that I truly got to know who Mark Forester was. Thad told

me about Mark's extensive military training; we talked about what a Combat Controller was, and how Thad felt when Mark was deployed to Afghanistan. When Thad and I talked on the phone over the next year, our conversations often turned to Mark and his welfare as he fought on the front lines.

On September 29, 2010, our hearts were broken with a phone call as we learned the devastating news that Mark had been killed in action. Our souls ached for the loss of one so young, intelligent, and good as Mark Forester.

With Mark's death, a new learning process began for us, a process that is generally reserved for those who lose a loved one in war. We learned what an Angel Flight is. We learned who the Patriot Guard Riders are. We witnessed thousands of acts of love as citizens from Mark's beloved Alabama, as well as folks from all over the United States, shared their love and support with the Forester family. We learned how Mark touched the lives of countless individuals as stories poured in about Mark's sense of humor, his skills as a Combat Controller, and his devotion to his God and Country. We learned to love and care about those who trained and fought beside Mark. We learned of the burdens and sacrifices that the survivors endure upon their return.

With this learning, stirring questions began to rise from within. With this knowledge that I now have, how do I honor Mark? How do I show my appreciation for the ideals he stood for? What can I do to honor the hundreds of thousands of brave men and woman, who have paid the ultimate sacrifice for me? How do I honor the heroes?

About this time, I had the sacred privilege of visiting Arlington National Cemetery. This experienced forever changed my life. As we walked those hallowed grounds, reminders of the price of freedom were everywhere, and Mark was at the forefront of my thoughts. While at Arlington, I came across a quote that touched my heart and soul in a way I had never felt before and it clarified those questions that had arisen.

"It is from numberless diverse acts of courage and belief that human history is shaped. Each time a man stands up for an ideal, or acts to improve the lot of others, or strikes out against injustice, he sends forth a tiny ripple of hope, and crossing each other from a million different centers of energy and daring, those ripples build a current which can sweep down the mightiest walls of oppression and resistance."

-Robert F. Kennedy, Arlington National Cemetery

With the awareness I now have, my duty and obligation is to live the best life I can. It is to be grateful for the gift of freedom granted to me by Mark and millions of others who have served. It is to serve those around me. It is to fly an American Flag. It is to show respect to those who I see in uniform. It is to thank a veteran. It is to show more gratitude. It is to exemplify more charity. It is to rise when an American flag passes in a parade. It is to be a better husband, father, son, brother, uncle, and brother-in-law. It is to live a life of purpose.

In short, I will be an epicenter of a tiny ripple of hope.

With the knowledge that you now have, dear friend, I now pass the torch on to you and ask:

How will you honor the heroes? What actions and attitudes will you commit to build the mighty current as it rolls forth?

Thanks to these reflections, we added a section on Mark's site called "Honor the Heroes" for people to share how they honor our heroes.

Mark lived great and he died great. Some have asked me if I thought Mark knew he wouldn't come home alive. We've talked about this in the family and here are my thoughts: I think he had a feeling, even before he deployed, that he would seal his example of commitment with his blood in Afghanistan. He, of course, didn't plan for it, but he had a feeling. I base this on multiple conversations he and I had, and that he had with others. He started telling me that he loved me more frequently as his time in Afghanistan ticked away. I noticed this and so did Joseph. He told one close family friend a few days before deploying, "If I come home, I'll be fine. If I don't come home, I'll be fine." I think he is fine now.

I've often wondered if he had time to process what actually happened when he was shot. He probably didn't, but if he did, his final thought was most likely about his momma and how this wasn't supposed to happen. Or, maybe he exclaimed "SERENITY NOW" (*Seinfeld* reference) before he took his last breath. Regardless, he went down fighting and moving forward. And we may console ourselves in this point: that he died in the cause of his country and of his God, and he is happy.

Recently, Rozlynn took a picture of Mark into a Hobby Lobby for framing. The guy helping her asked about Mark, what he did, how he died, how the AF notified us, etc. He hadn't heard of Mark before, but was touched and told Rozlynn to thank us all for Mark's service. Shortly after Mark's death, Rozlynn was on a similar errand. When the guy saw the picture, he said, "Is this *the* Mark Forester?" He was a UA student about to graduate and join the Air Force. He said Mark's story had helped motivate him to join.

These two small events are typical of the countless experiences we've had since Mark left us for his current mission, on the other side. Many have heard of Mark and others haven't; but all are consistently respectful, grateful and inspired. This is his legacy, and it has become my legacy as well. He's influenced more people since his passing than he could have in life. And because of his sacrifice (our sacrifice too, really), my family and I have the opportunity to do more good for others than we otherwise could have. I wish it weren't this way, but it's what we've been given. He did what he did, so I can do what I do. And I will always do my best to follow my younger brother's example. I hope you are inspired to do the same.

In Memoriam

Tribute to Calvin Harrison

On 29 September 2010, we lost another great American. Besides Mark, we lost Sgt. First Class Calvin Harrison, from Coldspring, TX. Calvin was one of Mark's Special Forces teammates--a Green Beret Medic. Mark and Calvin were in day two of a very successful mission, along with their other teammates, and were advancing on a suspected enemy ambush site when they were killed in action.

In a speech by Texas Congressman Ted Poe, he shared that when Calvin worked in a grocery store at a younger age, a customer one day walked in and looked him right in the eye and said "You're never gonna be nothin." Calvin remembered this moment and even brought it up to his dad his last time home. Sounds like he used this as positive motivation to help him achieve what he did.

The picture above is Calvin and Mark, taken on 29 September 2010 - the day of that fatal battle. We have been told by numerous people that Calvin was a fantastic father to his two girls, excellent soldier and medic, and well-liked by all teammates. We keep in touch with his mom and have a picture of Calvin and his girls in our home. After all, he was fighting alongside Mark. One of Calvin's high school friends told us that Mark couldn't have had a better man fighting alongside him. We know from their teammates that they were good friends and trusted each other completely.

We are grateful to Calvin for his sacrifice, for his example, and for his family's support while he served our country. Rest in peace Calvin. May you and Mark protect us from the other side.

Remembering Danny Sanchez

When I heard that SrA Danny Sanchez had been killed in Afghanistan on 16 September 2010, it struck me hard. I didn't know Danny, but knowing he was a Combat Controller, I realized even more that Mark's life could easily be taken as well. It was a tough day for my family and me.

Danny was from El Paso, TX. When he was five years old, his dad died in a car accident at the age of 23. His mom always told him she wanted him to live a long, happy life—longer than his father lived. Well, Danny turned 23 on August 30, 2010, and was killed 17 days later. His mom said he died doing what he loved, just as Mark did.

His mom, Yvette, also said Daniel loved life and had a never-ending smile. She has received overwhelming support and honor to help her conquer any negative feelings. She has a drive to keep Daniel's memory alive, as well as honor those who have and are serving for our freedoms. We feel this is very important.

We first met Yvette and her young son, Dakota, at the CCT reunion in Ft. Walton Beach, FL in October 2010. It's sad to think Dakota, only a young boy, will grow up without his big brother. At least he'll have his example to look to.

Tattooed on Senior Airman Daniel R. Sanchez's torso was a quote that defined his short life. *"It is not the critic who counts; not the man who points out how the strong man stumbles or where the doer of deeds could have done better. The credit belongs to the man who is actually in the arena, whose face is marred by dust and sweat and blood ..."*

At age 4, Sanchez was already seeking adventure, as the excerpt from his memorial website below describes:

"He invented his own scuba gear," said Yvette Duchene, the Airman's mother, during a Sunday interview at her East El Paso home. "He put socks on the ends of his feet like flippers. He had a big set of goggles and he had a backpack on his back."

Jumping off the roof gave him the sensation of flying, relatives said.

One day he appeared wearing a makeshift cape, imitating Darkwing Duck, a favorite Disney cartoon character. When the boy disappeared, a grandmother, Irene Sierra, became suspicious. "I told (his mother), 'You'd better go check him. I bet he's going to go to the roof,'" Sierra said.

Despite his adventurous nature, he never broke any bones, Duchene said. However, in one family photo, he has a smear of blood on his forehead, which he banged jumping off a wall. "He was a small Superman," Sierra said.

Sanchez liked to pull his brother and cousins into the excitement as well. One day, when there apparently was little else to do, he duct-taped his younger brother, Dakota, to a gate, where their mother found him upon her return home. Dakota, now 10, was a willing participant. Duchene laughed and scolded them about damaging the paint. "Most of it he didn't get in trouble for because of his smile," Dakota said. Andee Olivares, a cousin who called Sanchez "Baby Daniel," was a few years older and felt responsibility to make sure no one got hurt during those escapades. "I was picturing us growing old," Olivares said, tears clouding his eyes. "I wanted to meet his kids."

Sanchez liked going to school to play with friends, his mother said, but had trouble studying. He loved science, which was why he tattooed the solar system on his arm.

When he joined the Air Force at 18, he already was set on becoming an elite warrior. His childhood dreams of flying and scuba diving were fulfilled in the 23rd Special Tactics Squadron. He looked at the military as a career and planned to become an instructor.

"That's my saving grace," Duchene said. "I couldn't imagine him sitting behind a desk." During the grueling 10-week training in San Antonio, Sanchez called his mother to tell her he would not quit. In the end, he was among eight graduates in a class of about 200 men.

Sanchez was proud of his many tattoos, including a quote by Theodore Roosevelt. It proved prophetic:

"The credit belongs to the man who spends himself for a worthy cause, who, at the best, knows, in the end, the triumph of high achievement, and who, at the worst, if he fails, at least he fails while daring greatly, so that his place shall never be with those cold and timid souls who knew neither victory nor defeat."

After losing Danny, his mother wrote the following poem after his memorial service, "Because I wanted to say so many things I didn't know how to say."

Big blue ocean waves came crashing ashore,
A sea of Red Berets walked right through my door.
Many solemn faces that I didn't know,
Knelt down around me and held me just so.
"Your son died in combat", are the words I still hear
as the blue ocean waves whispered in my ear.
"He made the ultimate sacrifice" he continued to say...
"Our Brother, Your Son, wouldn't have it any other way."
Those big ocean waves continue to stir
In my head, the confusion and turmoil... still all a blur.
But now the waves whisper stories of hope, love and faith
They're those of your Brother, My Son, Daniel Ray.
His smile felt by ALL, not just his family
But those blue ocean waves of the Red Beret Sea.
He is loved by so many and I've come to understand,
The blue ocean waves are a Brotherhood of Man.
His fortitude, guts and bravery show through,
Just as the waves of the ocean inside each of you.
But in spite of the swell of the tides from this sea
It all just makes sense and is so clear to me.
The Red Beret Sea fills this hole in my heart
It's his way of showing that he'd never depart.
He holds us and guides us and will show us the way
We love you so much my baby Daniel Ray.

Yvette Sierra Duchene

Acknowledgements

This book, Mark's book, would not have been possible if not for generous, dedicated support of many others. I am pretty sure I've thanked each one of you personally, and I want to reiterate my unending gratitude here. Not only did you share of yourselves in being Mark's friend, mentor, commander, teammate, etc., but you shared what that relationship means to you, how losing him hurt you, and how his example inspired you.

I knew for certain in late September 2010 that I would write a book about Mark. So it was never a dream and I never doubted its completion. However, without the help from all included in this biography, it wouldn't be the quality work it is today. Each one of you knows your name is in our hearts and in this book, whether in ink or not. I don't think I overstate anything to say my family will appreciate and remember you for generations.

My wife Rozlynn has put up with me talking about the book almost daily and spending many hours each week working on this project. I am very thankful for her support and for providing a listening ear. She was a rock to me during this tragic time and continues to be; as well as being the perfect committed mother to our son Jackson Mark.

It also hasn't been easy for my parents and siblings to discuss their memories of Mark. I thank them for contributing and for helping verify stories and facts. Each family member helped make Mark the warrior he was.

Afterword

Posted on Matthew Glencoe's Facebook page on Saturday, 13 April 2013:

It's late and I've been working on Mark's book for many hours today. In the background, my mind mulls these thoughts:

All my life I've had a knack for words. More than meanings, words have flavor and texture that one can savor and enjoy as much as any of the finest food. I've mastered a second language and I hold a Bachelor's degree in Journalism from one of the best J-schools in the country. I've spent a huge portion of my professional and personal life striving to clearly and powerfully communicate information, ideas and trust.

Despite all that, I stumble and grope whenever I attempt to describe the effect this man—and all who knew him—has had upon my life.

I am humbled that provenance has favored me so.

I was introduced to Mark Forester sometime in mid-2011. Several months earlier I had reconnected, via Facebook, with Melanie (Hansen) Davis, an old friend from my high school days. I noticed she consistently posted comments and images relating to our veterans and service members. I finally asked what was behind her interest. She replied that in addition to being very patriotic, she was working on a book of history focused upon the first person stories of veterans titled, *The Triumph Book: HEROES*. I offered to help with editing and some ghost writing.

As she collected stories for her book, Melanie heard about Mark from a friend who knows the Foresters. Through that friend, Melanie connected with Thad, explained the project and Thad eagerly gave her an interview over the phone.

At the time, I was still a corporate road warrior, working in sales for a food manufacturer. I have a clear memory of sitting on a regional jet, heading home after a long week away. I had the row to myself, so I spread out with my laptop, computer bag and notes as I edited Mark's story. I was touched and impressed by this brief introduction.

Several months later, the opportunity developed for me to get off the corporate train and redirect my career. I gained some amazing experience in that world, but I hungered for more independence and the opportunity to make a bigger difference in the lives of those around me. I remembered Melanie mentioning that Mark's family wanted a book about him, and that Thad was looking for someone to collaborate with him to write this book. I raised my hand and after some long discussions, I got the opportunity of a lifetime.

Long before any meaningful writing could begin, I had to become deeply familiar with Mark's world. The process took longer than either Thad or I would have liked, but a friend reminded me: "Research *is* writing." And I reminded myself of something a writer friend, Michael Yon, once said to me, "Whenever the writing gets hard, it's because your research is lacking. Get back to digging and learning. Then, the words will flow."

And flow they did, more than 90,000 of them. Most are Thad's and the people who knew Mark personally. My focus and contribution was to establish an organization to tell the stories, massage them for readability— without sacrificing the teller's personal voice—and thread it all together to be interesting and compelling.

The one thing I find most remarkable about Mark is his continuing ability to inspire others to expect more of themselves and to strive for it. For myself, I find I am motivated to emulate Mark's love for others. I am intrigued that someone could be so committed to his values (sometimes to the point of being called "opinionated"), but could express that commitment in ways that encouraged and motivated, rather than alienated.

Although he gave up his life on that battlefield at Shah Mashad, the effect lives on. It is still there. I witness it repeatedly in others and I feel it myself. I consider it nothing less than a sacred duty to perpetuate that effect. If, after reading Mark Forester's story, you feel inspired to be a better version of yourself, then I have done my duty.

Very respectfully,

Matthew Glencoe
Lendum Enterprises L.L.C.

THE MARK FORESTER
FOUNDATION

Shortly after Mark's death, our family created The Mark Forester Foundation to honor an American Hero. Our desire is that Mark's example be shared with the world. First and foremost, we do this by providing a college scholarship to at least one Haleyville High School student each year. The city of Haleyville and the school district have provided wonderful support to our family since Mark's death, and we want to give back to our home town. We also want students to understand that freedom does not come without a price. We take awarding this scholarship(s) very seriously.

So far, we have donated to other charitable organizations including: Special Operations Warrior Foundation, Soldier's Angels, The Welcome Home Heroes Traveling Tribute, The University of Alabama Campus Veterans Association and Wounded Warrior Project. We will continue to support worthwhile organizations so long as we have the funds to do so.

A portion of the sales of this book will be donated to The Mark Forester Foundation. Thank you for your support. To learn more about Mark, his foundation, and other great American Heroes, please visit:

www.MarkAForester.com

CPSIA information can be obtained at www.ICGtesting.com
Printed in the USA
LVOW05*2203221113

362513LV00002B/25/P